Beyond the Trees

Beyond
THE Trees

STORIES OF WISCONSIN FORESTS

Candice Gaukel Andrews

Wisconsin Historical Society Press

Published by the Wisconsin Historical Society Press
Publishers since 1855

© 2011 by Candice Gaukel Andrews

For permission to reuse material from *Beyond the Trees: Stories of Wisconsin Forests* (ISBN: 978-0-87020467-8), please access www.copyright.com or contact the Copyright Clearance Center, Inc. (CCC), 222 Rosewood Drive, Danvers, MA 01923, 978–750–8400. CCC is a not-for-profit organization that provides licenses and registration for a variety of users.

Front cover photo of the Chequamegon-Nicolet National Forest by John T. Andrews

Maps by John T. Andrews

Frontmatter photos, all by John T. Andrews: page ii, Chequamegon Land Base: Northern Region; page viii, Kettle Moraine State Forest–Southern Unit; page xiii, Nicolet Land Base

Photographs identified with WHi or WHS are from the Society's collections; address requests to reproduce these photos to the Visual Materials Archivist at the Wisconsin Historical Society, 816 State Street, Madison, WI 53706.

Printed in Wisconsin, USA

Cover and interior designed and typeset by Jane Tenenbaum

27 26 25 24   2 3 4 5

Library of Congress Cataloging-in-Publication Data

Andrews, Candice Gaukel.
Beyond the trees: stories of Wisconsin forests / Candice Gaukel Andrews.
   p. cm.
   Includes index.
   ISBN 978-0-87020-467-8 (pbk. : alk. paper) 1. Forest reserves — Wisconsin. 2. Forests and forestry — Wisconsin. I. Title.
   SD428.A2W627 2011
   508.7750915'2 — dc22

                                                                    2010039305

To John, who encourages me to keep reaching for my best, while showing me how to stay grounded.

Contents

Acknowledgments

If I were doing this book truly alone, getting to know even a small portion of a single Wisconsin forest would take more than my one lifetime. Fortunately, I had the support and assistance of many people.

Thank you to John T. Andrews, my fellow forest adventurer. Your ability to find your way when I am hopelessly lost constantly astounds me, as does your artwork and photography. You also have my gratitude for creating all of the maps in this book.

Shane Andrews, you have always been my moral and ethical compass, pointing the way to the correct and true path for every situation I throw at you. Travis John Andrews, you show me what dedication, hard work, and passion for a dream look like. I am thankful for you both. You two keep me smiling through it all.

My sincere appreciation goes to my friend L. B. (Bud) Kuppenheimer, who agreed to contribute two pieces for this book. He is a man of the forests, whom I met in a canyon.

I'm grateful that a twist of fate sent me to Kate Thompson at the Wisconsin Historical Society Press, who expressed her enthusiasm for this book upon reading it in its first incarnation. The keen eyes and "reader's ear" of John Motoviloff, editor extraordinaire, then took over, keeping these stories going in the right direction when they sometimes strayed off the track. At the same time that he was building his Kickapoo Valley cabin from the foundation up, he helped raise a book from the manuscript provided to him. Kate, John, and the rest of the Society staff, my thanks for making this book a reality.

Lowell Klessig, professor emeritus of natural resources at the University of Wisconsin–Stevens Point, provided a careful review of the facts in this text; and Professor Eric Anderson and Professor Richard Hauer, also associated with the University of Wisconsin–Stevens Point, never failed to give me expert and thoughtful responses to my many questions. Adrian Wydeven, mammalian ecologist at the Wisconsin Department of Natural Resources, was quick to answer every query.

And thank you to all of the people whose names you'll see in these pages, who were kind enough to take the time to share their forest stories with me.

Most of all, my heartfelt thanks to all of you readers who live in the forests, who work in the forests, who strive to protect them, or who just love them for what they are.

Introduction

In the Company of Distinguished Individuals

One bunch of trees looks pretty much like another, right? It was the first thought that came into my mind when I was originally asked to write a book about experiencing all of Wisconsin's forests. Just how, in such a book, I wondered, would describing walking through the woods in chapter 1 appear to be any different from hiking through another patch of trees in chapter 2? In other words, how do you distinguish standing in the thick of northern Wisconsin's Chequamegon-Nicolet National Forest, let's say, from finding yourself surrounded by trunks in the southern Kettle Moraine?

I believed then — and believe even more so after writing this book — that Wisconsin's woods are some of the most beautiful places on Earth. But to really *see* each forest as a distinct entity and discover its unique personality, I knew I'd have to look beyond its trees, to borrow liberally from the old maxim.

With some trepidation, then, I agreed to take on the challenge. But before setting foot into any of the forests, I decided to make their initial acquaintance by reading what others had already written about them. The hope of finding the individuality I sought was soon squelched, however, by what seemed to be a common history.

Soon after the first wave of white European descendants arrived in the state, the destruction of our Wisconsin woods began. Loggers, sweeping across the country from the East Coast to the West, were charged with the task of felling trees to supply a growing nation with wood for building towns and cities, bridge supports, railroads, furniture, and fence posts. The loggers were followed by farmers, who cleared what little remained for cropland.

By the mid-1920s, the great pines and profitable hardwoods of Wisconsin's once-mighty Northwoods were almost gone. Most of the farmers had failed, too; by 1927, almost 25 percent of the land in Wisconsin's northern counties had become tax delinquent.

To make matters worse, the lack of tree cover had dangerously reduced the soil's water-holding capacity, causing riverbanks to wash away and headwaters to erode. Slash left on the ground after logging provided the fuel for the raging fires that now could roar across the denuded land.

By 1930, the scars were so evident that they could no longer be ignored. Soon after President Franklin D. Roosevelt took office in 1933, he proposed a Civilian Conservation Corps (CCC) as part of his New Deal legislation. By 1937, the CCC was formally established. Fifty CCC camps were created in Wisconsin's Chequamegon-Nicolet National Forest alone. Nationwide, forestry schools were founded, textbooks on the new science of forest management were written, and fire control efforts were put in place.

Today, forests are managed by principles that are designed to restore wildlife, to maintain the water-holding capacity of the soil, and to provide greenbelts for campers, hikers, and hunters. After an area has been logged, seed trees are left to regenerate the woods. Now, finally — following three hundred years of indiscriminate cutting — instead of losing our woodlands, our American forests are growing more timber each year than is being cut.

While this common history I read about provided an overarching theme that linked our forests together, the time had come to lace up my hiking boots and go out to meet them one by one. I needed to discover firsthand just what made them different.

For months, I journeyed through our forests. At first, the great physical differences were striking. In the north stands the mighty Chequamegon-Nicolet National Forest, covering more than 1.5 million acres. In the east is tiny Point Beach State Forest, a mere 2,903 acres; while in the west is the hidden Coulee Experimental State Forest, which I almost couldn't find at all. I explored a forest whose main purpose is to protect a river and then one that has virtually no permanent water. I hiked an "interpreted" trail explaining sustainable forestry practices and then drove through a clear-cut. I walked through city forests, such as Havenwoods, that are more prairie than forest; and wild and remote ones like the Brule River, where the vegetation is so thick I wondered if I'd ever get out. I investigated a forest that was born just a few years ago and one that went back to 1925.

But beyond those physical differences I first noted when I actually got out

into Wisconsin's woods, it was another kind of history — one that I could see with my own eyes and touch with my own hands — that made the forests start to take on their distinctive shapes. And this in-your-face history reached much further back than the logging era I had read about in books.

In the Chequamegon-Nicolet National Forest, for example, I saw the

Penokee-Gogebic Range, which forms the Great Divide running east to west through northern Wisconsin and upper Michigan. The range is thought to be billions of years old. In the Kettle Moraine, I gazed at formations left behind by a relatively "recent" glacier, just ten thousand years ago. And on a single day in the Brule River State Forest, I walked on a trail that was at least three centuries old — but then stopped along the way to read a forest logbook with entries dated just the day before.

However, it was the personal stories and histories I encountered in each forest that finally brought them into the sharpest focus. On my explorations, I met with politicians and postmasters; former fire tower lookouts and forest supervisors; lawyers and lodge dwellers and lumbermen; river guides and resort owners; skidder drivers and winning wood ticks. I sat and listened to the tales about bigger-than-life characters, such as Smokey Bear, Skunk Frank, and the Video Man of Mellen. I walked through the remains of miners' camps and loggers' camps and CCC camps. On a dam, I ran my hands over the same hand-cranked gears that river men used in 1878 and, in another forest, felt the foundation of a missile site from the 1950s. On a hike in the Brule River State Forest, my boots traversed seven stones, each inscribed with the name of a former traveler who passed by the same spot — people such as Daniel Greysolon, Sieur du Lhut, who wrote about his journey here in 1680; English cartographer Jonathan Carver, who went through in 1768; and Henry Schoolcraft, the man credited with discovering the source of the Mississippi River, who walked by in 1820. I trod trails with names honoring the legacies of John Muir and Aldo Leopold. I ran into a mountain rumored to be a site for space aliens, and then strolled in fields containing alien invaders. I brushed up with the spirits of Sauk and Ho-Chunk; Ojibwe and Potawatomi and Menominee.

Oh, and I also ran into those trees that, at first glance, I thought I wouldn't be able to see around. I learned that some of them, like a much-loved grandfather, are so venerable that they have been given their own names: the Big White Pine, the MacArthur Pine, or the Treaty Tree.

Now, come and explore Wisconsin's forests with me. You'll be in the company of some distinguished — and lofty — individuals.

C.G.A.
Sun Prairie, Wisconsin
March 2011

Wisconsin's State and National Forests

Brule River
State Forest

Northern Highland-
American Legion
State Forest

Chequamegon-Nicolet
National Forest
Northern Region

Governor Knowles
State Forest

Chequamegon-Nicolet
National Forest
Eastern Region

Flambeau River
State Forest

Chequamegon-Nicolet
National Forest
Nicolet

Chequamegon-Nicolet
National Forest
Southern Region

Peshtigo River
State Forest

Black River State Forest

Coulee Experimental State Forest

Point Beach
State Forest

Kettle Moraine State Forest
Northern Unit

Havenwoods State Forest

Kettle Moraine State Forest
Southern Unit

Great biodiversity exists within the Black River State
Forest. More than four thousand acres here have been
designated as parts of State Natural Areas. *John T. Andrews*

1 Black River State Forest
NEARLY DRIFTLESS ON A RED BLACK RIVER

A Standout in the Neighborhood

There's a children's game that originated on the TV series *Sesame Street* called "One of These Things Is Not Like the Others." Playing it, a youngster is asked to pick out the one of several things that has nothing in common with the other items in the group. That's what stepping into the Black River State Forest is like. It's not like anything else around it; it's paradoxical, individualistic. "Expect the unexpected" applies.

The Black River State Forest lies on the edge of Wisconsin's glaciated central plain, poised on the edge where the farthest reach of the glacier's icy fingers lightly tickled — but just missed grasping — the rugged "driftless" or "coulee" region. In fact, standing on top of 180-foot-high, unglaciated Castle Mound in the forest's detached, western section and looking east, you can see what was once the bed of "Glacial Lake Wisconsin." This is a land where towering buttes, sandstone hills, soaring bluffs, and flat lake beds could have been carved by the last advance of the Wisconsin Glacial Episode — or not.

Great biodiversity exists *within* this forest, as well. Here is one of the wildest places in Wisconsin. The forest covers 67,070 acres, backed up by 120,000 acres of the Jackson County Forest. Scores of animals and plants have noticed the rolling low hills and impressive spikes of limestone and sandstone, and have decided that this is a good place to grow and be left alone in. Deer and rare butterflies, turkeys and grouse, and gray wolves and black bears may spend their whole lives here and never be discovered or seen by us. Like them, we, too, can get lost in the Black River State Forest; it's easy to drift and to become driftless, all at once.

Aldo Leopold, known as the father of wildlife management, restored a worn-out, eighty-acre farm near Baraboo. His observations about the farm are recorded in his classic *Sand County Almanac*. Both Leopold's farm and the Black River State Forest are located in Wisconsin's Sand Counties.
WHi Image ID 2290

About four hundred million years ago, the area that is now this forest was submerged under a large sea, which left layers of sand deposits up to four hundred feet thick. These sand layers compressed and melded together to form what we now call "Cambrian sandstone." When the sea receded, sandy plains emerged, and wind and rain sculpted the sandstone into knolls, such as today's Castle Mound. Then came the human handiwork of logging, farming, and Civilian Conservation Corps remodeling. Oaks and maples now cling to the mounds and ridges, while white pine run through boggy lowlands.

But it's those sand deposits that define this area and stick in the mind for most of us. In 1935, ecologist, environmentalist, and forester Aldo Leopold bought a "sand county" farm northeast of Baraboo, "worn out and then abandoned by our bigger-and-better society," as he wrote, and "selected for its lack of goodness and its lack of highway." The Leopold family spent twelve years there, on and off, restoring their eighty acres into native Wisconsin habitat.

Leopold's 1949 book *A Sand County Almanac* described the natural happenings on his farm month-by-month and his thoughts on developing a "land ethic." The book was published by his son Luna a year after Aldo's death from a heart attack while fighting a brush fire on a neighbor's farm. Aldo Leopold is now considered to be the father of wildlife management in the United States, and *A Sand County Almanac* is recognized as a landmark book in the American conservation movement. More than two million copies have been printed, and it has been translated into nine languages.

Here is the small "kingdom" of Castle Mound, marked by a thirty-foot rock monolith.
John T. Andrews

It's not surprising that seas and sands play a role in a state forest named Black River. But true to the character of this place, the Black River cuts through the forest only in its northwest corner and along the western edge of its detached section. The majority of the forest is without a river at all. Another paradox.

Even more contradictory is the color of the Black River itself. It enthralled me from the moment I set eyes on the forest. It's burgundy. And that alone would make this forest stand out from its fellows.

At the Castle

Castle Mound is a formidable presence in the Black River State Forest and one of its most known icons. It was there I started my explorations.

The area surrounding Castle Mound is almost a small kingdom all by itself. Located about a mile southeast of the town of Black River Falls on Highway 12, it stands in the portion of the forest that is detached from the main area, which begins four miles north and east of Black River Falls on Highway 54.

More than four thousand acres of the Black River State Forest have been designated as parts of State Natural Areas, and the Castle Mound Pine Forest State Natural Area takes up eighty of them. My 1.5-mile route following the hilly Castle Mound Nature Trail will lead me to the top of the butte that projects almost two hundred feet above the surrounding sand plain.

This early June morning is bright, but rain is expected this afternoon. It's hard to tell what the weather is like anywhere else but along this path, though. The thick, rich forest canopy keeps me protected above, and the forest floor beneath my hiking boots is a soft mat of green and brown leaves. It's cool in here among the trees. On the northeast slope, white and red pine, red maple, white oak, and paper birch stand above the heart shapes of the large-leaved asters and the sharp-toothed pipsissewas. Toward the southwest, I can see yellow-green jack pine and more sturdy oaks.

Suddenly, to my left, on the narrow spine at the top of the butte, a wrinkled, thirty-foot-high rock monolith appears, jutting out of the forest floor without warning. It is unexpected — a vertical stone wall on top of an already lofty knob.

Swinging around to the other side of the craggy extrusion, I climb a path that narrows between wet, cool rock and the gnarled trunks of thick trees. As my hand grips the stone, I realize I am holding onto four-hundred-million-year-old sand, chiseled by winds long gone and water long ago receded. Ferns sprout from the rock, as if drawing their very life from it.

On the top of Castle Mound, I sit down to catch my breath. All around me, boulders tip against one another, in random, casual, and crazy ways, and pine trees have their feet firmly entrenched in rock bases. This is obviously a place where rocks and trees keep easy company with each other. Black-throated green warblers and red-breasted nuthatches — usually found much farther north — hold court with each other here; but again, in contrast, it is a place for "solitary" vireos.

From my vantage point at the long, narrow, flat top of Castle Mound, it is easy to see the marked difference in the landscape between the east's flat, glaciated central plain and the west's rugged, coulee region. Where I sit right now could be the wild, unruly line between glacier and no glacier, drift and driftless. This is definitely a forest that stands astride two opposing worlds.

On my way back down from the top of Castle Mound, I stop to feel the unique contours in the giant boulders that are strewn alongside the trail. *Strewn* is the only word imaginable for the haphazard way in which they sit in the forest. But the trees have a good relationship with them here, too; hugging them with their roots, as if protecting them from some danger. The rocks, in thanks, have tried to take on the look of the trees, adorning themselves in green mosses. I wonder what it would have been like to watch these huge boulders migrate here. There must have been some mighty, thunderous crashing noises.

One giant rock near the trail looks like the hull of a sinking ship. It appears as if it had succeeded in sailing across the forest this far, but then was suddenly reminded of just how heavy it really was.

The Black River Runs Red

The long roots of the trees along the nature trail in Perry Creek Park are the makings for myths.
Candice Gaukel Andrews

It seems logical that because places like Castle Mound are so astounding, the Black River would have to do something equally spectacular and dramatic to stand out.

It did. It turned red.

Perry Creek Park sits prettily on the shores of the Black River, just south of Castle Mound. It is here that I get my first close-up look at the Black River and its tributary creek. A nature trail runs along Perry Creek into a quiet gorge filled with waterfalls, rooty trees, and flat rocks that stretch out into the middle of the stream. Despite all that, the color of the water is the main attraction. Under this June morning sun, its burgundy hue flashes a bright red.

I ask Jamie Dahl, who has been a law enforcement ranger on the Black River State Forest for more than ten years, about the water's unusual color. "We get a lot of questions about that," says Jamie. "People think because of the color that this water must not be clean or safe. I submit water samples from our two swimming areas, and the test results have always been very good. The water is stained from the run-off of oak and tamarack tree tannins."

The Perry Creek nature trail invites me into the gorge, and soon I'm being transported deeper and deeper into the scene of a gnome glen straight out of a fairy tale. The trail lies next to the red waters of the creek, and it shows me the way by means of a pine needle path that acts like a big, orange arrow

Red-tinted Perry Creek runs into a quiet gorge filled with waterfalls and flat rocks that stretch to the middle of the stream.
John T. Andrews

pointing me onward. The water bubbles and gurgles over little rock-falls next to my feet.

The rocks in the creek are polished and shiny. Fallen tree trunks crisscross over the water like enchanted bridges. Ferns teeter on the shore, clamber down over the rocks, and slip into the creek. The gaping underside of a tipped tree gives insight into another mythical world, exposing a tangled network of root highways into what is usually a secret universe. Slabs of layered rock protect and enclose the whole place.

Just before exiting the gorge, I walk over the small bridge that traverses Perry Creek. Down below, on the sand, there are some large canine tracks; I wonder if they are those of a wolf or of a very large dog. It's hard to tell from up here.

But no sooner is my attention drawn below my feet than it is called into

ONLY MANLY MEN NEED APPLY: RECRUITING FOREST RANGERS

Men Wanted!

A ranger must be able to take care of himself and his horse under very trying conditions; build trails and cabins; ride all day and all night; pack, shoot, and fight fire without loosing his head . . .

All this requires a very vigorous constitution. It means the hardest kind of physical work from beginning to end. It is not a job for those seeking health or light outdoor work . . .

Invalids need not apply!

IN 1905, POSTERS FROM THE NEW U.S. FOREST Service with the above text served as the recruiting call for rangers. Once the men applied, they were given written and field examinations. The written test contained questions on basic ranching techniques and assessed knowledge on surveying, lumbering, mapping, cabin-constructing, and livestock practices.

The outdoor field examination required that the applicant demonstrate his practical skills on saddling a horse, riding at a gallop, packing a mule by "throwing" a diamond hitch to keep baggage in place, pacing the distance around a measured course and computing the area in acres, and taking compass bearings and following a straight line. Potential rangers were also asked to bring a rifle and pistol to the test site and asked to shoot accurately at a target. Sometimes, they were told to cook a meal and then eat it. If he passed the test successfully, a ranger could expect to earn sixty dollars per month. But he was required to furnish his own equipment, horse, and pack animals.

Today, in order to become a full-time enforcement ranger in a Wisconsin state forest, you must complete sixty fully-accredited, college-level credits (before or within the first five years of employment) and pass the Wisconsin State Civil Service Examination. You then become eligible for employment as a law enforcement ranger and, depending on your ranking on the examination, will be invited to interview as positions are opened. Certification as a law enforcement officer is required prior to completing your probationary period.

According to ranger Jamie Dahl at the Black River State Forest, "The law enforcement training Wisconsin forest rangers are required to have — and then that they receive on the job — is equal to that of any county or city police department. I am a credentialed officer, and I carry a firearm. In my position, I get to do a little bit of everything. I go out on patrols in the forest, making arrests and issuing citations when necessary. I manage the forest's recreational revenue account. In the off-season, I also have public contact and maintenance duties, such as registering campers and cleaning restrooms."

Historically, a ranger was a "keeper, guardian, or soldier who ranges over a region to protect the area or enforce the law"; the *range* part of *ranger* meaning to "travel around an area." And sometimes, as we've learned since 1905, the best man for that job is a woman.

focus overhead. A sandhill crane rises into the sky from somewhere in the forest backing up the creek. Aldo Leopold wrote of cranes — and of paradoxes — in his *Sand County Almanac*:

Thus always does history, whether of marsh or market place, end in paradox. The ultimate value in these marshes is wildness, and the crane is wildness incarnate. But all conservation of wildness is self-defeating, for to cherish we must see and fondle, and when enough have seen and fondled, there is no wilderness left to cherish.

Some day, perhaps in the very process of our benefactions, perhaps in the fullness of geologic time, the last crane will trumpet his farewell and spiral skyward from the great marsh. High out of the clouds will fall the sound of hunting horns, the baying of the phantom pack, the tinkle of little bells, and then a silence never to be broken, unless perchance in some far pasture of the Milky Way.

Back to the Black

While the shallower Perry Creek flashes a bright red in the sunshine, its larger "parent" body of water, the Black River, looks a bit darker. In fact, early French traders named the river "Black" due to its duskiness, which is caused by two factors: tannic acid leaching in from places where tamaracks, oak trees, and sphagnum moss grow; and the high iron content of the soil.

The approximately two-hundred-mile Black River originates in the Chequamegon-Nicolet National Forest in Black Lake in Taylor County. It flows southwesterly to empty into the Mississippi River near New Amsterdam, Wisconsin. The section of the river that runs from Clark County to Black River Falls has cut a steep channel through the sandstone, exposing a much older bed of granite. Called the inlier, this forty-mile, naturally formed trench is a favorite with canoers.

The Black River and the East Fork of the Black River flow for just twenty-four miles along the northwest edge of the forest from Lake Arbutus to the forest boundary about a mile south of Hall's Creek. Between the town of Hatfield and Black River Falls, where the Driftless Area begins, the Black River makes its greatest descent in elevation. It's also where some of the best fishing in the forest is done. Muskie, northern pike, walleye, bass, catfish, and pan fish are all found in the riffles and pools created by the drop in altitude.

Mostly slow flowing, the Black River contains a few rapids on its forest section. There are four canoe landings within the forest, located at East Fork Campground, Hall's Creek, Perry Creek Park, and Mason's Landing. There are two canoe campsites south of Black River Falls.

The East Fork of the Black River forms the forest's northern border for its

The city of Black River Falls suffered its worst flood in 1911, when two upstream dams on the Black River failed. Wood houses and businesses were rebuilt using stone. *Courtesy Jackson County Historical Society*

last two miles; the rest of the fork runs through county forest. There are several small rapids along the ten-mile, half-day route between the Pray Road Canoe Landing outside the forest and the East Fork Campground within the forest.

The Black River has very few lakes and is subject to flooding. One of the most severe floods since white settlers arrived occurred in 1911 during the month of October, when forty-two acres of the Black River Falls business district were washed away. Since that time, hydroelectric dams and new woods on formerly denuded land have helped to prevent any more such disasters.

The Black River has been included on the list of Wisconsin's Land Legacy Places: places that the Wisconsin Department of Natural Resources and the public have deemed critical in meeting Wisconsin's future conservation and recreation needs because of their unique, pristine condition. And as ranger Jamie Dahl will attest, rivers as clean and natural as the Black River are becoming more and more difficult to find.

A Place of Pines Anew

As usual with the places in Wisconsin noted for their natural beauty and features, the land that is now the Black River State Forest has been used by different peoples for centuries. The Ho-Chunk saw the land as a hunting and meeting grounds. The distinctive sandstone bluffs served as important travel landmarks for not only the Ho-Chunk but for European explorers, traders, and settlers.

The Black River valley once held white and red pine that soared to the sky and that stood watch over the buttes and dark-tinted waters. In fact, the valley contained one of the densest concentrations of pine trees in Wisconsin when the first permanent sawmill opened on the Black River in 1839. Eventually, more than fifty sawmills would whir away twenty-four hours a day in Jackson County, processing 4.9 billion board feet of lumber. One colorful statistic states that in a forty-year period more than enough lumber was sawed to build a plank road nine feet wide and four inches thick around the world. By the end of the nineteenth century, the forest had been mostly cleared.

The land was soon passed off to settlers as farmland. Some farmers prospered for a few years, but most found that the land was unsuited for agricultural purposes. Infertile, sandy soil and early frosts soon bankrupted them. In the 1930s, the United States Resettlement Administration purchased much of the "useless" land on which the farmers were unable to produce enough to earn a living and moved them elsewhere in Jackson County. This is when Aldo Leopold and his Sand County farm enter in again. He wrote in *A Sand County Almanac:*

> Higher up the creeklet I encounter an abandoned farm. I try to read, from the age of the young jack pines marching across an old field, how long ago the luckless farmer found out that sand plains were meant to grow solitude, not corn. Jack pines tell tall tales to the unwary, for they put on several whorls of branches each year, instead of only one. I find a better chronometer in an elm seedling that now blocks the barn door. Its rings date back to the drought of 1930. Since that year no man has carried milk out of this barn.
>
> I wonder what this family thought about when their mortgage finally outgrew their crops, and thus gave the signal for their eviction. Many thoughts, like flying grouse, leave no trace of their passing, but some leave clues that outlast the decades. He who, in some unforgotten April, planted this lilac must have thought pleasantly of blooms for all the Aprils to come. She who used this washboard, its corrugations worn thin with many Mondays, may have wished for a cessation of all Mondays, and soon.

The Civilian Conservation Corps was called in to reforest the area, and in 1940 the U.S. Forest Service entered into an agreement with the Wisconsin Conservation Commission (now the Wisconsin Department of Natural Resources) to manage the area for wildlife and forestry purposes. In 1957, the federal government conveyed fifty-nine thousand acres to the state's conservation department, and the Black River State Forest was established. Over the next two years, service and public facilities were built.

Today, the Black River State Forest is a transitional zone in many ways, including between glaciated and unglaciated landscapes, and between the northern and central hardwoods forests. The majestic white and red pine in the highlands and tamaracks in the lowlands prior to the logging days of the nineteenth century have now been replaced with mainly aspens in the lowlands and jack pine in the highlands, along with some white pine reproduction from the few remaining seed-producing trees. Various species of oaks and birches fill the spaces in between.

But it is the comeback of the white pine — the largest conifer in Wisconsin — that is particularly exciting. Says Eric Epstein, a former ecologist with the Wisconsin Bureau of Endangered Resources who is currently writing a handbook entitled *The Ecological Landscapes of Wisconsin*, "The fact that the white pine have grown back to the degree that they have does teach us a lesson about the potential for ecosystem resilience that is important."

White pine are known as the Monarchs of the North and are favored by nesting bald eagles. They were also preferred by another famous Wisconsin conservationist, Senator Gaylord Nelson, the founder of Earth Day. I once had the pleasure of meeting Senator Nelson, when I served as an art director on a photo shoot of which he was the subject. He was to be photographed holding a tree seedling, and he made the request that it be a Wisconsin white pine.

The Black River State Forest is currently managed for timber — but now in a sustainable way — as well as for wildlife and recreation. And just as the Ho-Chunk have known for hundreds of years, it is a prime hunting grounds, especially for white-tailed deer.

Phantom Wolves, Black Bears, and Blue Racers

But it is another predator of deer whose tracks intrigue me today. I don't know if the tracks I see below the bridge over Perry Creek are those of wolves or not. It is rare to actually see a wolf; tracks are usually the most visible evidence of their presence. But whether or not they are truly wolf tracks, several packs are known to roam within the forest boundaries. I ask law enforcement ranger Jamie Dahl and ecologist Eric Epstein if they have spotted the elusive animals.

"I have seen many hawks, foxes, coyotes, and deer during my rounds in the forest," says Jamie. "And I know there are northern flying squirrels, otters, beavers, and mink. As much as I'm out and about, though, I can count on one hand how many times I've seen a wolf or a bear."

Eric Epstein has had almost the same experience: "I've seen wolf sign frequently, but I've not yet actually set eyes on them. I think the reason that the wolves are attracted to the Black River State Forest is because they're relatively free from persecution; they can't get into as much trouble in that landscape as they could get into in more heavily settled areas; and there's a very, very high deer population," he postulates.

"Black bears aren't common, but they're here," Eric continues. "Rarely but occasionally I see bobcat sign. An animal that isn't rare but which few people expect in this part of the state is the porcupine — sometimes you have to swerve to avoid them."

It is these smaller, perhaps less widely charismatic animals in the forest that Eric talks about the most. "Snowshoe hares have not been faring too well lately in our milder winters," he says. "The hares turn white even if the ground remains dark in a winter of little snow, so they are extremely vulnerable to predators."

Also capturing Eric's interest are the reptiles, not often thought of as "foresty" creatures. Says Eric:

The Black River supports several species of turtles that are now quite rare in the state but common on parts of the forest. One is the Blanding's turtle. It has a bright-yellow neck and chin and likes prairies, pine barrens, and oak savannas. Along the East Fork of the Black River and on some of the high-gradient tributaries of the Black River, you can find wood turtles. They have a sculpted shell and like very clean, rocky-bottom streams.

The massasagua rattlesnake is very rare, and we're not sure it still occurs on the Black River State Forest. It hasn't been seen here for almost twenty years. Occasionally, though, you can still find the ring-necked snake and a snake I used to call the "blue racer." It's called the yellow-bellied snake now, but I do prefer the more dynamic blue racer name!

Birds of a Forest Feather

As engaging as snakes with racy names are, the subject that really gets Eric going is the Black River State Forest's avian residents and visitors. He says:

> The forest is a fantastic area for birds. It has very strong populations of a number of what we collectively call neo-tropical migrants, especially the wood warblers. They are very well represented in the Black River State Forest by many different species; some of them are quite rare this far south in Wisconsin.
>
> There's another set of birds that are associated with sand prairies, pine barrens, and oak savanna habitats. Sharp-tailed grouse, the common nighthawk, and the whippoorwill have declined in many areas in the state. The common nighthawk is no longer so common. I live about forty-five miles south and west of the Black River State Forest. I used to be able to sit on my porch and listen to the whippoorwills. But I haven't heard them where I live for more than twenty years. However, one of their strongholds is in the Black River State Forest.

Ever the ecologist and now on a roll, Eric tells me about one of his favorite forest residents:

> One of the birds that is most characteristic of certain forest types found on the Black River State Forest is called the Canada warbler. It's got a very lovely song and is one of my potential poster children for the Black River area. The Canada warbler falls into the category of neotropical migrant. Finding that it even occurred here at all was surprising — this is a bird that was thought to nest only in the northernmost parts of the state. But I've found quite a few nesting here. The males sing from low shrubs near eye-level, where you can actually watch them do it. Part of what makes seeing them so special is the setting: often in magnificent stands of older pines with a beautiful, lush floor of mosses, ferns, and skunk cabbage and scattered patches of winterberry and bog holly — with these little, yellow-and-black jewels flitting through the understory.

At Dike 17

Eric's enthusiasm for watching birds is catching. Luckily, in the east-central section of the forest is the 3,700-acre Dike 17 Wildlife Area, a place of grasslands, marshes, and flowages that is a bird haven. I decide to spend the rest of the afternoon there.

The Dike 17 Wildlife Area was purchased from local farmers in the 1930s. Civilian Conservation Corps crews then developed the land to attract waterfowl, mostly by building earthen dams. There are now two dozen flowages located on or near the property that provide a thousand acres of waterfowl habitat.

The curving waterways of the Dike 17 Wildlife Area are attractive to waterfowl on their journeys along the Mississippi Flyway. *John T. Andrews*

During the fall and spring migrations, thousands of ducks and geese rest here during their journeys along the Mississippi Flyway. As many as four hundred sandhill cranes frequent the flowages. Scarce species find solace here, too; bald eagles, ospreys, Cooper's hawks, and red-shouldered hawks have been known to make appearances. And northern goshawks, broad-winged hawks, pileated woodpeckers, wild turkeys, and ruffed grouse hunt the dragonflies, beetles, and grasshoppers in the marshes and grasslands.

Prescribed fires maintain the grass and brush landscape for species such as sharp-tailed grouse. And an annual draw down of some of the flowages stimulates vegetation growth to feed waterfowl.

I walk the half-mile trail to the Dike 17 observation tower, wishing I'd encounter a short-eared owl, an otter, a beaver, or a white-tailed deer. Surrounding me are flat, green fields, ribboned with curving and circular waterways. On the far horizon are forested mounds. Again I am struck by the contrasting sides to and landscapes in the Black River State Forest.

I climb the wooden stairs to the top platform, hoping to photograph some wildlife. But all is still. It seems I'm the only one out here this early evening. I put the camera away and finish the day just looking out over the flowages as the sun sets. True to the weather prediction, it begins to drizzle lightly. The view and colors go hazy and muted in the raindrops, and I think of the old masters, of Claude Monet paintings.

Among the grasses, the palmy leaves of wild lupine shiver when beads of jewel-like raindrops land on them.

Better for Butterflies

These wild lupines provide an important service for one of the Black River State Forest's most well-loved natives. They are the only host plant for the endangered Karner blue butterfly. And this delicate insect has very special needs.

Karner blue caterpillars eat *only* one thing: the leaves of wild lupine. The adults feed on the flowering plant's nectar. The Karner blue is extinct in some of its historic locations, such as Massachusetts and Pennsylvania. Wisconsin is one of the butterfly's last refuges. Their existence has not gone unnoticed or unappreciated here.

Wild lupine grows quickly in areas recently cleared by fire or other disturbance. During the last thirty years on the Black River State Forest, natural fires have been partly substituted for by forestry practices such as timber harvesting, followed by soil scarification for tree planting and natural seeding. In the fall of 1994, thirty-eight acres of oaks and jack pine were clear-cut on the forest. In the summer of 1995, the clear-cut site was prepared for seed; and that fall, twenty acres were hand-planted with lupine.

Lupine plants were observed at Dike 17 during the growing season of 1996. By 2002, the monitoring of Karner blues had begun. Since then, annual counts have shown that the numbers of Karner blue butterflies at the site are increasing slightly.

The Black River State Forest takes extra steps and special care when it comes to its Karner blue butterflies and timber management. All proposed timber sale areas that include the butterfly's habitat, lupine, or are likely to support populations of the butterfly must be surveyed first by forest personnel. If an area is found to contain lupine and Karner blues, forest managers will design the timber sale to avoid old log landings and openings along logging roads. Thick lupine patches in these openings provide a safe place for the butterflies to live in until the timber harvest opens up the forest floor to sunlight. Then, new lupine will spring up, creating new habitats for the Karner blues to colonize.

In addition, whenever possible, timber harvests are planned for the winter months, when the snow cover protects the butterflies in their dormant egg phase. Thus, the Karner blue has been able to flourish in the Black River State Forest.

Every year in July, the city of Black River Falls celebrates the endangered and indigenous butterfly with its Karner Blue Butterfly Festival. A young princess — who must be a resident of Black River Falls between the ages of ten and twelve — is crowned. She must represent the butterfly and her city in parades and promotional events for a year.

Staying Power

A Karner blue butterfly lives on average for six days. I think of the many, many generations of this small, blue creature that have *only* ever seen this forest in their lifetimes.

On Smrekar Road, in the southern portion of the forest, there is another

BLUES IN THE BLACK

FORESTS OFTEN IMPRESS US WITH BIG THINGS: towering trees, large acreage, or high numbers of pristine, natural areas. But the Black River State Forest has one very small item of note: the Karner blue butterfly (*Lycaeides melissa samuelis*).

Measuring about an inch across its wingspan, the diminutive Karner blue was placed on the federal endangered list in 1992 and declared extirpated in Canada in 2000. In Wisconsin, however, the tiny insect is deemed only a "species of concern." In fact, our state supports the largest and most widespread Karner blue butterfly population in the world, and they live mostly in central Wisconsin. The Black River State Forest, with its sandy soils and wild lupine, is one of their favorite habitats.

The Karner blue's lifecycle depends on the blue lupine flower (*Lupinus perennis*), which blooms in late May. Karner blue caterpillars eat *only* the leaves of the lupine plant, while adults feed on the nectar of wildflowers. This severely restricts where they can survive. Natural disturbances in forests, such as wildfires and grazing by large mammals, maintains the butterfly's habitat of sandy oak savannas and pine barrens by periodically clearing the forest's floor and encouraging flowering plant growth. Unfortunately, agriculture and land development have elsewhere caused most of the Karner's habitat to be destroyed.

The attractive males and females have their own special looks. The topside of a male's wings is colored deep sky blue. A female's wings are darker blue and brown on top, with orange, crescent-shaped spots on the edges of their hind wings. Underneath, both males and females are gray with a band of orange spots along the wing sides.

The Karner blue butterfly usually has two annual hatches. In April, the first group of caterpillars hatches from eggs that were laid the previous year. By mid-May, the caterpillars pupate. In late May or early June, they become adult butterflies. These adults mate, laying their eggs in June on or near wild lupine plants. Their eggs hatch approximately one week later, and the caterpillars feed for about three weeks. They then pupate, and the second generation of adult butterflies appears in July. These adults mate and lay eggs that will not hatch until the following spring.

Most Karner blues, especially the females, will stay near their home lupine patches during their five- to seven-day lives. Males may travel over a mile to find a new territory.

The beauty and rarity of the Karner blue makes it desirable to collectors. Today, fortunately, collection is illegal without a permit from the U.S. Fish and Wildlife Service.

In September 1999, the Wisconsin Department of Natural Resources and the U.S. Fish and Wildlife Service approved the Karner Blue Butterfly Habitat Conservation Plan, which allows Wisconsin land managers to continue operating in and around areas where the Karner blues are found, provided they modify activities to minimize the incidental "take" of the butterflies.

A better "take" of the Karner blues is one of the "take a look" variety. Watch for them in the Black River State Forest, near the wild lupine patches.

reminder of lives fully lived in what is now the Black River State Forest. Here, I stop to walk through the old Sullivan Cemetery, dating back to the 1800s. There are settlers here who came to farm — those who stayed and then passed away, rather than just passing through.

One of the stones I stop to read lists a birth date of 1854. How peaceful it must be to rest for a hundred years in a Wisconsin forest.

It is another unusual spot in a most extraordinary place.

An Industrious Nature

Some of these old stones in the Sullivan Cemetery have been here roughly since the time of the Civil War, and a certain air of spirituality comes from this. It was also at just about that time that this area was found to hold large stores of sphagnum moss.

Although sphagnum moss is no longer actively harvested in the forest, commercial processing of this "green gold" does still take place in Jackson County. In fact, this pocket of western Wisconsin is one of the largest production areas of sphagnum moss in the nation.

Sphagnum moss rejuvenates itself rapidly in the boggy and marshy peat areas of the Sand Counties after harvest. It is ready to be pulled again every three years. Because it can hold twenty times its weight in water, the moss is used to keep nursery plants and flowers alive during shipping and for hydroponic gardening. And because it is sterile, it can be used in surgical dressings and in seed germination to prevent fungus attacks.

If you travel anywhere in Jackson County from spring through the first freeze, you're sure to see moss being pulled and baled. More than three hundred thousand bales are pulled annually for shipment all over the world.

According to ecologist Eric Epstein, there are even more oddities of the flora variety here:

> There are a number of plants that occur in moist, sunny, sandy habitats in central Wisconsin that are most common in the Atlantic Coastal Plain of the Eastern United States but very limited in their distributions farther west. Yet you'll find many of these on the Black River State Forest. It's kind of an anomaly that you have these plants that are so disjunct from the core areas of their range.

For Eric, there are more "things-not-like-the-others" happenstances. One of them is the high representation in the forest of native prairie plants. Says Eric:

> Along the main stem of the Black River, there are a number of terraces that are just laced with springs and seepages, and these areas have a fantastically diverse flora. It's very unlike anything on other state or public lands in this part of Wisconsin. There are also a number of plants here that occur almost entirely in central Wisconsin but not in other parts of the state. Plant geographers still argue among themselves about why they're here, but it is probably related to some postglacial events that happened ten to twelve thousand years ago.

Traveling south from Dike 17, I stop at Pigeon Creek in the southern half of the main section of the forest. Here I come upon yet another unique industrious aspect to this forest — a cranberry bog. While the forest itself does not conduct any cranberry farming, there are some cranberry growers on private land within the boundaries of the state forest.

As with sphagnum moss, Wisconsin is one of the country's leading producers of cranberries. Annually, about 350 million pounds come from our state, or about 50 percent of the total U.S. cranberry crop.

Cranberries have been grown in Wisconsin since the mid-1850s. The time coincides with the date etched in my mind from seeing the stone in Sullivan Cemetery. In fact, it was settlers — seventeenth-century German and Dutch ones who arrived on the East Coast, where the berry also grows — who gave the cranberry its modern name. They thought that the pink blossom resembled the head of a crane and called them crane berries. Eventually the name was shortened to cranberry. In 2004, the cranberry was designated the Wisconsin state fruit.

The Story of an Understory

My second day in the Black River State Forest starts as the first day ended, with a gentle rain. Today, I'll hike the Norway Pine Trail in the south-central section of the forest. I'm hoping it is aptly named.

"We have a twenty-four-mile system of trails — hike, bike, and ski — that may be accessed from two trailheads," ranger Jamie Dahl tells me. "One is

A lush floor of ferns tells the understory story on the Norway Pine Trail.
John T. Andrews

the Wildcat Parking Lot on North Settlement Road and the other is the Smrekar Parking Lot on Smrekar Road. I think some of the most breathtaking scenery is in those two areas. From the trails, you can get up to the top of the bluffs and look out over a canopy of white pine trees. It's beautiful! Out on these trails, you feel like you're in the middle of nowhere. Backpackers report that they rarely see anyone else while camping in the forest," she says.

In addition to those twenty-four miles of trails, there are twenty miles of horseback-riding trails, fifty-one miles of snowmobile trails, and thirty-four miles of ATV and motor-cycle trails. "ATVs are big in this part of Wisconsin," says Jamie. "Our trails get a lot of use. There aren't many places where ATVers can ride, particularly in our adjoining states. I hear that a lot from our out-of-state ATVers."

But it is the cross-country ski trails that first called Jamie Dahl to the forest. It is said that the Black River's ski trails are some of Wisconsin's finest. Among snow-covered buttes and bluffs, competitive classic and skate skiers train and amateurs are challenged, all while being treated to vistas and overlooks of white-blanketed trees and frosty hills.

"I'll never forget the first time I cross-country skied in the Black River State Forest," laughs Jamie. "I'd go up one hill, ski down the other side, and still have enough momentum to get up the next hill. I couldn't believe it!"

Actually, that ski trip was the very first time Jamie visited the Black River State Forest. She explains:

In 1990, I was working as a ranger at Potawatomi State Park in Sturgeon Bay. That winter, a friend of mine and I went over to the Black River area to cross-country ski. I remember driving through the forest on our way to the trailhead parking lot, and I was just in awe: the snow-covered pines; the peacefulness; the remoteness of it all just off a busy highway. At the time, I didn't think that I'd ever get a chance to work here. When I was presented with the opportunity to transfer to this forest in 1993, I didn't even have to think twice about whether I would.

I set off on my hike on the Norway Pine Trail, a loop that begins from the Wildcat Parking Lot. The trail twists up and down several steep hills, and I can imagine how difficult this would be on skis in winter. But keeping on the rolling trail rewards me with an entry into a perfect, full, fern forest. Above me, the tall trees obliterate the clouds. I can hear the rain, but the drops can't find their way through to get to me below.

It seems I have stumbled into what Eric Epstein had told me about the forest: "Pine forests usually occur in dry, sandy places. But on the Black River, there are pine forests that develop on sites that are quite wet, often where there is an understory of wetland plants such as skunk cabbages, sphagnum moss, and robust ferns that can grow four, five, or even six feet high. That's a forest type that really doesn't occur in many places in the state. And it's by far more common on the Black River than on any other property that I've ever been on."

The Final Juxtaposition

You could pick from any of a number of things that make the Black River State Forest "not like the others" and a paradox: that it contains both glaciated and unglaciated terrain; that it is named for a river, but very little of it actually flows through the forest; that the Black River's color is red, not black; that there are birds, animals, and plants here that usually are found somewhere else; that spotting reptiles is just as likely to excite forest ecologists as seeing wolves; that there are marshes, flowages, and bogs as well as tall stands of trees; that there are records of lives here spanning only six days to those that reach back more than a hundred years.

Perhaps that's why everyone can pick out something in this forest that speaks to him or her. For Eric Epstein, it's the "geology, pines, and peat."

Law enforcement ranger Jamie Dahl and one of her closest forest friends.
Courtesy Wisconsin Department of Natural Resources

Adds Eric, "The fact that you have this very large area in central Wisconsin that is still relatively undeveloped with so much native vegetation is key; that plays an important part in maintaining so many of our native plants and animals, some of which you are very unlikely to see elsewhere in southern Wisconsin. There is a very significant diversity here of rare and common mammals, birds, reptiles, amphibians, and invertebrates."

For Jamie Dahl, the Black River State Forest is about its solitude and remoteness. "There are so many areas you can go to and really feel like you've gotten away," concludes Jamie. "Things are spread out enough so that you don't have to see anyone else if you don't want to."

And what does Aldo Leopold say? He, too, wrote of his Sand County farm on a June day, much like mine today: "Sometimes in June, when I see unearned dividends of dew hung on every lupine, I have doubts about the real poverty of the sands. On solvent farmlands lupines do not even grow, much less collect a daily rainbow of jewels. If they did, the weed-control officer, who seldom sees a dewy dawn, would doubtless insist that they be cut. Do economists know about lupines?"

I wonder. I know ecologists and forest rangers do. I turn up my collar against the summer rain that I know will find me once I am out of this forest, and I walk back out the way I came in.

The Castle Mound Nature Trail narrows between wet, cool rock and gnarled trunks of trees.
John T. Andrews

LOST AND FOUND IN THE FOREST

FORESTS ARE ENTICING PRECISELY BECAUSE you can get "lost" in them and forget about the pressures of daily, urban life. That kind of getting lost in nature restores our souls in immeasurable ways. But physically getting lost is more stressful than soothing. In forests such as the Black River, where scenic bluffs and a red river beg you to explore, it's especially easy to get off-track. But with two simple tools — a good map and a handheld compass — you can navigate almost anywhere.

For hundreds of years, people have walked through unknown terrain with only crudely drawn maps and magnetized needles floating on water to guide them. This early type of compass can be traced back as far as China's Qin Dynasty (221–206 BC). At that time, Chinese fortune-tellers frequently used a mineral form of black iron oxide found in Magnesia, a district in Asia Minor, to fabricate their prognosticating boards (one of the precursors of Ouija boards). The mineral — which aligns itself in a north-south direction oriented to the Earth's two magnetic poles when a magnetic field is applied to it, such as when it's struck by lightning — was given the name magnetite, derived from the location of its source.

Eventually, when it was realized that magnetite (or lodestone, the name given magnetized magnetite) was better at pointing out real directions than predicting the future, the first rudimentary compass was born: a piece of the mineral that pointed north-south when allowed free movement in a bowl of water.

Soon, flat bits of iron were used instead, which, when polarized by stroking them with magnetite, indicated a north-south direction. These iron "needles" did not keep their magnetism permanently, so a piece of magnetite was also carried to rub against the needle whenever the magnetism wore off.

The first recorded instance of a compass being used in Europe was around AD 1190. By the end of the thirteenth century, however, the English mounted the needle on a pin — rather than floating it in water — creating the basic design of the compass we use today.

The compass did not change much between the 1600s and 1800s. When European settlers came to Wisconsin, their compasses, made in France or Germany — or sometimes in one of the New England states — came with them.

Since the 1990s, civilians have been able to add another tool to the time-tested compass and map. The U.S. Department of Defense's Global Positioning System (GPS) operates a network of satellites orbiting the globe, continually transmitting microwave signals giving their location, speed, direction, and time. By locking into at least four of those signals with a GPS receiver, you can pinpoint within a few feet where you are anywhere on Earth. In dense forests, however, receiving signals can be a problem. Then, it's best to either head for an open area to try again, or — just like the state's first explorers and settlers — use a compass and map.

Most of Wisconsin's forests have loop trails, and by staying on them, you'll end up where you started. But carrying a map and a compass in your backpack — and knowing how to use them — can give you added peace of mind while you achieve peace of spirit.

Black River State Forest

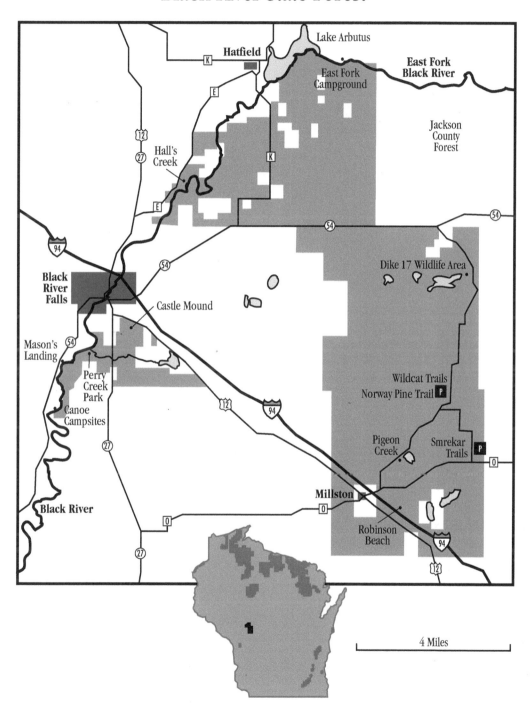

Lake Arbutus

Hatfield K

East Fork
Campground

**East Fork
Black River**

Jackson
County
Forest

Hall's
Creek

E

K

E

54

12
27

94

54

Dike 17 Wildlife Area

**Black
River
Falls**

Castle Mound

Mason's
Landing

54

Perry
Creek
Park

Wildcat Trails

Norway Pine Trail P

Canoe
Campsites

27

12

94

Smrekar
Trails P

0

Pigeon
Creek

Black River

Millston

0

0

Robinson
Beach

94

27

12

1

4 Miles

A continental divide causes the Bois Brule River
to run north into Lake Superior. *John T. Andrews*

2 Brule River State Forest

WRITING THE RIVER; WRITING THE WOODS

The Book

> *I am spending this beautiful, early spring day hiking several miles of the North Country National Scenic Trail.*
>
> *On this date twenty years ago, I put a backpack on for the first time in my life and began a seven-hundred-mile hike southward from Superior, Wisconsin, until I crossed the Wisconsin/Illinois border six weeks later at Dubuque. I have spent the last twenty years exploring the most remote areas of Wisconsin, Minnesota, and Michigan.*
>
> *I turned fifty years old this year, and I look forward to the next twenty years, experiencing places as lovely and historic as this!*

The entry was by a man from Superior, Wisconsin. He had written it into the Historic Brule to St. Croix Portage Trail logbook.

I'm sitting, in another spring, probably on the same spot where he had rested just a few years ago and put his thoughts down on paper. This section of the Historic Brule to St. Croix Portage Trail is part of the North Country National Scenic Trail, a 4,600-mile trek across seven northern states. When it is completed, the North Country will be the longest off-road hiking trail in the country, stretching from Upper New York State and ending in North Dakota. The man from Superior had chosen well — this certainly was an appropriate spot to celebrate twenty years of hiking.

There is a small bench here, constructed of wood, just at the crest of a hill. Across the path from the bench is a wooden post, with a small box nailed to

I take a moment to record my thoughts in the Historic Brule to St. Croix Portage Trail logbook.
John T. Andrews

the top. It looks a lot like a squirrel or bat house. Lifting the cover of the box, I reach inside to find the logbook — actually a spiral notebook — and a stub of a pencil. I carefully open the book and hold together its frayed pages that want to flutter away in the high winds on this hill. On the first page, there is a handwritten invitation to Brule River State Forest visitors. It asks them to stop here a while and write down their thoughts about the forest, about the world, about life.

I sit down and begin to leaf through the rest of the pages, jumping around from the beginning to the end to somewhere in the middle. I'm not searching for a chronology of visitors so much as a common feeling or experience of the forest that transcends specific days and months. The random thoughts and ramblings recorded here over recent years flit around, too, this way, just like the leaves of the quaking aspen shimmering and dancing in the trees surrounding me.

The Portage

Found just northeast of Solon Springs, Wisconsin, the narrow, two-mile Historic Brule to St. Croix Portage Trail is at least three centuries old. It runs between the St. Croix River and the Bois Brule River, and was once an important trade route between Lake Superior and the Mississippi River. Native Americans, trappers, traders, and missionaries once used this same track, carrying their canoes and baggage from the tip of the Bois Brule to Upper St. Croix Lake, or vice versa. The ancient path was first publicized by French

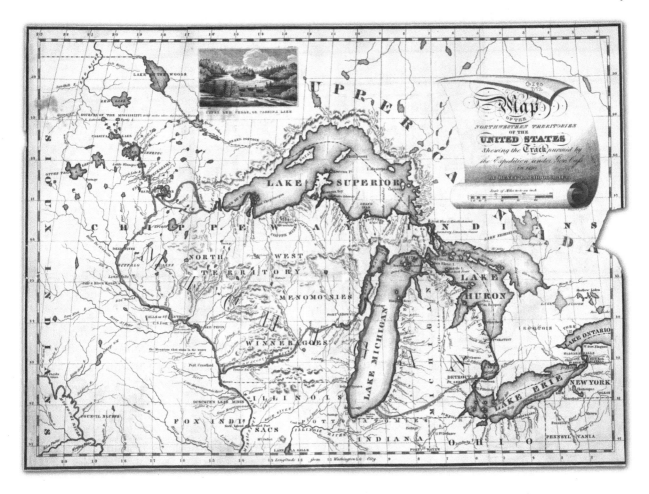

Henry Rowe Schoolcraft was one of seven great explorers who walked what is now the Historic Brule to St. Croix Portage Trail. Schoolcraft made this map in 1820, while searching for the source of the Mississippi River.
WHi Image ID 65966

explorer Daniel Greysolon, Sieur du Lhut, namesake of the city of Duluth, who wrote a record of his portage in 1680. The route then became so important to the French that they built forts at both ends for its protection.

The headwaters of the Bois Brule River spring from a large conifer bog forty-seven miles south of Lake Superior, while the St. Croix River originates half a mile southwest of the Bois Brule's beginnings in Upper St. Croix Lake. A continental divide between the two causes the St. Croix to flow south, eventually to join the Mississippi River, and from there to flow into the Gulf of Mexico. The same divide makes the Bois Brule River run north into Lake Superior, then into the other Great Lakes, through the St. Lawrence River, and then into the Atlantic Ocean. The two-mile portage trail connects these two great river systems.

I sit astride this continental divide as I ponder the trail logbook on the raw-boned bench on this breezy April day. Below my hill, the North Country National Scenic Trail falls away for sixteen miles through the forest, and from there on through into Minnesota and North Dakota. But my thoughts choose to keep following the Historic Brule to St. Croix Portage Trail, listed on both the Wisconsin Register of Historic Places and the National Register of Historic Places. From this high spot, it dips down to wind through bogs and then leads directly to the Bois Brule River.

The Bois Brule River cascades over rocks shadowed by tall stands of trees.
Candice Gaukel Andrews

Wild, Remote: The Brule

Described simply, the Brule River State Forest is where the Bois Brule River begins and ends. Only about twenty-six miles long north to south, the approximately 47,000-acre forest contains the entire forty-four miles of the moody river.

The river was called *Wiisaakode-ziibi*, meaning "a river through a half-burnt woods" in the Anishinaabe language (Ojibwe language group), which was translated into French as *bois brule* or "burnt wood." The Mascoutins, who are thought to have lived in the area in about 1600, were known as the "fire nation" or "people of fire," probably because the pine barrens through which the river flowed frequently caught fire. Today, forest has replaced most of those barrens, and the Bois Brule River is locally known as just "the Brule."

From its beginnings in the bog a little less than fifty miles south of Lake Superior, the Brule meanders gently for several miles downstream. The upper river, south of Highway 2, makes for an easygoing canoe trip, dropping just 3.5 feet per mile for the first twenty-six to thirty miles. On the four-hour river trip from Stones Bridge to Winneboujou (a name honoring an Ojibwe god), large cedars, spruces, tamaracks, and balsams shade dark pools in the river, where groundwater springs feed the cold, clear flow. The springs are

At Mays Ledges, you can walk out onto flat rocks into the rushing Bois Brule River, cascading between banks forested with aspens and balsam fir.
John T. Andrews

the result of earlier snowfalls and rains that fell on higher land, soaked in, and then found an underground route to the river. A few small rapids and a lake grace this part of the quiet Upper Brule.

Then the face of the river changes. It meets the Copper Range, a dramatic upthrust of volcanic rock, and drops sharply — 328 feet in the final eighteen miles (a drop of about eighteen feet per mile), with a hundred-foot drop occurring in just the three miles downstream from the Copper Range Campground.

Adventurous canoeists and kayakers who seek whitewater thrills like to tackle what is now known as the Lower Brule (from Copper Range Campground to Lake Superior). The river here carves its way through steep bluffs and red clay banks and cascades over rocks shadowed by tall stands of aspens, birches, and balsam fir. North of the Pine Tree Landing, a wild ride awaits.

The smelt run on Lake Superior usually takes place during the last two weeks of April. These smelt netters are taking advantage of its short peak, just after the ice goes out.
John T. Andrews

From there to the Highway 13 Landing, the river will put you through a nearly continuous run of riffles, rapids, and ledges.

In total, the north-flowing, forty-four-mile river drops 423 feet from its source to its mouth at Lake Superior. And even this is ever changing: the river flow (cubic feet per second) and water levels can fluctuate significantly. Winter snowmelt and spring and summer rains can raise the water flow and level quickly, creating fast and dangerous conditions. Many of the river's eighty-plus rapids (including some Class IV rapids, defined as "extremely difficult, requiring very strong paddling skills and the ability to quickly maneuver around obstructions and hazards") should be portaged by all but experts.

As the Bois Brule River finally empties into Lake Superior, it is surrounded by a boreal forest. As it slips into Superior's cold, blue depths, the river seems to change character again. This time, its steady, strong flow appears as a trickle against the great lake's vastness.

IN SEARCH OF THE HOLY STEELHEAD

FOR SOME, STEELHEAD FISHING IS NOTHING short of a religious experience, and a mecca for those anglers is the Bois Brule River. For more than a hundred years, these waters have called to fly fishermen from all over the world, experienced as well as amateur, famous — such as five U.S. presidents — and not.

Steelhead are a variety of rainbow trout. They were first brought from the Pacific Northwest and stocked in Wisconsin's Brule River in 1895. White-mouthed with a pinkish stripe on a black-spotted, silvery body, steelhead average about twenty inches in length and weigh from three to eight pounds.

According to Steve Petersen, former superintendent of the Brule River State Forest, "Steelheads are rainbow trout with a special lifestyle." They spend the first to third year of their lives in the Bois Brule River before migrating to Lake Superior, where they grow and mature. One to four years later, they return to the river to spawn. Unlike salmon, which die after spawning, steelhead rejuvenate and return to Lake Superior within three years to start the cycle all over again. "Some steelhead are able to spawn three or four times during their lifetimes," says Steve, "and they get big — really big."

That's why, during their spring spawning runs, steelhead offer top-notch fishing. From late March through May (with peak numbers occurring in early April), this hard-fighting game fish gives anglers a workout; steelhead are capable of gazellelike bounds in the air, torpedo-type runs, and crashes and thrashes on the red clay banks of the Brule.

The Brule River has been known as a trout fishing destination for more than a century. *WHi Image ID 2206*

In the fall, steelhead begin moving up into the Brule from Lake Superior, anywhere from mid-August to late November, with the largest runs usually occurring between mid-September and late October. The total Brule steelhead run, spring and fall, is between eight thousand and ten thousand fish. Salmon, brown trout, and brook trout also spawn in the Brule.

Every year, wildlife publications and outdoor magazines include the almost-obligatory fishing story on the Brule. And rumor has it that the ashes of many a fly fisherman have been spread over their beloved Bois Brule River. As fishing guide John Edstrom of the Headwaters Fly Fishing Company of Minnesota writes, "You fish other rivers to fill your ego. You fish the Brule to fill your soul."

Getting Away from Politics

I'm here, solo after my hiking pals had to go home (sad smiley face). I didn't — so this gorgeous stretch of trail that they didn't get to do, the dog and I did (happy smiley face).

Saw tons of grouse — and a bear being chased by hounds. Made it to Highway S — back now. Beautiful day.

In 1928, President Calvin Coolidge spent the summer fishing on the Brule River. Five U.S. presidents have fished the Brule.
WHi Image ID 44768

As I read this log entry, I am put in mind of others — famous people — who are often mentioned for having found this place "gorgeous" as well. Five U.S. presidents have fished the Brule's blue-ribbon trout waters: Ulysses Grant, Grover Cleveland, Calvin Coolidge, Herbert Hoover, and Dwight Eisenhower. I can't help but notice that the last of them left office in 1961, about the time that the majority of homes in the country started to contain a television set. That event seems to coincide with the time when presidents, like many children, stopped going outdoors for recreation. But Calvin Coolidge didn't have that diversion. It is said that he was so in love with the Brule that in 1928, four miles from Stones Bridge at Cedar Island Estate resort, he spent the summer and essentially relocated the White House there for the season. The Brule's "sound bite" for the past several decades has thus been "the River of Presidents."

But another man in politics who loved the Brule fires my imagination even more. I can see him, in my mind's eye, standing on the shores of this river holding a fishing rod, even more clearly than I can see a leader of the Free World here, dressed in fishing gear.

"My dad, Reino A. Perala, was a blind attorney from Superior who was also in the Wisconsin legislature," says Ron Perala, whose family has lived on the banks of the Bois Brule River since the early 1950s. "And he loved to fish. I remember a time back in the 1970s when we were fishing in front of our cabin here on the river. He made one cast, and he got a seven-pound steelhead. He said to me, 'I'm going to take this fish up to the cabin, have breakfast, and then maybe I'll come down again,'" recalls Ron. "About an hour later, my dad walks back to the river, makes one cast, and gets another steelhead — this one about eight pounds. He was remarkable," laughs Ron.

I ask Ron how his father, being blind, could fish so proficiently. After all, a pair of steelhead like this is a banner day for any fisherman.

"I think with him it was just desire," concludes Ron. "My dad had this *sisu*. Do you know what that is? It's a Finnish term that roughly translated means 'a fierce determination.' Being that he was handicapped, he compensated by developing this strength of will to succeed in whatever he wanted to do," says Ron. "He just *believed* he knew where to cast. And very seldom did he get his lure snagged on something. He ran on his own."

The forest itself also got up and running in the 1950s, after a much earlier start. In 1907, Frederick Weyerhauser, who had previously logged the area under the name of his Nebagamon Lumber Company, donated the initial

The forest got its start in 1907 when Frederick Weyerhauser, who had previously logged the area under the name of his Nebagamon Lumber Company, donated the initial acreage to the state.

John T. Andrews

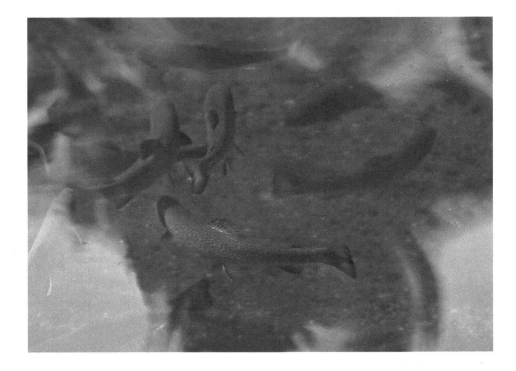

The trout at Bois Brule State Fish Hatchery are stocked in the Brule and other northern Wisconsin rivers.
John T. Andrews

4,320 acres to the state. But the forest wasn't officially established until 1932, and it took until 1959 to encompass the entire Bois Brule River.

Today, the Brule River State Forest protects the wild and remote nature of the Brule for all of us. In addition to the river and almost twenty-three miles of the North Country National Scenic Trail, the forest contains eight miles of frontage on Lake Superior, five State Natural Areas, and the Bois Brule State Fish Hatchery.

Wisconsin fishermen say there are only two types of trout rivers: "the Brule, and all the rest." Five U.S. presidents, apparently, would agree.

Bears on the Brule

Ron tells me another favorite story about his dad. "One time my father was fishing, and he could hear that there were some other people fishing close by," he begins. "My dad thought that a dog, perhaps belonging to the people next to him, had come up to see him. He called out to the dog to come close enough so that he could pet it, but he sensed the dog running away. So my dad walked

THE PRECARIOUSLY POISED WISCONSIN DEER

A belt of open farmlands that interweaves the forest supports one of the highest deer populations in northern Wisconsin.
John T. Andrews

WHITE-TAILED DEER MAY BE THE MOST powerful, graceful, and adaptable creatures on earth. They can leap seven-foot fences from a standstill, bound away on taut, muscular legs in a flash, and melt into the forest foliage right before your eyes.

Prior to hunting season, the Wisconsin deer population numbers between 1.3 and 1.8 million. If you live here — or if you're a Wisconsin forest — you can't help but be affected by them, especially if you are the Brule River State Forest, where a productive deer herd exists.

Before European settlement, this area had fewer deer. But with the clearing of agricultural lands adjacent to our great forests, favorable white-tailed habitat increased: deer like "living on the edge," savoring the abundant food of open croplands while depending on the shelter of woods. In more recent years, other factors have contributed to the growing herds: milder winters, baiting and feeding, and more and more land going into private ownership, reducing hunter access.

Deer in great numbers change a forest's ecology. At a density of twelve to fifteen deer per square mile,

(continued on next page)

over to the people and started talking to them. He said, 'Whose dog was that?' And one of the guys said, 'That wasn't a dog. That was a black bear!'"

It's hard to visit the Brule River State Forest and not run into any wildlife. Black bears, timber wolves, and deer populate the three distinct ecological land types here: the Lake Superior clay plain (with species such as aspens and balsam fir), the Mille Lacs upland (containing basswoods, sugar maple, and red oak), and the Bayfield sand plain (with plantations of red pine and jack pine as well as scrub oak). And a belt of open farmlands interweaving the three almost ensures that the Upper Brule valley will have one of the highest deer populations in northern Wisconsin. During my explorations of the Brule, I saw many deer haunting this northern forest. Often my early morning hikes and dusky drives were watched by dark deer eyes, and I could see that some of the surrounding uplands were heavily browsed.

THE PRECARIOUSLY POISED WISCONSIN DEER

(continued from page 37)

herbaceous plants, such as showy lady's slippers and white-fringed orchids, decline. At twenty to twenty-five per square mile, pines, oaks, hemlocks, and white cedar may stop regenerating. And at thirty-five deer per square mile, many bird species dwindle from lack of ground cover. Simply put, too many deer threaten a healthy forest.

Currently, the primary method for keeping the deer herd at carrying capacity (the maximum number of deer that can survive on the land under average habitat and weather conditions) is recreational hunting. Though Wisconsin hunters have harvested an average of three hundred thousand to four hundred thousand deer per year, the herd's ability to proliferate is sometimes still greater.

The return of Wisconsin's timber wolves, another deer predator, engenders as much controversy as the deer numbers themselves do. While Wisconsin

Department of Natural Resource studies show that wolves have only a limited impact on the size of the deer herd — and that wolves may help reduce over-browsing of forest lands and the spread of disease in the herd by eliminating sick and injured animals from the population — lots of deer make possible the sport of deer hunting, whose participants annually buy $900 million worth of goods and services, additionally creating close to $133 million in state and local tax revenue. Too, more than two million Wisconsinites are wildlife watchers, and two-thirds of them say that white-tailed deer are their favorites. Yearly, they spend about $500 million on their hobby.

Obviously, deer have a very complex relationship with our forests and with us. Toeing a line between the harmful ecological and biological effects they have on forests and the positive economic and aesthetic benefits they provide is the precarious spot we ask them to negotiate on their elegant limbs.

Deer, along with the forest's snowshoe hares and ruffed grouse, love the leaves, buds, and twig ends of quaking aspen, Wisconsin's most important paper-producing tree. Their spade-shaped leaves are carried on long, flat stems, keeping the foliage in constant motion with the slightest breeze. Forests, the lumber industry, and deer have a complicated, intricate relationship — as interwoven as the woodlands, bogs, and farmlands are in the Brule. It doesn't surprise me that we even have an economic slang term regarding deer: *buck* originated with the custom of using deerskins as currency, with one skin having a value of roughly one dollar in trade.

Like deer, ruffed grouse love to eat the leaves of the quaking aspen. In spring, you can hear the males drumming their wings on logs, increasing the cadence to attract females and doing their best to proclaim their territories. In fall, the music of the forest changes from the drumbeats of grouse to the trumpeting of migrating geese. And in winter, the sopranos take over as bald eagles screech overhead. The snowy owls remain silent, drifting soundlessly on some of the longest wings in North America.

It's possible to see more than 180 bird species in this very linear forest. Even a partial listing reads like the checked-off register in a birder's journal: ovenbirds; rose-breasted grosbeaks; red-eyed vireos; thrushes; black-backed, three-toed, and pileated woodpeckers; boreal chickadees; upland sandpipers; saw-whet owls; great blue herons; kingfishers; red-breasted nuthatches; winter wrens; golden-crowned and ruby-crowned kinglets; northern parulas; golden-winged, Nashville, Backburnian, and chestnut-sided warblers; and ravens.

Beavers, river otters, and muskrats cling to their native shores here, while coyotes, foxes, and fishers move through the forest. Rare wood turtles trek along the sandy shores of Lake Superior at the top of the forest, and the elusive bobcats, which prey on the abundant snowshoe hares, leave tracks in the snow — as do the wolves.

"I'm happy the wolves are here," says Ron Perala about the controversial canid. "I'd like to see all the animals that were originally here in the forest come back." Ron holds this feeling, even though a wolf may have killed one of his much-loved Saint Bernards.

"I assumed a wolf killed the dog," says Ron. "But there was no proof. It was our fault for letting the dog get loose. My wife took our two dogs for a walk on the river. The two bolted for some reason, and then only one came

BACK IN THE BRULE: TIMBER WOLVES

THE LONG, EERIE HOWL on the wind. The quick, dark shadow through the trees. The "fierce green fire" in wild eyes that Aldo Leopold once wrote about. All of these sensory descriptions immediately call to mind only one thing: wolves.

No other animal in Wisconsin signifies its wilderness areas more or strikes in our hearts a deeper connection to the primordial world. Wolves and Wisconsin have been together since the time the glaciers melted; by 1800, as many as five thousand may have lived in

Wolves are the iconic symbol of the Wisconsin wilderness. *Gary Kramer/USFWS*

what is now the state. But because of a fear that wolves were killing too many deer, a territorial bounty law on wolves was passed in 1839 and a state bounty law was passed in 1865. The last of Wisconsin's wolves were killed by 1960.

However, gray wolves (*Canis lupus*), also referred to as timber wolves, have made a remarkable comeback: about seven hundred now call Wisconsin home again, and some of those reside in the Brule River valley. Currently, they are concentrated in five packs, with an average of three to six adult members each in spring: Casey Creek, Lake Nebagamon, Moreland Lake, Orienta Falls, and Muck Lake packs.

While the likelihood of seeing one of these powerful, mysterious, and elusive creatures is slim, hearing them or finding evidence of them can be just as chill inducing. Wolf tracks are most easily spotted on freshly fallen snow; but in the Brule River State Forest, you

could discover them on the sandy roads south of U.S. Highway 2.

The tracks of wolves and coyotes are different from dog tracks in that they are generally in "direct registration," meaning that the hind feet step in the same line as the front feet. But wolf tracks usually dwarf those of coyotes. The average pad size in wolves is 4.5 inches long (including the claws) and 3.5 inches wide. A coyote's pad measures about 2.75 inches long (with the claws) and 1.5 inches wide. Wolves stand two and a half feet at the shoulder and weigh fifty to one hundred pounds; coyotes are about half that size.

If you should hear a wolf howl in the Brule River State Forest, resist the temptation to howl back. Heard up to five miles away, wolf howls serve as a long-distance defense system, allowing packs to announce their locations to prevent accidental meetings, which often result in harm to their families and food supply. On the other hand, wolves have to weigh the dangers of howling back, revealing their whereabouts. Thus, howling by people can interrupt the intricacies of wolf communication and inadvertently make a negative impact on a pack.

Do wolves really howl at the moon? Researchers say the phase of the moon doesn't affect howl rates at all. But the image of a wolf with his neck stretched up in full moonlight on the banks of the Bois Brule River is one of those sensory images we should never let go of — just like the wolves themselves, ever again.

back. There was a lot of wolf sign around, so I just assumed that's what happened. But I never did find my dog. He didn't have very good teeth, so he wouldn't have been able to defend himself," says Ron.

If it was a wolf, it could have been a loner, or a member of the Casey Creek pack, one of several packs currently in the forest.

The Old Bayfield Road Trail

A place to ponder. What measure of people who came before us! Some stopped to live here and survived, others kept following those who knew the way. Some crossed the continent, the St. Lawrence River, the Hudson Bay, the McKenzie River, the Fraser River, and the Gulf of Mexico.

The ravens still call as they did then, and I hear them as I write. I know the wolves still hunt here as they did before. Of those people, inhabitants and travelers, I would like to think that there is still some of them in us.

What was the measure of those people, as this log writer asks? They were tough. There's no question when you look at the Brule River State Forest. Then as now, this area was bears and wolves; thick woods and raging waters; cold Lake Superior winters and cool valley-floor summers.

It was the ghost of a mine and a miners' camp on the Historic Bayfield Road Hiking and Snowshoe Trail that I was soon to encounter that made me ponder the toughness of this forest and the people who braved it. Is there some of them yet still in us — in me?

Today I have resolved to walk that 2.25-mile trail, a thickly wooded path that partially follows the route of the first road between Superior and Bayfield built in 1870, which was replaced by a railroad in 1885. A few boardwalks help today's hikers along the course, a luxury those in the 1800s didn't have. They, I'm sure, had to hack and slog their way through, when the forest often took back what they were trying to carve out.

About half a mile into the trail, I pass the old Percival mine, sectioned off by a small fence. Old newspaper reports indicate that in 1845 someone reported a copper vein only fifteen feet down from the surface. It is presumed that the American Fur Company, under John Jacob Astor, hauled steam-driven drills and pumps here but failed to locate the mineral. Later newspaper articles mentioned that the mine was being worked again in the 1860s through 1899 and was producing "promising" amounts of copper. Today the shaft that once stretched down ninety feet is all but lost in the undergrowth.

I cross a small stream and look for the foundations of the miners' quarters, which I'm supposed to be able to see, but they have been quietly reclaimed by the conifers. This forest is tough.

The trail eventually leaves the old Bayfield Road route to climb to the top of Sugar Camp Hill. At the top of the hill, I lose the trail completely. It's close to 80 degrees on this April day here, and I've worked up a good sweat. Luckily, at the top of the hill are the Clevedon Fire Tower and a small clearing surrounding its base. Here, at least, I am able to get a look around, and I pause to retrieve my bearings.

Just as I determine that the correct way to go to pick up the trail would be to walk down the gravel road leading out from the fire tower on the other side of the clearing, a Wisconsin Department of Natural Resources ranger in the tower's cab at the top yells down to me that I'm going the wrong way. The risk of fire was high that day, and he had climbed the tower for a look around. After directing me to get off the road and go back into the woods to follow the blue paint marks on the trees, he reports that he can see a fire burning, just twenty miles away.

A Place Lost in Time

I could feel it then. In the Brule — despite the fact that today almost all fire surveillance is conducted from airplanes — you can actually still run into a lookout in a fire tower. Not only was I lost in place, but in time.

"The Brule River State Forest feels like a forest from thirty years ago," Steve Petersen, the Brule's former forest superintendent, had told me before I came to visit. "It's at that kind of pace. It's about primitive camping, hand pumps, and pit toilets." Yes, this forest is tougher than some of its Wisconsin brothers.

Ron Perala would place the forest even farther back. "Most people come to the forest to fish," he says. "But I like to walk on the Lake Superior beach, between the cliffs and the world's largest lake. I like looking for fossil rocks that the glacier brought here from Canada. It's a pretty sweet place to be," he says.

In between the forest time frames of Ron Perala and Steve Petersen, I remember the small boulders I saw on the Historic Brule to St. Croix Portage

Trail. There were seven stones, each with the name of a former trail traveler, people such as Daniel Greysolon, Sieur du Lhut, who wrote about his journey here in 1680; English cartographer Jonathan Carver, who passed through in 1768; and Henry Schoolcraft, the man credited with discovering the source of the Mississippi River, who walked by in 1820.

Tomorrow, I'm going to go back to that trail and open the logbook one more time. I'll take out the short, stubby pencil and write:

I came up to northern Wisconsin this weekend from the Madison area. I wanted to find out what the Brule River State Forest was all about. I got lost. In time, in place.

But I think I found something, too. The story — the soul — of this forest here, on this spot.

Thank you, to all of you woods walkers, who took the time to write.

Brule River State Forest

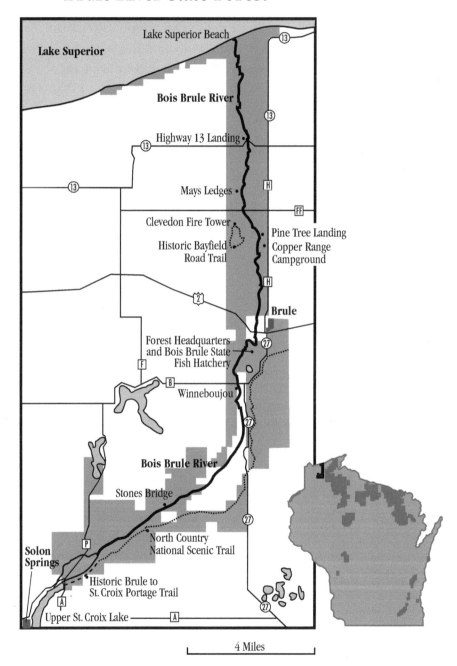

Lake Superior

Lake Superior Beach

13

Bois Brule River

13

Highway 13 Landing

13

13

Mays Ledges

H

FF

Clevedon Fire Tower

Pine Tree Landing
Copper Range
Campground

Historic Bayfield
Road Trail

H

2

Brule

Forest Headquarters
and Bois Brule State
Fish Hatchery

27

F

B

Winneboujou

27

Bois Brule River

Stones Bridge

Solon
Springs

P

North Country
National Scenic Trail

27

Historic Brule to
St. Croix Portage Trail

A

Upper St. Croix Lake

A

27

4 Miles

A young tree stands in a patch of sunlight, new growth in the wild, remote Brule River State Forest. *John T. Andrews*

Manny Stein got to see the forest from a bird's-eye perspective from perches such as the Fifield Fire Lookout Tower, now on the National Register of Historic Places. *John T. Andrews*

3 Chequamegon-Nicolet National Forest– Chequamegon Land Base: Eastern and Southern Regions

FOREST FOOTPRINTS

Alone, Above the Treetops

Manny Stein was totally alone, just sitting and watching. He was at work, and that's all he could do, really. That's all his boss would allow him to do.

"I was a lookout in the Chequamegon fire towers in the 1950s and 1960s," explains Manny by phone. I had called him after reading a newspaper story about an upcoming ceremony the U.S. Forest Service planned to hold in the Chequamegon-Nicolet National Forest. According to the article, Manny and his sister, Betty, would be in attendance at the September 2006 commemoration for the Fifield Fire Lookout Tower in the eastern region of the forest's Chequamegon Land Base. Betty had been a fire tower lookout, too, and the brother-and-sister pair promised to be some of the prime storytellers at the shindig.

"When I first started as a lookout," says Manny, "it was pretty much a no-no to take up a book or a radio or any of that stuff. You were supposed to be watching for smoke, and that's it."

The whole idea of being a lookout intrigued me: working in a dense, green, natural setting surrounded by precious solitude day in and day out, and seeing the forest from a bird's-eye perspective that most of us will never be able to arrange. But while a job where you're paid to just sit and watch sounds like a breeze to me, Manny quickly corrected my thinking. Watching for hours in a forest fire tower with absolutely no distractions is a bit harder than it sounds. And breezes were just one of many challenges.

"The wind constantly whistles through those towers, the tin, and the antenna," says Manny with an eerie tone in his voice when I ask him to tell me what a typical day was like up there. "It was kind of a weary sound, you know? You couldn't get away from it. Very seldom do you have a calm day at one hundred feet above the ground. You kind of had to talk to yourself and tell yourself to ignore it. If you let it get to you psychologically, it would start to bother you."

The more Manny talked about the lonesome, moaning steel giants in the forest and the tricks they liked to play, the more I got bothered. I had to go and see the Fifield Fire Lookout Tower — and Wisconsin's only national forest — for myself.

An Unfamiliar Vastness

There is something a little unsettling when you first come face-to-face with the breadth of this forest. The total acreage of the Chequamegon side of the combined Chequamegon-Nicolet National Forest is a vast 849,000 acres, with the isolated eastern portion accounting for 150,000 of them. State Highway 70 takes you right through the heart of this region. Totally alone is how I am — and I'm not even in a tower.

The two-lane highway runs like a straight cut through tall, beefy trees on either side — for miles and miles and miles and miles. Although I know that just beyond these trees there must be trails and tracks, raccoons and ruffed grouse, squirrels and snowshoe hares, black bears and white-tailed deer, I can see nothing but the trees and the road even on this January day when the woods should be more bare. I am forlorn. And *forlorn* isn't a word I've used or even thought of for a very long time.

I feel what Manny was talking about, even from ground level. I can see how getting lost alone in this forest or having your car suffer a mechanical break-down somewhere on this stretch of asphalt could, after a few hours, start to play with your mental state.

The Tower

Although the Chequamegon and Nicolet forests were once separate entities, they were officially joined as the Chequamegon-Nicolet National Forest for administrative purposes in February 1998. When speaking of them, the U.S. Forest Service either uses the combined official name or refers to them as the Chequamegon Land Base and the Nicolet Land Base.

Of the thirty-eight original fire lookout towers built in the 1930s in the Chequamegon-Nicolet National Forest, only nine remain today. Seven stand in the Chequamegon, and two are left in the Nicolet. They are:

- Clam Lake Fire Lookout Tower (Sawyer County, Clam Lake vicinity)
- Fifield Fire Lookout Tower (Price County, Fifield vicinity)
- Iron River Fire Lookout Tower (Bayfield County, Iron River vicinity)
- Jump River Fire Lookout Tower (Taylor County, Westboro vicinity)
- Laona Fire Lookout Tower (Nicolet National Forest, Forest County, Laona vicinity)
- Long Mile Fire Lookout Tower (Bayfield County, Grand View vicinity)
- Mountain Fire Lookout Tower (Nicolet National Forest, Oconto County, Mountain vicinity; interpreted and open to the public)
- Perkinstown Fire Lookout Tower (Taylor County, Perkinstown vicinity)
- West Fork Fire Lookout Tower (Sawyer County, Hayward vicinity)

Typically one hundred feet high, these forest overseers were constructed on the highest points to ensure that smoke could be seen over the treetops.

My journey today along Highway 70 leads me to the Fifield Fire Lookout Tower, just five miles east of the town of Fifield. Manny Stein worked here many hours. This tower was built in 1932, when wildfires, fueled by logging debris, raged across the cutover forests of northern Wisconsin. The metal giant's frail and slender appearance is deceiving; she's made of galvanized steel. Metal brace-supports between her skinny legs allow her to bend and sway to the music of a strong wind, keeping her from breaking off at the base. A small, seven-foot square lookout cab at the top has a pyramid-shaped, steel roof, a wooden floor, and 360-view windows.

I stand dead center, just beneath the tower, and throw my head back as far as I can to look straight up. I feel like a child watching a balloon that was accidentally let go, rise into the upper atmosphere. I know I could never climb up this behemoth. Manny had told me, "Not everybody can. Some of the new lookouts-in-training would get twenty feet off the ground, and their legs would start to shake. Some of them just couldn't do it and had to give up." I knew I would have been among them.

The ones, like Manny, who did get to the top, though, would watch all day for signs of smoke. In the early years, lookouts in the towers communicated with the ground-level ranger stations by a single-wire telephone system. The wire ran through the woods or alongside the roads and was fastened to trees; reminiscent, I think, of the two-tin-cans-and-a-long-string science experiment running between the backyard of one child's home and that of his or her best friend's. The Federal Communications Commission approved the use of ultra-high frequency radios in 1938, and the old technique soon fell by the wayside.

The Fifield Fire Lookout Tower was in operation until the 1970s, when all of the Chequamegon's towers were closed. Today, airplanes conduct fire surveillance, and pilots replace the forest service lookouts. There are vestiges once in a while, though, of humanity still within the steel skeletons. The Wisconsin Department of Natural Resources occasionally staffs some of the towers during peak fire season.

The Fifield Fire Lookout Tower is now listed on the National Register of Historic Places.

The Creation of Wisconsin's National Forests

There are 155 national forests in the United States, and the 1.5-million-acre Chequamegon-Nicolet is one of them. The Chequamegon Land Base consists of three, noncontiguous sections. The eastern portion, which contains the Fifield Fire Lookout Tower, is in Price County, with a bit of overage in Vilas County. The southern section lies in Taylor County; and the northern part is located in Bayfield, Ashland, and Sawyer Counties (see chapter 4).

By the mid-1920s, the great pines and profitable hardwoods of Wiscon-

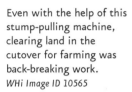

Even with the help of this stump-pulling machine, clearing land in the cutover for farming was back-breaking work.
WHi Image ID 10565

sin's once-mighty Northwoods forests were almost gone. Farmers had tried to make a living on the land cleared by the loggers, but most of them failed. By 1927, almost 25 percent of the land in Wisconsin's northern counties had become tax delinquent. This, with the dwindling timber supply and growing unemployment, convinced state leaders that the forests needed to be restored and protected if they were ever going to be profitable again. Legally establishing national forests would mean jobs for the neighboring communities and a benefit for local governments: they would receive 25 percent of the gross receipts from the sale of forest resources, with an additional 10 percent for road construction.

In 1925, the state passed the Wisconsin Enabling Act, giving the federal government permission to purchase, control, and administer Wisconsin state lands as national forests. The act limited purchases to one hundred thousand acres and required approval of purchase areas by the governor, the Wisconsin Board of Commissioners of Public Lands, and the Wisconsin Conservation Commission (precursor to the Wisconsin Department of Natural Resources). Three subsequent amendments raised the limit: in 1927 to five hundred thousand acres; in 1929 to one million; and in 1933 to two million acres. The 1933

Restoring Wisconsin's National Forests: The "Soil Soldiers"

Twenty-eight million Americans — 20 percent of the workforce — were jobless in 1932. Soon after President Franklin Roosevelt took office in January 1933, he introduced his "New Deal" to Congress. Among other goals was the restoration of six hundred million acres of forested land, under the auspices of the Emergency Conservation Work program, which evolved into the Civilian Conservation Corps in 1937.

Within four months, 275,000 young men had signed up for work in the nation's parks and forests. Ninety percent were between the ages of eighteen and twenty-five (age limits changed to seventeen and twenty-eight in 1935), unmarried, and from families on relief. Enlistment lasted for a six-month period, but additional six-month terms for up to a maximum of two years were allowed.

The U.S. Army provided clothes, food, housing, and medical care for the enrollees, while the U.S. Forest Service administered the work program. In addition, the workers received thirty dollars per month, twenty-five of which was sent directly to their families.

After basic training at a "conditioning camp," the CCC "boys" (known also as "Roosevelt's Tree Army" or "Soil Soldiers") were sent to a work camp near their assigned project. From April to October 1933, the Wisconsin national forests had twenty-one CCC camps. By the time the CCC had peaked, the Chequamegon included twenty-seven camps, with about two hundred men per camp, and the Nicolet contained twenty-three camps. During the almost ten years that it was active, the CCC constructed hundreds of roads and recreation areas, and improved thousands of fish and wildlife habitats. Pines planted by the CCC are providing bank stabilization in the Chequamegon-Nicolet National Forest yet today.

amendment also added the county board of each county in which a purchase area was located to the approval process.

In December 1928, the U.S. Forest Service, a branch of the U.S. Department of Agriculture, bought lands in Oneida, Forest, Vilas, Bayfield, Ashland, Taylor, and Price Counties and designated them the Moquah, Flambeau, and Oneida Purchase Units. The service added the Mondeaux and Chequamegon Purchase Units in May 1931. One year later, the Oconto Purchase Unit was created and the Oneida Purchase Unit was expanded. On March 2, 1933, President Herbert Hoover officially proclaimed the units to be the "Nicolet National Forest." In July 1933, the forest was split into "Nicolet East" (which later became the Nicolet National Forest) and "Nicolet West" (what subsequently developed into the Chequamegon National Forest).

The reason Wisconsin's national forest lands are not contiguous is that they were bought at different times from different sellers and not created from large blocks of public land. To manage them, these purchased parcels were

Restoring Wisconsin's National Forests: The "Soil Soldiers"

Like the CCC, the Works Progress (later Projects) Administration provided labor for national forest work. Established in 1935, the WPA held to a minimum age of eighteen, but there was no maximum age, and employment was limited to one person per family, usually the family head.

The Medford ranger station was one of the projects in the southern section of the Chequamegon that both CCC and WPA workers helped construct. Between 1934 and 1935, they built the office, a warehouse, an oil house, and a dwelling. The enrollees completed the rough construction work, with carpenters doing the finish work. From 1937 to 1941, the CCC built the station's stone terraces and planted its lawns, shrubs, and trees.

As the nation prepared for World War II, however, the need for relief programs lessened. By 1941 the last of the fifty Civilian Conservation Corps camps in the Chequamegon-Nicolet National Forest — located at Perkinstown in the southern section of the Chequamegon — closed. On June 30, 1943, Congress officially shut down the WPA and CCC. In total, the CCC had employed 92,094 men at Wisconsin camps, with sixty-four thousand of them from Wisconsin.

THE CCC — A YOUNG MAN'S OPPORTUNITY
to work
to live
to learn
to build
— and to conserve our National Resources

The Civilian Conservation Corps gave young men good jobs and a chance to help restore our forests. *WHi Image ID 5762*

subdivided into ranger districts, located in towns that were situated near the portion of the forest administered by that district. Today there are five ranger districts. The Nicolet National Forest, with its headquarters in Rhinelander, was divided into the Eagle River-Florence Ranger District and the Lakewood-Laona Ranger District. The Chequamegon National Forest was divided into the Great Divide Ranger District and the Washburn Ranger District in the northern section, and the Medford-Park Falls Ranger District in the southern and eastern regions. The Chequamegon's headquarters is in Park Falls.

Around the Round Lake Logging Dam

While fire lookout towers and their companion fires seem to have given the eastern portion of the Chequamegon the look of a land walked by the last of a breed of metal colossuses, there is another earth-element that can't be counted out when defining this place: water.

Back across Highway 70 away from Fifield, at the other end of Chequamegon's eastern forest parcel, is Round Lake. In the 1870s, this area was full of winter's hardy loggers and spring's agile river men.

In the late nineteenth century, with one-sixth of all the white pine growing west of the Appalachian Mountains, Wisconsin was producing billions of board feet of lumber. Around Round Lake in winter, the forest echoed with the long, drawn-out shouts of "T-I-M-B-E-R!" Horse-drawn sleighs on roads of ice hauled freshly cut pine logs to the lakeshore to await the spring thaw.

When the ice on the South Fork of the Flambeau River began to break up,

Originally constructed in 1878, the Round Lake Logging Dam stands strong again, restored with its historic timbers and original iron hardware.
Candice Gaukel Andrews

With log-mark hammers like this one, workers pounded their camp's mark into the cut ends of logs, making sorting logs easier at the end of a drive.
Courtesy Wisconsin Historical Museum

the logs could begin their journey downstream to Chippewa River and Mississippi River mills. Lumberjacks stamped end marks on every log to ensure that they were accounted to the correct lumber company.

Wooden turnstiles on the Round Lake Logging Dam once unleashed a pure power from the wilds of this forest.
John T. Andrews

Originally constructed in 1878, the wooden Round Lake Logging Dam was one of about a hundred dams that harnessed the power of the Chequamegon's lakes. At the dam, hand-cranked gears wound chains to raise the sluice gates. Balancing themselves on a timber frame, men pike-poled logs through the sluiceway into the holding pond. Once the holding pond had filled with logs, the gates were shut. Spring lake levels rose behind the dam to create a ten-foot head of water.

During the spring river drive, men cranked the turnstiles open, and the floodgates released a thunderous explosion of water. As the shallow South Fork of the Flambeau flooded, the logs were herded and flushed to the next dam twelve miles downriver, the Sugar Bush Dam, where another burst of power propelled the logs on to Fifield. There, the river widened. Logs from the South Fork of the Flambeau were joined by those from the North Fork, and by other logs from tributaries of the Chippewa. Sure-footed and daredevil "drivers" guided these "rafts" of logs to the mills.

I hear no shouts around Round Lake on my January day here. The forest is quiet. I take my time walking the Round Lake Logging Dam Interpretive Trail. Crossing the dam, I stop to touch the wooden turnstiles that were once so capable of unleashing a forceful, pure power; of harnessing just a little bit of the wild nature of this forest. About ten years ago, this dam was rebuilt using its historic timbers and original iron hardware. It stands here strong again, but — like the forest on this winter day — silent this time around; a keeper, no doubt, of many untold logging and river-drive stories.

A Land Called Leopold

Those stories may be lost forever. But farther south in the Chequamegon, another man's story is well told.

Aldo Leopold is one of my heroes. A professor and the chair of game management in the Agricultural Economics Department at the University of Wisconsin–Madison from 1933 to 1948, he outlined a "land ethic" before anyone else and inspired a conservation conscience long before Al Gore and "going-green" advocates. His book *A Sand County Almanac* has been read by millions of people around the world.

Leopold loved to walk in the early morning across the open landscape on his farm near Baraboo. These walks informed his writings on nature. Walking the southern Chequamegon's Aldo Leopold Interpretive Trail, you become a little closer to the man and the land.

"A thing is right when it tends to preserve the integrity, stability, and beauty of the biotic community. It is wrong when it tends otherwise," wrote Leopold, according to one of the trail's interpretive signs. Hiking on this esker near the Mondeaux Dam, I can't help but take a page from Leopold's book and try to blend poetic prose with my own observations of the natural world I see around me here:

> Broken stumps, gnarled roots, and tangles of shed bark from once-tall trees jut up from the frozen surface of the flowage below me. They are the bones of long-ago, robust, living organisms, still beautiful in their stark-ness and in the statements they still make on this forest community. And the thing they say is right: "Like me, you, too, have passed this way and now are part of us."

From Leopold, again: "It is fortunate, perhaps, that no matter how intently one studies the hundred little dramas of the woods and meadows, one can never learn all of the salient facts about any one of them."

I may not know the salient facts. I don't know if Aldo Leopold ever walked here in the Chequamegon. But his words are present, just as surely as the essence of what he believed in thrives.

A Bear Named Smokey

Aldo Leopold once served as forest supervisor of the Carson National Forest in New Mexico. But he is not the only New Mexico persona whose influence can be felt in Wisconsin's Chequamegon today.

By the early 1900s, a tremendous tide of lumberjacks had completely scoured Wisconsin's central and northern forests of its timber, demanded by the state's growing furniture, paper, and tanning industries (see chapter 14 for more on tanning industry history in our state). The fellers left in their wake thousands of acres of stumps, brush, and bark — slash that was very dry. By the time of the Dust Bowl era, from 1930 to 1934, close to three thousand fires burned 336,000 acres annually in Wisconsin. Many forest service workers at the time reported that the sun would be gone for hours — or days — hidden by clouds of smoke and ash.

With the establishment of Wisconsin's national forests in 1933, fire suppression became a major concern. The Civilian Conservation Corps, started in the same year, provided the manpower needed in the forests to fight fires. But with the start of World War II, that workforce of young men disappeared for the Chequamegon-Nicolet. With pared down staffs, foresters realized they needed to turn to the general public for help in preventing forest fires. But how to convince ordinary citizens to offer their aid was a challenge.

Then, in the spring of 1942 off the coast of southern California, a Japanese submarine fired on an oil field near Santa Barbara, close to the Los Padres National Forest. The event provided the impetus the foresters were looking for. Fear that an enemy could set off raging forest fires that could compromise the country's lumber supply started to grow. With the help of the Wartime Advertising Council, the U.S. Forest Service organized the Cooperative Forest Fire Prevention Campaign to solicit the public's help.

The campaign created colorful posters with headlines such as "Forest Fires Aid the Enemy" and "Our Carelessness, Their Secret Weapon." When Walt Disney released the cartoon motion picture *Bambi* in 1944, his studio loaned its lead character to the general education effort for one year.

Smokey Bear may have done his job a little too well, according to naturalist Eric Rock.
John T. Andrews

Bambi proved a success in drawing the public's attention to the fire prevention message. But the forest service now needed to find another "spokes-animal," one that could be used long-term. A black bear was chosen to be the new symbol for the country's number one firefighter.

"Smokey Bear" made his first appearance on August 9, 1944. A poster by Albert Staehle featured him in a ranger's hat and firefighter's dungarees pouring a bucket of water on a campfire. The Wartime Advertising Council introduced his well-known slogan, "Only You Can Prevent Forest Fires," in 1947.

A few years later, an unfortunate event brought the Smokey Bear character "to life." On a spring day in 1950, a wildfire engulfed a section of the Lincoln National Forest in the Capitan Mountains in New Mexico. Forest rangers, civilian volunteers, and army soldiers who were working to contain the blaze reported seeing a black bear cub wandering near the fire line. Thinking his mother might come for him, they left the little bear alone.

Several soldiers just barely escaped the firestorm by lying face down on a rockslide for over an hour until the fire burned past them. The bear cub fled to a tree, but he badly burned his paws and hind legs. The soldiers carried the bear out of the fire zone and gave him to a local rancher. A New Mexico Department of Game and Fish ranger heard about the cub and subsequently flew the bear to Santa Fe, where a veterinarian treated his burns.

The United Press and Associated Press picked up the story, and the public fell in love with the little survivor. The New Mexico state game warden presented the cub to the U.S. Forest Service chief with the understanding that the bear would be dedicated to spreading a conservation and fire prevention

FOREST FIRES: WAS SMOKEY BEAR AN OVERACHIEVER?

Not all fires in the forest are bad. Some plants and trees need periodic fires to grow. *Candice Gaukel Andrews*

SMOKEY BEAR MAY HAVE DONE HIS JOB A little too well. The awareness he brought to the public about the dangers of forest fires undoubtedly saved many lives and thousands of acres of forest. But without natural fires, a forest cannot live and grow.

After a forest fire, immediate, phenomenal growth takes place. Fire rapidly breaks down organic matter and releases nutrients, such as phosphorus, potassium, calcium, and magnesium, which are ordinarily locked up in the living trees and plants or in the decomposing matter on the forest floor. These nutrients enrich the soil, giving plants a burst of energy. Fires can, then, accelerate the work of years of bacterial decomposition. And partial or complete clearing of the forest canopy by fire permits intense photosynthesis on the floor, causing sun-loving plants to push up and through.

Not all the trees in the forest are damaged by a natural fire. Some have evolved to survive blazes. Mature red and white pine have thick bark that protects their cambium from the fire's heat. With their foliage at the top of their tall trunks, they are immune to anything but crown fires. And even if a particular stand of pines is burned, there is almost always a small number of survivors whose seeds, falling to a floor now burned clear of the thick, inhibiting needle litter, can germinate to begin the building of a new pine forest. Some plant species, such as jack pine, need fire to release their seeds, which are sealed in pitch. Without fire, seeds of other various plants may lie dormant in the soil for years.

According to naturalist and worldwide guide Eric Rock, who has been taking eco-travelers to remote and wild locations such as the forests on the North Rim of the Grand Canyon for more than ten years, "if a forest goes for forty to fifty years without a fire, when the fire does finally come, it will most probably burn *everything*. When natural fuels — such as needles, leaves, and brush — build up over decades, the resultant fire will be larger, far more intense, erratic, and more dangerous to fight. That kind of fire can burn everything from roots to treetops." He concludes, "Entire eco-systems can disappear in that kind of fire. Smokey Bear made people fear all forest fires and made them think all fire in the forest is bad. He should have stipulated 'accidental, manmade fires.'"

message. Little "Smokey Bear" was relocated to the National Zoo in Washington, D.C.

Three Wisconsinites, Neal Long, Frank Brunner, and Ada Hart, constructed the first Smokey Bear suit that a person could wear. The costume was made from bear hides and first appeared in the Logging Congress Parade in Wausau in September 1950.

In 1952, a congressional act was passed taking Smokey Bear out of the public domain and placing him under the control of the secretary of agriculture. All royalties and fees collected from his use were to be earmarked for continued education on forest fire prevention. Later that year, Steve Nelson and Jack Rollins wrote a song about the woodsy icon. In order to maintain the tune's rhythm, the composers added a *the* between *Smokey* and *Bear*. However, his name was never officially changed, and the correct way to refer to him remains "Smokey Bear."

Making Tracks in the Woods

While black bears definitely do make their living within the Chequamegon, there is another animal of formidable strength that may be a new — or longtime but invisible — resident. Cheryl Olesen, who also lives in the forest's vicinity, told me about it.

"I've owned the Deer Trail Cabins in the southern part of Taylor County and lived in or close to the forest since 1994," says Cheryl. "On a fall day in 2006, I was on County Highway A about two miles from the cabins. Just down the road, I saw an animal that looked like something I'd never seen before. It was crossing the road about a quarter of a mile in front of me. I was coming over a hill doing fifty miles per hour, so I got a pretty good look at its silhouette," she states. "It was bigger than a bobcat and had a long tail that it swooshed. The Department of Natural Resources claims there are no cougars in the woods, but I know what I saw."

It would take a year and half before another run-in with a large, catlike creature would convince the public — and the Department of Natural Resources — that Cheryl's story was factual. On January 18, 2008, a trapper and welder from Rock County had a feline encounter of the big kind — in his barn.

In a hayloft in a dilapidated building near Milton, the forty-four-year-old

A Call for Cougars

Many Wisconsinites have claimed that cougars have been here for several years now. The WDNR is collecting reports on cougar sightings in the state. This cougar is in captivity. *John T. Andrews*

With the recent confirmation of at least one cougar in Wisconsin, it doesn't take much imagination to believe that others are here — and perhaps always have been.

Historically, the cougar, the largest cat in North America, roamed throughout Wisconsin and the Great Lakes region. Since its primary prey was white-tailed deer, cougars found the wooded portions of northern Wisconsin extremely favorable and the oak savannas of the southern part of the state to their liking. Known also by the terms puma, panther, catamount (short for catamountain), American lion, mountain lion, or the Ojibwe name *mishibijn*, the large cat was probably extirpated from the state during the early 1900s — or so it was thought. At about that time, the last reports of cougar sightings came in from Marinette County, and it is believed that the very last Wisconsin cougar was taken in Douglas County in 1908.

Reports of the presence of cougars in the state started up again in the 1930s and 1940s, but most of those were suspected of being that of escaped cap-

tives or released pets. There has been no definitive evidence — carcass, track, scat, or photograph — of a cougar in Wisconsin until the Milton occurrence in January 2008.

In 1991, the Wisconsin Department of Natural Resources began keeping track of reported cougar sightings as part of their Rare Mammal Observation Program. From 1994 to 2003, 404 cougar observations were reported. "Probable" sightings accounted for only 9.2 percent of the total, however; the most common species misidentified as cougars were dogs, coyotes, wolves, bobcats, fishers, and bears.

(continued on next page)

welder, who runs trap lines as a hobby, unexpectedly ran into a cougar. The cat took two strides toward him, then gracefully leapt — or "floated," according to the welder — through a hole in the barn's siding twelve feet below and vanished. The man estimated the cat to be more than six feet from his nose to his tail tip. It would become the first confirmed sighting of one of the big cats in Wisconsin in a hundred years.

Measurement of the Milton cat's paw print suggested the animal was a young male, weighing approximately 120 pounds. Later genetic analysis of a urine sample from where the cat had left its mark and a small drop of blood inside one of the paw prints from a cut foot identified the cat as a wild one from North America. It is thought to be a member of the Black Hills, South Dakota, population, which is eight hundred miles away.

Cheryl Olesen is not surprised in the least. She's known about the cougars in Wisconsin for a few years now. "In December 2005, my husband David and our neighbor Carmen were in his woods cutting Christmas trees when they spotted some huge, catlike prints along a fallen tree," she says. "There were about twenty fresh paw prints in the snow. Not having a firearm for protection, they hurried out of there and bought their trees at the gas station."

A CALL FOR COUGARS

(continued from page 61)

Cougars are brown or tawny-yellow in color with long, black-tipped tails that are twenty-eight to thirty-eight inches in length. They have dark patches on the sides of their muzzles and on the backs of their ears. From nose to tail tip, the cat may measure six to eight and a half feet in length and weigh 75 to 265 pounds. At the shoulder, adults stand about twenty-seven to thirty-one inches high.

Secretive and solitary hunters, adult cougars have enough power to bring down a large deer. If a deer hunt is successful, the mountain lion may return to the kill several times, loosely covering the carcass with leaf litter to hide it between feedings. They also eat birds and smaller mammals, such as raccoons, beavers, hares, rabbits, and mice. Attacks on humans are rare, but a mountain lion will attack if it is particularly hungry or if it feels cornered with no obvious means of escape.

The tracks of cougars in mud or snow are usually round and often wider than they are long. They measure about 2.7 to 4.0 inches in length and 2.8 to 4.5 inches in width, showing no claws.

The WDNR is still collecting reports on cougar observations in the state. A Rare Mammal Observation Form can be found on the Department of Natural Resources Web site at http://dnr.wi.gov.

The Smith Rapids Covered Bridge, in the eastern region of the forest, spans ninety feet of the South Fork of the Flambeau River. *John T. Andrews*

Making Good First Impressions

Cheryl's cougar encounter in the forest reminds Manny Stein of two memorable meetings he's had in the Chequamegon, in another fire tower.

"I was working in the Sentinel Point Lookout Tower, and a guy that was selling encyclopedias came to my house one day," reports Manny. "My wife told him, 'The only way you're going to sell that set of books to us is by talking to my husband, and he's in a lookout tower.' Lo and behold, the guy comes to my tower, and he climbs up a hundred feet to see me! He brought a couple of his encyclopedia books up in a little backpack. I think he was secretly more interested in looking around at the world up there than selling me the encyclopedias," confesses Manny. "But he gave me his best sales pitch. And I did buy a set for the kids. I could hardly refuse him after he went to all that effort," he laughs.

I ask him about his other favorite moment in that small cab at the tower's top.

"The Sentinel Point Lookout Tower was in view of two lakes to the north," Manny starts, after a quiet moment of thought. "An eagle was very interested in the ducks, of course, and he had built a nest in a tree between the two lakes. Well, one day he was soaring around, and he started coming at the tower. He landed right on the roof. He sat there for a second, and then I could hear his claws kind of screeching as he began to slide down on the steel. So I went to the edge of the window and looked out. Just as I did that, his head came around the corner, and our two beaks came together, about six inches apart!" Manny exclaims.

"He was looking at me with his big, golden eyes in that huge, white head. He was staring right in at me, and I was looking right out at him! Then he just kind of let loose and drifted away. He wanted to see who was in that box, I guess. There isn't a lot of excitement going on up there, so if you get an eagle to fly in on you, it's something you never forget," says Manny.

Big Shoes to Fill

Eagle talons on fire tower roofs, and cougar paw prints in the snow. The steel legs of lookout towers anchored in the soil, and the muscular lower limbs of river men controlling enormous rafts of weighty timbers. Aldo Leopold's ethics born in the earth, and Smokey Bear's burned hind feet. That unsettled feeling I had when I first stepped into the Chequamegon metamorphosed into a notion of being very grounded. And if you look closely on the Chequamegon's forest floor, you might see yet another set of impressive tracks.

"I was born and raised in these woods," says Manny, "and I still live here, in a log home on the South Fork of the Flambeau, which is right in the middle of the national forest. My dad was a logger, and my son's been a logger for thirty-five years. He lives in the forest, too, in a log home I built. I go out and help him sometimes," Manny says with pride. "Still being able to work in the woods with my son, well, that's kind of neat because the forest is a big part of my life.

"After I retired," Manny continues, "I was offered some timber inventory work. I was able to walk farther into places I hadn't been in for years and even into some little spots I hadn't ever been in. I must have covered sixty thousand acres after I quit my U.S. Forest Service job. I have flashbacks now of where I've been to in this forest, of certain locations, lands, roads, and swamps. It's humbling to know that my boot tracks are all over this beautiful place."

Manny's final reflection reminds me of something else Aldo Leopold once wrote in *A Sand County Almanac:* "Now we face the question whether a still higher 'standard of living' is worth its cost in things natural, wild, and free. For us of the minority, the opportunity to see geese is more important than television, and the chance to find a pasqueflower is a right as inalienable as free speech."

I guess Manny, in that fire tower all alone, without benefit of books or radio or television, came to know that, better than anyone.

Chequamegon-Nicolet National Forest–
Chequamegon Land Base: Eastern Region

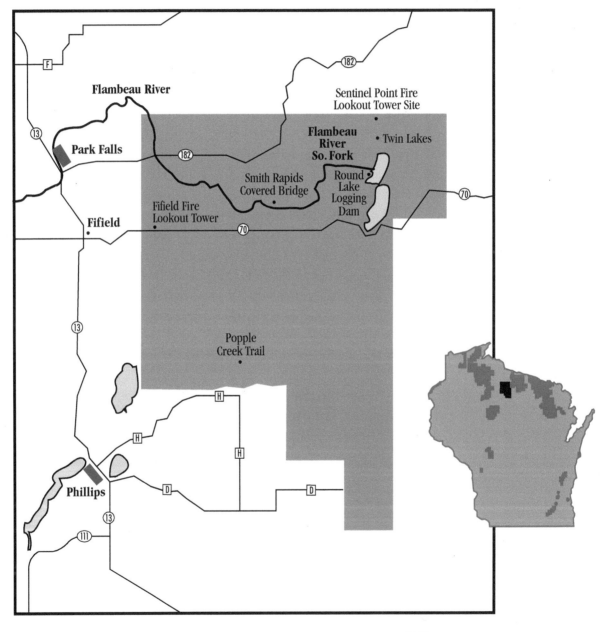

Flambeau River

Park Falls

Fifield

F

13

182

Sentinel Point Fire
Lookout Tower Site

Twin Lakes

Flambeau
River
So. Fork

Smith Rapids
Covered Bridge

Round
Lake
Logging
Dam

70

182

Fifield Fire
Lookout Tower

70

Popple
Creek Trail

13

H

H

H

D

D

Phillips

13

111

6 Miles

Chequamegon-Nicolet National Forest–
Chequamegon Land Base: Southern Region

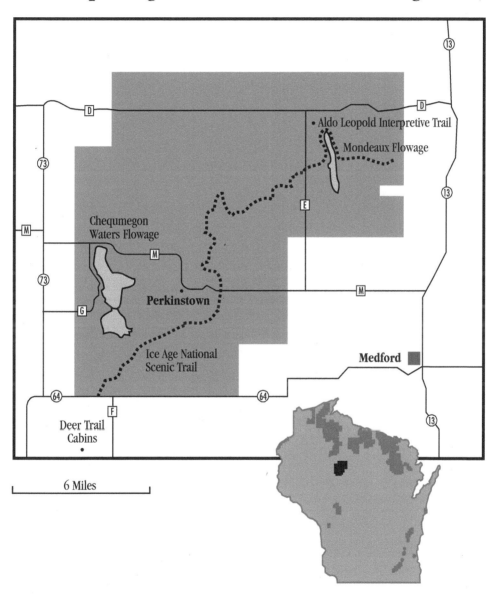

Aldo Leopold Interpretive Trail

Mondeaux Flowage

Chequmegon
Waters Flowage

Perkinstown

Ice Age National
Scenic Trail

Medford

Deer Trail
Cabins

6 Miles

Hundreds of animals, birds, and turtles are drawn to Martin Hanson's ponds at Camelot North, and they often wind up as the subjects of photographs and videotapes. *John T. Andrews*

4 Chequamegon-Nicolet National Forest– Chequamegon Land Base: Northern Region

THERE, ON THE FOREST EDGE

Camelot North

"They call me the 'Video Man of Mellen,'" says Martin Hanson proudly as he hands me three videotapes he'd like me to take home and view.

I'm in Martin's combined living room/dining room on this breezy, summer day, surrounded on four sides by his floor-to-ceiling windows. Conspicuous in the room is a video camera poised on a tripod, pointed outside to the two ponds in front of his house — ponds that Martin himself built. The June sun pours in through the windows and floods around the camera, a computer monitor, a TV, overflowing bookshelves, and a table strewn with papers and open volumes.

Martin Hanson was eighty years old when I visited him. A well-known and respected conservationist, he was once dubbed the "The Last Lord of Camelot North" by Paul G. Hayes in the February 20, 1994, *Milwaukee Journal Magazine*.

I found Martin's kingdom at the end of Beaver Dam Lake Road at the eastern edge of the northern section of the Chequamegon side of the Chequamegon-Nicolet National Forest. His house was built in 1967 and

Among his many achievements, Gaylord Nelson is perhaps best known as the founder of Earth Day. Less known but equally important is his role, while a U.S. senator, in winning protection for the Apostle Islands National Lakeshore and St. Croix National Scenic Riverway.
WHi Image ID 48016

designed by a protégé of Frank Lloyd Wright, Herb Fritz from Spring Green. Martin calls the house "the best blind in northern Wisconsin," and from here, he videotapes the wildlife coming to the grounds from three directions. Deer, black bears, and hundreds of other kinds of animals and birds are drawn to Martin's ten and a half acres of ponds and eight acres of openings. The site is part of the 1,240 acres west of Mellen in Ashland County that his father, an avid fisherman, bought in 1926.

Shortly after moving to Mellen, Martin and his brother, Louis, became friends with then–Wisconsin governor Gaylord Nelson, soon to become the state's junior senator in Washington. Famous as the founder of Earth Day, Gaylord Nelson and his environmental accomplishments are legendary. Nelson was a frequent guest at Martin Hanson's "Camelot North" — as were many other Democratic governors and congressmen and almost every environmentalist of national significance. At the Hanson dining table, debates and discussions on conservation issues were served as freely as the food and martinis.

Today, I'm sitting with Martin at his busy table, perhaps the very same one over which the strategy for naming the St. Croix and Namekagon a National Scenic Riverway was hammered out and where part of the campaign that led to a ban on DDT in the state was fashioned. I feel humble just to be in Martin's — and history's — presence.

Here, where I sit, is also the place where the Apostle Islands National Lakeshore Act of 1970 was hatched. In the late summer of 1963, Martin Hanson got aboard a military helicopter with President John F. Kennedy, Senator Gaylord Nelson, Wisconsin's Governor John Reynolds, U.S. Secretary of the Interior Stewart Udall, and Secretary of Agriculture Orville Freeman for a tour of the islands in Lake Superior. Martin Hanson was the president's personal guide on the trip. Less than two months later, President John F. Kennedy was killed in Dallas, Texas.

That was more than forty years ago. Yet, today, Martin is still at it — perhaps the last living knight of the Round Table, carrying on the environmental tradition of Kennedy's "Camelot" administration and Senator Gaylord Nelson's Earth Day. In fact, I have just missed Tia Nelson, Gaylord's daughter, and seven members of the River Alliance by a day. They came out to Martin's place to discuss an effort to designate another state waterway, the Brunsweiler, a National Wild and Scenic River. They were seeking Martin's opinion and advice.

The Road to Elk

Perhaps one of the reasons Martin Hanson's father was drawn to the northern Chequamegon so many years ago was that according to statistics, it has the forest's highest concentration of lakes — especially around the Clam Lake area — and good fish populations. But for the past decade and a half, it is another forest population that has identified the Clam Lake vicinity more than anything else: elk. And Martin Hanson played a pivotal role in bringing this native animal back home in 1995.

"I went every place I could to learn about elk," recalls Martin. "I visited Pennsylvania and Arkansas, where they had been replanted; then I went West to Yellowstone, Glacier, and Wind Cave National Parks to study elk. I even read the bible of elk," he says to me, pointing to one of the books stacked on his dining room table, *Elk of North America*, a huge tome by Jack Ward Thomas, written in 1982.

"I read that whole thing — until I got to too many Latin names," he says with a twinkle in his eye. "Then a few of us proponents of bringing the elk back to Wisconsin went to numerous town boards. I brought with me several videotapes I made of elk in the different places I visited and feasibility reports on introducing them back into the state. About ten town boards surrounding Clam Lake gave us their support. Then we got Governor Tommy Thompson's support, and that got us started," he says.

Twenty-five elk from Michigan were brought into Wisconsin in 1995. Unfortunately, one died right away. A few others were later to succumb to one

MOVING INTO THE NORTHWOODS: WISCONSIN'S ELK

Once native to Wisconsin, elk were reintroduced to the state in 1995 when twenty-five of them from Michigan were brought to Clam Lake. *John T. Andrews*

WISCONSIN HAS ITS OWN VERSION OF THE famed Yellowstone National Park Wolf Reintroduction Program. Our edition involves elk (*Cervus elaphus*), Wisconsin's largest native mammal, which was extirpated from the state in 1886.

During February 1995, twenty-five elk were trapped in Michigan's lower peninsula, held in quarantine for ninety days, and shipped to the Great Divide District near Clam Lake. After a two-week acclimation period in a holding pen, the elk were released into the Chequamegon-Nicolet National Forest on May 17 of that year.

Historic records indicate that elk once inhabited at least fifty of the state's seventy-two counties. A previous attempt in the 1930s to bring elk back failed because of illegal hunting; the last four of these elk were killed by poachers in 1948.

In 1989, the Wisconsin Department of Natural Resources and conservationists such as Martin Hanson explored the possibility of reintroducing elk, moose, and caribou. The resulting feasibility reports stated that while elk might again succeed here, moose or caribou probably would not due to their vulnerability to brain worm, a nematode that causes a nervous system disease often resulting in death.

Elk are about five times the size of their cousins the white-tailed deer. Weighing between five hundred and nine hundred pounds, elk stand up to five feet tall at the shoulder. In the winter, an elk's head, neck, and legs are dark brown, while its sides and back are much lighter. Its summer coat is a deep, reddish-brown color. Both males and females have heavy, dark manes extending to the lower chest and a yellow rump patch.

Each year male elk grow large, multitined antlers —

of our state's predators. Says Martin, "Michigan has fewer wolves, so their elk reproduction rate is high; I think their population currently stands at a thousand or so. But we have a pack of wolves in Clam Lake, and they are protein-hungry in June. And elk tend to have their calves in the same area year after year. So the bears and the wolves learn where the elk go to give birth every two years, and we lose several of them," he explains.

Martin has me hoping my trip to this vast, 575,465-acre northern region of the Chequamegon will result in at least one elk sighting out of the 125 now estimated to roam here. I can't wait to get out on Highway 77, the state route that runs through the heart of Clam Lake.

Our Great Divide

Highway 77 is an appropriate first trail for me on this northern adventure, apart from its elk connection. Between the town of Glidden and Lost Land Lake near Hayward, this twenty-nine mile stretch is known as the Great Divide National Forest Scenic Byway.

The byway gets its name from its location on a high point of land called the Great Divide. This north-south, continental dividing ridge separates the watersheds of the Great Lakes and the Mississippi River. Water flows down the north slopes of the highlands into the Bois Brule, White, and Bad Rivers and continues through the Great Lakes to the Atlantic Ocean. Water flows

MOVING INTO THE NORTHWOODS: WISCONSIN'S ELK

with a four- to five-foot spread and weighing up to forty pounds — that they use for dominance displays and for combat. Elk are herbivorous; on the Clam Lake range, they eat woody browse and a wide variety of grasses, shrubs, and seedling leaves. The Chequamegon's forest openings, natural meadows, and clear-cuts provide attractive foraging areas.

Today, if you drive along Highway 77 between Hayward and Clam Lake, you'll see several roadside posts with flashing lights and signs that read "Elk Crossing Area." Transmitters on collared elk that may be a mile or more away trigger the lights, warning motorists to slow down. If you're lucky, you may spot one of these native Wisconsinites.

The Clam Lake elk herd is far from the goal set for it at fourteen hundred animals, or one to two elk per square mile of their Chequamegon forest habitat. However, after an absence of more than a hundred years, elk bugles are again carried on September winds in a Wisconsin wild land.

down the south slopes into the Chippewa and St. Croix Rivers, then into the Mississippi River, and eventually the Gulf of Mexico.

The rugged Penokee-Gogebic Range, just north of Highway 77, forms the Great Divide, which runs east to west for about eighty miles through northern Wisconsin and upper Michigan. The range is thought to have been created billions of years ago by the folding, faulting, and the pushing up of volcanic material to the surface, making it one of the oldest formations in the United States. About 1.6 billion years ago, the Penokees stood almost four miles above sea level, higher than the Swiss Alps. They have since been eroded by crushing glaciers, wind, and water.

The Penokee-Gogebic Range held one of our country's greatest concentrations of iron ore. Underground chasms are still thought to harbor the planet's most comprehensive reserves of untouched taconite ore — 3.7 billion tons. Atop these minerals and rocks lies the residue of millions of years of marine sediment.

Looking at my map of the Great Divide National Forest Scenic Byway, I see that there is a still lot of "marine" activity in the area. At least eight bodies of water lie adjacent to this stretch of Highway 77 blacktop. Although Lost Land Lake and Dead Horse Slough sound enticing, I decide I can't go home without investigating the waters known as Ghost Lake.

Summer clouds, like sheets blowing in the wind, are reflected on the surface of Ghost Lake.
John T. Andrews

Ghost Lake is located toward the Hayward end of the byway. Although you'd never suspect it by looking at the U.S. Forest Service's map, the narrow access road to it off Highway 77 seems to go on forever. I keep angling down through stands of mature conifers and pass one opening filled with huge glacial erratics. I feel like an ant looking up from my grass-level perspective at a human-size game of lawn bocce.

Finally arriving at the boat ramp, I see Ghost Lake materialize before me. White, billowy, summer clouds are reflected on Ghost Lake's cool, barely moving surface, like sheets gently blowing in the wind. Dragonflies with spiritlike, translucent wings land by my feet.

The Mountain's Edge

If yesterday ended with the lighter, more ephemeral face of the Great Divide at Ghost Lake, today my adventures will be grounded in a much more solid foundation. I'm off to the Penokee Overlook, three miles west of Mellen on County Highway GG, to get a close-up look at what makes up the Great Divide.

I walk the wooden-planked trail and stairs through thick forest to the top of the Penokees, which now stand one-third of a mile above sea level, a shadow of their former stature. Still, from the top, I can see over the conifers and deciduous trees; eye the ridge-and-valley pattern to the landscape. Below my hiking boots, on the other side of the wooden floor planks, is the ancient mountain range, overlaid by marine drift, dropped off nearly two billion years ago by a long-gone sea.

The Penokee peaks weren't the only things to be smashed down here. When news of the vast iron ore deposits spread in the 1880s, scores of miners flocked to this region. Some mining companies did strike it rich; most individual miners did not and left with their dreams flattened.

At first, an endless stream of railcars filled with several hundred thousand tons of iron ore traveled north to Ashland each year. There, the load was put on ships bound for the industrial cities on the Atlantic Seaboard.

As more and more ore came out of the Penokees, new mining companies, backed by speculators in the East, continued to spring up. Newspapers and investment prospectuses reported ore of "unparalleled magnitude" in the Penokee-Gogebic range. In 1912, however, production began dropping, and

In the late 1880s, scores of miners came to the Penokee-Gogebic Range near Hurley. These men worked at John E. Burton's iron mine. *WHi Image ID 23380*

the bottom soon fell out of the mining industry here. Get-rich-quick hopes faded.

In less than fifty years, nearly three hundred million tons of iron ore were extracted from the mines in the Penokee-Gogebic Range. Of this total, seventy-one million came from Wisconsin, the rest from Michigan.

But what I find intriguing today is that more than signifying mineral wealth, the Penokees represent at least one hard edge to the Chequamegon side of this vast, combined national forest known as the Chequamegon-Nicolet. It's hard to find anything with a boundary when you're somewhere deep inside its seemingly limitless acreage. At least the Penokees are a wavy line that could be drawn on a black-and-white map of this forest, a dividing mark of sorts on an immense white page.

Art Alfresco

This afternoon, I'm visiting another man whose roots push deep into the forest, one who can give me some perspective on finding other edges to grab onto in such an overwhelming space.

Artist Greg Alexander has a studio in Ashland, a large classroom in a former school building. The studio is filled to near-capacity with cabinets and easels; paintings and props.

After high school, Greg had enrolled in an art college in St. Paul, Minnesota. But he found his true calling in painting wildlife, something the college's curriculum did not offer. He moved to the South Shore of Lake Superior and spent the next four years in a remote log cabin near Herbster, Wisconsin. Says Greg:

> I lived on the other side of the forest from civilization, which from Herbster is Ashland and Washburn. Cutting through the forest was a great commute by motorcycle or my old truck. At certain times of the year, I'd pick blueberries all the way through, or hunt grouse or whitetail with a bow and arrow. In those travels through the woods, I learned about animal habitats and the forest's microenvironments and how they changed during the seasons. That was my four-year education. I paid $150 a month for rent, and I decided that that was cheap tuition.

Greg soon realized that the Chequamegon was a place where he could paint for a lifetime and never get tired of or run out of subjects.

> For example, I can go north and find a pine-barrens-sand forest in the Bayfield Peninsula. I can go south an equal distance and find a boreal forest with dense, granite outcroppings covered in mosses, cedars, and a lot of hilly, watershed areas. Both have a very different type of soil; different types of habitats. And in the mix, there are a lot of agricultural lands, which help the wildlife to flourish.

His years of traveling through, living with, and painting in this forest have given him insight into something else going on in the Chequamegon.

> I think what's unusual here is that a lot of animals migrate out of the forest to the edges. If you take a look at the topography of the Bayfield Peninsula, it's one big hill. In the early wintertime, toward late November, the evaporation off Lake Superior turns to snow in the higher elevations. At that point, animals will migrate twenty to twenty-five miles out of there. I've found a migration route of one population of white-tailed deer that comes through every year. It's in a bottleneck area, and the deer — and animals I've never seen before coming from who knows where — all congregate at a ridge before they go down the hill. But it doesn't turn on until that first snow.

I ask Greg where he prefers to paint in the forest. "I look for water edges," he says without hesitation. "Mostly stream bottoms, because they are natural corridors for wildlife. Black bears travel the creek bottoms. I look for where conifers open up to a meadow, or where natural edges come into each other. I also look for the edges of a season," he tells me. "In the winter, a lack of color makes cool tones in the woods. Starting in March, a spring-fed stream will bring up those rich, warm tones. It's an edge of time."

Falling Down and Climbing Up

I discover another watery edge to this region of the Chequamegon on the western end of the Penokee-Gogebic Range, off Forest Road 199. But this one is vertical.

The trail to the seventy-foot-tall Morgan Falls is flat and pretty, bordered by full, leafy ferns and woodland flowers. I walk across the very shallow and emerald Morgan Creek, strewn with mossy rocks that give the water a soft, bubbling sound as it separates gently to get around them. The old Civilian Conservation Corps campground I pass by is quiet now, marked by a stone fireplace that I imagine being stoked up in the 1930s by men whose faces are as hard as iron ore and whose bellies hunger from a day of hard work and walking in the woods.

Just a little more than a half a mile in, I enter a high-walled, rock glen. Skinny Morgan Falls slides down slick rocks in a series of steps from someplace up high; more rocks obscure its top. But down here, on the slab canyon floor, the falls' fresh droplets cool my arms and face in a light misting.

Among the highest waterfalls in the state, Morgan Falls culminates in a small splash pool. Those rich, warm tones Greg talked about are all around me in this invigorating brown canyon, with its orange butterflies drying their wings on the stony floor.

Backtracking along the short spur into the canyon, I hit the main trail again, which leads to St. Peter's Dome, or "Old Baldy" as some local people call it. It's a 3.6-mile round trip to the dome, but after the respite at the waterfall glen, I feel game to give it a go on this sweltering, ninety-degree summer day — even though I've left my water bottle in the car. Twenty minutes later, I'm regretting my decision. As easy as the trail to Morgan Falls was, the path to Old Baldy is three times as hard.

The emerald-colored Morgan Creek is shallow, shiny, and strewn with mossy rocks. It's bordered by leafy ferns and woodland flowers.
John T. Andrews

Not far beyond the spur, the main trail narrows and almost immediately begins its climb to 1,565 feet above sea level. "Sea level" makes me think all the more about the water I don't have with me. But not wanting to waste energy going back, I forge ahead, trying to channel the determination that must have fueled that steely CCC crew.

A great deal of the way up is a jumble of roots and rocks, constantly grabbing at my hiking boots, almost as if they seem to enjoy tripping me up. The slopes continue to get steeper as I go, but now well into it, I feel it would be cowardice to turn back short of seeing the highest point in the Chequamegon.

I cross another rocky streambed and marvel at the giant, exposed roots of the trees here. While they seem to be roughly toying with me, they are gentle with the boulders at their bases, reaching tentacled arms around them as if holding them in a caring embrace. This dichotomy in a tree's personality makes me smile.

I'm sure by the time I'm done, the 3.6 miles will feel more like 60.3. An hour and a half later, after passing a granite outcrop, the trail gets seriously steep. It makes two switchbacks, and finally takes me to the grassy opening on top. The view — as was the trail to it — is breathtaking. I can see clear over to Chequamegon Bay and even to what I think are some of the Apostle Islands, twenty miles to the north. I sit on Old Baldy's north face for a while, looking *out* at the incredible horizon and trying to avoid looking *down* to the sheer drop-off below me.

Seeing the bay from on high here makes me think of the origin of the name *Chequamegon*, which is an Ojibwe word for "place of shallow waters." Some say it is a reference to the body of water I see sparkling out before me; others say it reflects the abundant wetlands and more than eight hundred lakes created by glaciers that now rest within the Chequamegon's confines. After talking with Greg Alexander, I think it could refer to where the water meets a lowland forest. Filled with plants, predators, and prey, such an edge environment would have been significant to Native Americans.

A few paces away from the ledge, there is a brass U.S. Geological Survey marker embedded in the rock. I stand over it and take a photo, just to prove I made it up here. Thirsty, tired, and hot, yes; but if I haven't spent the last few hours hiking right up to the Pearly Gates, at least I made it to St. Peter's Dome.

A Barren Start

There is a story much grander than mine of survival in this forest. In fact, it is a story of survival of the state's first forest *within* a forest — that wasn't even a forest to begin with.

The sandy soils of the 14,907-acre Moquah Barrens (13,640 acres of which are in one large area, with the remaining acres in several "satellite" barrens), situated on the far north end of the Chequamegon in the Washburn District, are parting gifts from the giant glaciers that scraped over Wisconsin more than ten thousand years ago. Red and jack pine, aspens, oaks, and especially some species of grasses favored the low-nutrient environment of this outwash plain and thrived.

The loggers who first arrived here in the 1800s saw a nearly continuous woodland when they gazed upon the vast areas of pine trees, some almost one hundred feet tall and nine feet around. They observed immense hemlocks at least four hundred years old, huge stands of big sugar maple and yellow birch, some open bogs and tangled swamps, and large areas of flattened timber, burned or leveled by wind. They could hear wolves and see signs of mountain lions.

But by the late 1800s, the loggers had cut most of the mature red and white pine. Then wildfires, fueled by the slash that was left, raced across the area. Once the fires had subsided, speculators began their quick moves on the landscape and sold this stump-studded terrain as "the finest agricultural lands on Earth" to unwary buyers.

Families came by the thousands to purchase these "dream" farmlands at relatively high prices. Once some of them had a chance to assess what they had bought, they left, never clearing a square foot. But others took to heart the advice they were given: just begin sowing and prepare to reap an abundant harvest.

Most of those who stayed to farm lasted only a few decades before going bankrupt. In 1929, the federal government began purchasing these tax delinquent lands to form a national forest. The Moquah, then, at its most barren, became the first portion of the Chequamegon National Forest, which was finally established in 1933.

In the 1930s, the Civilian Conservation Corps was directed to replant the trees the loggers had taken. In fact, the Brinks Camp in the Moquah was the

While initial harvests like this one were sometimes impressive, the cutover's sandy soil — together with its abundant stumps and short growing season — makes for very difficult farming.
WHi Image ID 1979

first CCC camp to be designated in Wisconsin. To encourage the sharp-tailed grouse population, the CCC first planted buckwheat patches for their food. Later, they planted jack pine and red pine, which eventually closed the open barrens, making the habitat ultimately unsuitable for the grouse.

The CCC-planted jack pine can still be seen today in cornlike rows on the hills and valleys of the barrens. As the jack and red pine plantations flourished, however, other native plant species dwindled.

Today, the U.S. Forest Service is removing most of the pine plantations in the barrens to encourage the original prairie grasses and brush to grow. Periodic low-intensity prescribed burns and timber harvests are being used to keep the area from reverting to forest. Restoring the Moquah Barrens to a landscape approaching its original state will improve habitats for sharp-tailed grouse, upland sandpipers, grassland sparrows, brown thrashers, and eastern bluebirds — the bird, as Henry David Thoreau wrote, that "carries the sky on its back."

The Moquah Barrens became the first portion of the Chequamegon National Forest, officially established in 1933. The open environment attracts hawks, deer, badgers, and woodchucks. *John T. Andrews*

This open environment is also now attractive to red-tailed hawks, coyotes, white-tailed deer, woodchucks, badgers, and plains pocket gophers. Gray wolves and black bears occasionally use the area, since it now is ripe again with wild strawberries, blackberries, Juneberries — and blueberries.

Because the Moquah Barrens' sandy terrain is hundreds of feet deep, only the hardiest of plants can survive. Blueberries and bracken fern are two who love it here. The prescribed fires enhance the yield of the berries. Early Woodland (before 1000 BC) Native Americans burned the area to promote berry growth much the same as the U.S. Forest Service does today. Blueberries were cooked down, shaped into patties, and dried, providing an easily transportable source of fruit for the entire year.

In other efforts to return the Moquah Barrens to its natural condition, the U.S. Forest Service constructed a pond in an old wetland that had filled in with vegetation over time. Today, the pond is home to salamanders, turtles, frogs, and insects and is a watering hole for deer, bears, and coyotes.

Although the Moquah Barrens has a self-guided, twenty-mile auto tour that begins on Forest Road 236 off Highway 2, it is best seen by walking some of its many side roads, where spring and summer wildflowers cover the meadows like a brilliantly colored, brand-new bedspread.

In contrast to this area being managed by timber harvests and prescribed burns, in 1935 the U.S. Forest Service set aside a separate, one-square-mile unit (648 acres) where fire is being eliminated from the ecosystem. In this Moquah Barrens Research Natural Area, nothing has or will be done to alter nature's work except to protect the area from wildfire. The research area was designated a National Natural Landmark in 1980.

Moquah is a derivative of the Ojibwe word *makwa*, which means "bear."

FRUITS OF THEIR FOREST LABOR

WHEN MOST OF US THINK ABOUT RECREATING in our state's forests, we think of activities such as cross-country skiing, hiking, swimming, hunting, fishing, camping, and biking. But there is another "-ing" activity that is extremely popular, especially with those who are lucky enough to live close to the woods: foraging.

From June through September, there are pickers in the forests and once-forests, seeking wild berries, such as strawberries, raspberries, and blackberries. But for those like Kelly Illick, whose grandparents lived at the edge of the Moquah Barrens, it's the taste of wild blueberries that call her back to the cutovers every year.

"When I was a child," says Kelly, "I really looked forward to blueberry-picking days. My parents had an old station wagon. On the way out to the berry patches in the barrens, I remember grandpa barreling over the 'tickle bellies' — the hills on the sandy roads — and on the way

Berry picking has long been a Wisconsin rite of summer — in the Moquah Barrens and elsewhere. *WHi Image ID 49372*

back in, the back of the car would just be loaded with twenty ice cream buckets full of blueberries from one day of picking," she recalls.

Places like the Moquah Barrens provide a perfect habitat for native wild blueberries. In fact, blueberries often proliferate after a fire or a logging because the plants benefit from the removal of competing vegetation. Blueberries also like sunlight and sandy soil — things the Moquah Barrens has plenty of.

"My grandparents lived on Cherryville Road," explains Kelly, who now owns the Second Wind Country Inn Bed and Breakfast in Ashland. "They had the last house before entering the barrens. The soil in my grandpa's garden was mostly sand. I don't know how he got things to grow, but he did. Today, my aunt and uncle farm his homestead, and his asparagus patch is still going strong. My aunt's first picking is a full, five-pound pail — this from the patch my grandpa planted sixty years ago!"

Barrens blueberry pickers need that kind of asparagus-fortitude. Picking is hard, hot work.

Meeting Black Bears

Whether it's because of the edgy creek bottoms Greg Alexander mentioned, where rich nutrients course, or the wild blueberries that grow in the Moquah, black bears seem to find the Chequamegon inviting territory.

"I'm a quiet observer when I go out, and a lot of times animals don't know what to think of me," says Greg.

> That's gotten me in trouble with a few different black bears over the years. Once, I was fishing for rainbow trout on the Cranberry River in the Chequamegon on a day late in spring. Luckily, I had my dog with me. I was walking along in camouflage clothing, and I began to hear some grunting in front of me. My chocolate Labrador retriever was right behind me, and I was just about to the stream. I sent my dog out in front of me, she took about five steps, and her hackles went up. I knew what that meant: bear.

No sooner had the dog gotten about twenty-five yards ahead of him on the trail when Greg was surprised by something from behind.

> I was watching the dog, when all of a sudden, I heard something coming down the bank behind me. It was a 350-pound bruin. He startled me so much I jumped. And when I jumped, he saw me. He waited, looked at me, and I looked at him. But when my dog saw the bear on the other side of

FRUITS OF THEIR FOREST LABOR

"My grandma would drape herself with big kerchiefs so the flies wouldn't bite her," says Kelly. "It was grueling work, but we loved it. I was one of those who never ate when I picked; my reward was going home with buckets of blueberries."

What you can do with those blueberries once you get home — and the ailments they are reported to fend off — reads like the "shrimp list" from the movie *Forrest Gump*: there's blueberry muffins, blueberry cobblers, blueberry pie, blueberry jam, blueberry pancakes, and blueberry cheesecakes; and blueberries are said to have a beneficial effect in preventing cancer, Alzheimer's disease, urinary tract infections, strokes, and high cholesterol.

Berry pickers should expect a little competition in their chosen sport. Black bears are known to gorge on berries in July and August. Berries are mid-summer delicacies for bears, and they eat them at the rate of eleven to eighteen pounds per day, right in the patch.

Perhaps Kelly is missing out on something good.

me, she took off after him. They went up the bluff, and I lost sight of them because of a plateau. So, I started fishing. Fifteen minutes later, I saw my dog up on the bluff, just sitting there, calmly watching me. I look again, and there's that bear standing behind her. She spins around and takes off after him again. My dog grew up in that log cabin where I basically got my education, so she was really good around bears. I had no worries for her. But I wondered why that bear came back.

It took several minutes for Greg to figure out why the bear was acting so strangely, decipherable only because of the knowledge he had gained from his closeness to the forest.

I knew the bear was a male because when he came down the bank, I could see his big "mane," where his shoulders come right up to his jawbone. And I knew he meant business. When the dog was tangling with the bear the second time, I could hear her going around and around with him. This time, the bear wasn't leaving. I thought I had better get out of there; I was about thirty-five yards downstream. After several minutes, my dog came running back to me. I looked back upstream — there the bear is again! This time, he's waving his head back and forth, and I can see he's really annoyed.

Greg watched the bear, who continued to walk around in a big circle for twenty minutes.

At each half circle, he'd stop, sit down, and wave his head back and forth. All of a sudden a bell went off in my head. This is the time of year the fawns are being born. He's got a fawn buried right in the ground in the middle of that circle. And I was right in his kitchen! No wonder he was angry.

It wasn't the only time Greg would run into a black bear at the edge where forest meets stream.

Last year at this time, I was down at the river painting with my field easel. The sun was just tracking up the riverbed, and it was pretty bright in my eyes. I'd been reading a black-bear-encounter book, and I was thinking about it. I thought to myself, *with this river rushing by me like this, I can't hear a thing.* I was concentrating only on three things: my palette, my board, and the light in front of me. For almost three hours, I hadn't turned around. You know how your ears go back, and you think something could

MOVING OUT OF THE NORTHWOODS: WISCONSIN'S BLACK BEARS

THE BLACK BEAR (*URSUS AMERICANUS*) IS the only bear species in Wisconsin. As a symbol of Wisconsin wilderness, it runs a close second to the timber wolf.

The community of Glidden, about twenty-six miles east of Clam Lake, calls itself the "Black Bear Capital of the World" due to a ten-foot, seven-inch, 665-pound black bear shot five miles east of the town in 1963. It's believed that the black bear population around the town is still among the highest in the state. And according to recent Department of Natural Resources statistics, Wisconsin's black bear population — formerly confined to the northern third of the state — is both growing and spreading.

The WDNR estimates that there are about twenty-six thousand black bears in the state, up at least thirteen thousand from the number previously thought. This means that black bears are most likely on the move, expanding into new territories. While most bears still reside in the upper third of the state, they are increasingly being spotted in Wisconsin's west-central woods, and "pioneer bears" will probably continue to push southward. Bears have even been sighted around Madison, and in 2005, a jogger ran across a black bear in a Cedarburg park, a twenty-minute drive from downtown Milwaukee.

Adult male bears average 4.5 to 6 feet in length and weigh from 250 to 500 pounds. Females weigh from 225 to 450 pounds and measure 4 to 4.5 feet long. Black bears have a round, short body and sturdy legs. Their rounded shape comes from a thick layer of fat under the skin and dense, coarse hair. Their fur is usually glossy black (although some black bears may be brown, tan, or cinnamon in color), with a tan patch across the nose. About 25 percent of Wisconsin's bears

Black bears continue to move into new territories in Wisconsin. *Emery Orlikowski*

have white patches on their chests. They walk on the soles of their feet — as do humans — and have five toes with nonretractable claws. Black bears can run more than thirty miles per hour and can climb a tree in a flash.

Black bears tend to be shy and solitary animals and will typically leave when they hear or smell people. At certain times of the year, however, particularly in the spring, when they emerge from their winter dens and food is scarce, they will become opportunistic feeders. Bear attacks on humans, however, are very rare — occurring usually only after a person has startled a bear.

If you see a black bear while exploring the forests, make noise and wave your arms. Let the bear know you are there so you don't surprise him. If you should unexpectedly encounter a black bear at close range, back away slowly but do not run. Assure him that you respect him and his right to live in Wisconsin.

be standing right behind you? Well, at that moment, I turned around, and there was a black bear; a small female. She was across the river, but the river was only about twenty-five yards wide. I was surprised she hadn't smelled my paint; she was just totally unaware. She put her nose on the water. If she had crossed the river there, she would have been seven feet away from me. Bears have really poor eyesight. But they can smell incredibly well. Why she didn't detect me, I'll never know.

Got It on Tape

Before I left Martin Hanson's home a few days ago, he had asked me to take him on a car ride around the neighboring forest roads. While we were driving, Martin pointed out to me some of the places he remembered from his many years in the Chequamegon. Places where people he knew had once lived and places where his family had built many memories.

After that tour, I said my thanks and good-byes to Martin. On the long drive home, I felt sad that I didn't see a single elk in my explorations. But I realized it would probably take several trips to the forest to earn the reward of seeing one.

Back at home now, I pop one of Martin's three videos into the tape player. The TV screen lights up with scenes of does, bucks, and fawns cautiously checking out Martin's feeders; black bears at the edge of the trees vying for beaver carcasses with bald eagles; fishers sliding on their bellies across the snow-filled yard; badgers digging dens with their signature front-left-paw-back-right-foot and front-right-paw-back-left-foot manner; and wood ducks gathering by the hundreds on his ponds.

It looks like a wildlife heaven — a Wisconsin forest from an olden time. You could almost say it looks like Camelot.

Sadly, Martin Hanson passed away on October 22, 2008. On February 24, 2009, the state legislature designated a ten-mile segment of the Brunsweiler River within the Chequamegon-Nicolet National Forest as a State Wild River. Wisconsin Act 7 of 2009 Senate Bill 6 states that "this portion of the Brunsweiler River shall be known as the 'Martin Hanson Wild River.'"

Chequamegon-Nicolet National Forest –
Chequamegon Land Base: Northern Region

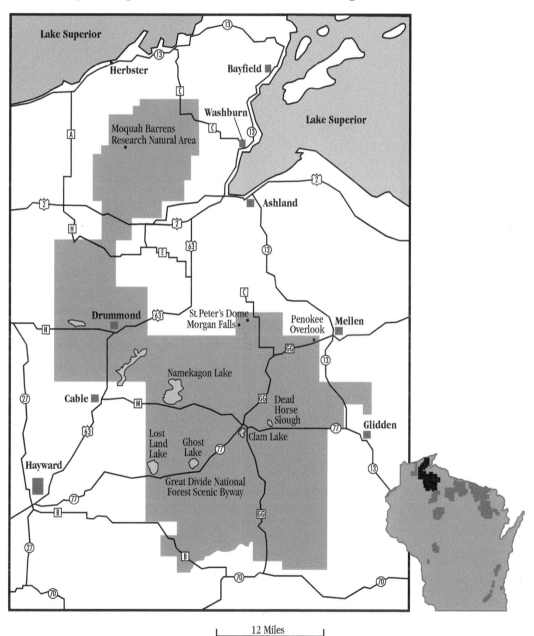

12 Miles

Prairies managed by prescribed burns, like Berg Prairie in the Coulee Experimental State Forest, often see a resurgence of native plants. *John T. Andrews*

5 Coulee Experimental State Forest

RESEARCHING THE FOREST, QUIET AND DEEP

The Wild West

With the exception of six years I spent in Los Angeles after graduating from college, I have lived in the Madison area for my whole life. I am used to lakes and isthmuses, flat fields and wetlands.

So driving into the southwestern part of our state is always a shock to my visual system. As I roll into La Crosse County on I-90, things get strange. Once I hit the Driftless Area, the unglaciated region, the unfamiliar ridges, valleys, and rolling green hills hit me full-on with that Dorothy-like feeling of "I'm not in Madison anymore."

Out the front windshield on this early Saturday morning in August, I can see a range of mounded hills and bluffs on the distant horizon. This is like a new country to me. Green slopes and red barns dot the spaces below the rounded projections that look so odd; grazing, brown beef cattle add to the complementary colors of the bucolic scene.

My destination today is the Coulee Experimental State Forest, about fifteen miles east of La Crosse and four miles south of Bangor, Wisconsin. It is our only state forest with the word *experimental* in its name, deriving from the research that has been conducted there since the first day of the forest's inception. The word *coulee* comes from an old French word meaning "ravine." It accurately describes the deep gulches formed by water erosion in this part of the state.

Unlike the Black River State Forest that stands astride the two worlds of Glaciated and Unglaciated, the Coulee Experimental State Forest is totally within the Driftless Area. And that would still be apparent if you didn't know anything about Wisconsin topography. To even get to this very hidden and secretive place, you must drive up County Highway II — and I literally mean "up." The road is long and curving and climbs to a ridgeline summit, and my ears were popping just motoring along *to* the forest.

But keeping my ears pressure free, it turns out, isn't the only sensory challenge to getting there. I can't *see* where the forest begins. There are no big, friendly-looking, wooden signs on County Highway II or on Antony Road, the route that intersects II and is supposed to lead me into the 2,972-acre forest.

Just as I'm ready to give up on finding the forest from its eastern edge and about to head west to approach it from its access off Russlan Coulee Road on its western boundary, a small gravel driveway mostly hidden by trees and at a right angle to County Highway II catches my eye. Although I must have passed this turnoff several times driving back and forth in my attempts, I hadn't seen it until now. The moment I make the quick right turn onto it and my tires hit the stones, I see a faded sign tucked into the overgrowth and undergrowth bordering the gravel drive: "Coulee Experimental Forest, Dept. of Natural Resources." It's obvious to me that this forest doesn't really want to be found.

Nonetheless, I have discovered it. The turnoff leads to a small, circular parking area. There are only three other cars here, with horse trailers hitched to their back ends. So few for such a warm, beautiful, late-summer Saturday morning.

I have the feeling I have found Wisconsin's Wild West.

Finders (and) Keepers

James Dalton, a forester for the Wisconsin Department of Natural Resources, has been the Coulee Experimental State Forest's property manager since 2002. I ask him if he truly didn't want me to find his forest. He laughs.

> I have heard that remark from other people, that the forest is kind of hidden back in there. But I can assure you that that is not intentional; we just haven't had an opportunity to update the signage yet. The Coulee Experimental State Forest is used mostly by locals. People like to hike with their dogs here, ride horses, or hunt in the fall. In winter, we have

Quiet might just be the defining characteristic of the Coulee Experimental State Forest. *Candice Gaukel Andrews*

cross-country skiers on the Coulee. In summer, berry pickers come; and in spring, the mushroom seekers. I'd say it's a place just for *quiet* recreation. Since there are no facilities here, it's definitely not "overused."

I have heard of "silent sports" before, such as canoeing and biking. But James's "quiet recreation" goes even beyond the typical meaning. Not only is motorized recreation prohibited on this forest, but bicycles are, too. And as far as paddling, the Coulee has no streams, lakes, or wetlands. Water on this forest is in the form of several small springs scattered throughout the property.

And, I later learn, keeping the Coulee forest quiet is something its keeper would like to do.

Defining an "Experimental Forest"

"Our Regional and Property Analysis states that the Coulee Experimental State Forest has 'found a niche supporting quiet, day-use recreation that is compatible with research and forest management,'" James tells me when I ask him what it is that sets this forest apart from Wisconsin's others. "And in the preparations for our writing our master plan, we did discuss alternatives. But in the final draft, we decided to stay with quiet recreation — the traditional foot-travel type of things, with the exception of horseback riding. I don't see that decision changing any time soon," he says.

But it's not the only characteristic that marks the Coulee as truly unique in the state. James explains:

This is the only experimental state forest in Wisconsin, although there are some other ones located across the country. In the 1950s, the U.S. Forest Service sought locations for "experimental forests" where they could conduct research on certain regional forestry issues. In the case of this forest, they were searching for a place to carry out forestry and watershed studies in the Driftless Areas of Minnesota, Iowa, and Wisconsin. The plan was then to share what they learned from their research with the region's landowners in an effort to reduce water problems and improve forest yields. In the 1950s and 1960s, the interface of agricultural land and forest was an unknown entity. The forest service wanted to study water movement off of different vegetative cover, such as cropland, pasture, and woods. No one knew for sure if certain crops or forestland could stop water from forming these big gullies that you see in the coulee regions of those three states. So they needed a place that typified the diverse topographical features necessary to study water runoff. That's how the forest got started.

In 1958, the U.S. Forest Service announced it had found a suitable tract of land for its studies in La Crosse County. Land purchases and acquisitions began and continued until 1964. The formal dedication of the Coulee Experimental State Forest was conducted in June 1960. Says James:

> Part of the attractive nature of the area was that there were forests with 150-year-old trees still standing on some hillsides even though the land had been in private ownership and farmed intensively with row crops and pastures. After the farms were purchased, the buildings were demolished or moved to other sites. There are no buildings on the property now except for one shed that the U.S. Forest Service used as their "shop" and that we use for storing machinery.

Today, the forest is owned and administered by the WDNR and not only managed for research, but for timber production, wildlife habitat, and that "quiet" recreation. James continues:

> The U.S. Forest Service has a fifteen-year lease on the property that they renewed in 2004. That allows them to formulate and carry out research projects here on the forest. The WDNR's obligation is to provide a variable land base for them where they can do that. But it is understood that their research will not inhibit management of the property, and we will be flexible in terms of the sites where they want to locate projects — and we won't do anything to wreck the research.

On the Forest's Trail

The Coulee Experimental State Forest has only two parking areas, and this small gravel turnout is one of them. From here, I can get to the forest's one designated trail, a twelve-mile cross-country ski trail that can be used for hiking and horseback riding in the spring, summer, and fall. The trail has no official name.

"When the state designates a trail," explains James, "that means that it is

Snowflakes aren't the only winter-white, lacey wonders found on the ski trail. Queen Anne's lace, or wild carrot, takes their place during August.
John T. Andrews

maintained according to set trail standards and that it can appear on maps available to the public. We mow the ski trail a minimum of once and a maximum of twice a year. I try to get it mowed in June, but the Coulee forest doesn't have its own budget for operations. So at times, it's a little 'rustic,' I guess," he says.

In winter, under a volunteer agreement, the trail actually is groomed by a local ski club for classical and skate skiing.

I don't plan to do the trail's whole twelve miles today, but I will try to hike into this forest as deep as time allows. The path starts at the edge of a cornfield that is high with stalks and tasseled ears on this early August day. This is one of those "interfaces" — that once "unknown entity" James mentioned — where agricultural land and forest meet, the kind of place the U.S. Forest Service wanted to study back in the 1950s. Again, I am struck by the feeling that this is a special and unusual landscape.

I'm lucky that the trail has been mowed at least once this year, and after rounding the cornfield, the landscape transforms into a thick, upland forest of central hardwoods, filled with red and white oak, shagbark hickory, basswoods, and elms. In some stands, the trunks of the trees are thick; in others, close and skinny trees stretch one on top of the other into the sky. There are some stately conifers here, too — white pine make up 2.3 percent of the forest's trees and grow on sixty-seven of its acres.

About a mile in when the forest opens up into a tiny clearing, a small group of equestrians passes me by. I'm sure my expression is a mirror of theirs; all of us a little shocked to actually run into someone else. We exchange hellos and pass on our ways. I think this is probably as crowded as the forest ever gets.

Shortly after seeing the horses and riders, about two miles in, I lose the trail completely in the ferny undergrowth, once mowed this year or not. Either experience or a map, I think to myself, is necessary to go farther. I have neither. I turn around and walk back out the way I came in, contemplating this

About a mile into the cross-country ski trail from the east entrance, the forest opens up into a small clearing.
John T. Andrews

mix of trees, clearings, and agricultural lands. I have read that coyotes frequent this portion of the trail, especially the forest fringes alongside the cornfield. The horses and I have most probably been too much of a disturbance for the coyotes to show themselves this morning, and I fail to see any. I have also missed seeing any long vistas of this coulee landscape, but James tells me "from the Bostwick Overlook, when the leaves are down, you can look up and down the valley."

Experimenting in the Coulee

That valley has sparked a lot of interest since the 1960s, not only from the U.S. Forest Service but also from the U.S. Fish and Wildlife Service, the Wild Turkey Federation, the Ruffed Grouse Society, the Wisconsin Woodland

COYOTES IN THE COULEE

Intent and skillful hunters, coyotes are now present in every county in Wisconsin. *John T. Andrews*

ONCE FOUND ALMOST EXCLUSIVELY ON OUR country's Western plains and prairies, coyotes (*Canis latrans*) are today residents in all of the United States. The extirpation of the gray wolf from much of its original habitat opened the country up to the highly adaptable coyote. In Wisconsin, coyotes are present in every county and have proven to be smart, skillful hunters. They now play an important role in the state's natural web of life.

Coyote was known as "the Trickster" by many Native American tribes. He amused, scandalized, or humiliated the people of prehistory in many of their tales, yet he was also believed to be the intelligent father of the Indian people and a conductor of spiritual forces in sacred dreams.

Coyotes are about half the size of wolves and have thinner muzzles. An adult male is 3.5 to 4.5 feet long, including its fourteen-inch bushy, black-tipped tail.

They have large ears and weigh between twenty-five and forty-two pounds. The animal's fur is tan, with black and orange highlights and a cream-colored belly. Running at twenty-five to thirty miles an hour, a coyote will hold his tail down, while dogs run with their tails held up and wolves with their tails held straight out.

Like a domestic dog, a coyote is playful and sociable. Even the adults will roll and tumble about like puppies. Omnivores, coyotes eat fruit, small mammals, reptiles, amphibians, birds, insects, and carrion. A coyote will hunt alone or in small groups. It uses its large ears to hear small mammals beneath snow or vegetation; then, standing over a spot, it will cock its head back and forth to pinpoint prey and pounce.

Secretive and nocturnal, coyotes are more likely to be heard than seen. Their doglike barking results in a chorus of high-pitched howling and yipping; a sound

COYOTES IN THE COULEE

different from the lower, deeper call of a timber wolf, which rarely yips.

Prior to 1900, coyotes were equally common throughout Wisconsin. But because coyotes were formidable competitors for the rabbits, grouse, and turkeys that pioneers also fancied on their tables — plus the coyote's penchant for raiding chicken coops and killing an occasional young farm animal — white settlers considered them pests and placed bounties on their heads. In fact, in an 1863 southern Wisconsin newspaper article, all readers were invited to take part in a "grand wolf hunt" (coyotes were then referred to as "prairie wolves"). A long line of hunters would spread out over a large area, walk in unison, and shoot coyotes driven out of their hiding spots. While their numbers were drastically reduced in southern Wisconsin due to such practices, coyote populations increased in the Northwoods.

Currently, Wisconsin's coyote count is deemed healthy. Year-round coyote hunting with no bag limits is allowed in the state, but a defined trapping season was instituted in 1981. Hopefully, these many-storied and wise canines will be part of Wisconsin's lore and forest nights for generations to come.

Owners Association, the Audubon Society, and Whitetails Unlimited. All have conducted research here.

Before white settlers came to La Crosse County, the forests covering the ridge tops held the soil in place with litter, humus, and tree roots. When farmers cleared much of the high forests, water runoff carried a lot of the soil down the steep slopes, piling up debris along the way or at the bottom. Because nonglaciated soils are mostly wind-laid silt loams, they are highly erosive.

By taking some of this land out of agricultural production and putting it back into woods, the remaining soil has been held in place. The results of the U.S. Forest Service's research over the years has pointed out the key role that woodlands can play in shaping the future of unglaciated areas. Soil and water values can be protected through rehabilitation of existing forest, by reforesting the slopes and abandoned farmland, and by special timber cutting and harvesting practices.

But while the primary mission of the research initiated on the Coulee was to investigate ways to manage steep land to control floods, soil erosion, and stream sedimentation, a secondary mission was to study the adaptability of various tree species and classes of planting stock to various conditions in an effort to guide landowners in their tree-planting programs. As a result of research conducted on the Coulee Experimental State Forest over the years, many reports have been published on runoff, soil erosion, soil freezing, spring flow and groundwater, evapotranspiration, and reforestation.

"When the U.S. Forest Service was doing research here, it was pretty intense," says James Dalton. "They had a field station located in La Crosse, with several scientists as well as some technical staff. They hired bulldozers and built berms and waterways, used to measure water flow. They really went at it pretty hard organizing these projects. They would study them for a few years, and then when their questions were answered, they would close down that particular project and publish the results."

Most of the forest service's projects were completed in the early to mid-1970s. However, the last experimental planting on the Coulee occurred in 1992, on 1.5 acres, when the U.S. Forest Service conducted a study on the growth rates of various strains of genetically improved poplars to meet a projected shortage in northern Minnesota. Since then, other groups have used the forest to conduct research; however, it has not been on the same intense level as it was in the 1960s and 1970s. For the most part, researchers with current projects on the state forest are made up of University of Wisconsin professors and graduate students in the field of forestry.

"For example," says James, "in 1987 a group of UW professors collaborated on a study of evergreen and coniferous species and published their results in 1993. All we require of the researchers is to give us a synopsis of what they propose to do and where they want to do it. We make sure that their projects don't interfere with something else going on in the forest," he says.

On the Town Road

Since my own experiment into going deeper into the Coulee forest on the eastern edge has come to a halt, I decide to make my next foray into this wild country from the west access point off Russlan Coulee Road, just east of the small community of Barre Mills. Although there are no trails on this side of the forest, just off the small western parking lot is the old Russlan Coulee Road.

"A lot of the paths in the forest are former logging roads or, in the case of Russlan Coulee, an abandoned town road," James tells me. "Until the 1980s, that was the road from Barre Mills to Bangor. But cars were having so much trouble getting stuck, that it was finally closed to motor vehicles. Some of the farmers that lived in the valleys used to have fields on top of the ridges. They had private, hill roads to get to their fields and to get the produce back down. So some of those roads are there yet, and people hike on them, too," says James.

This afternoon, the path I will follow is the old Russlan Coulee town road. Although now very much grown up into a forest, this side of the property seems sunnier to me, a bit more open. The trees look leaner, and I can almost imagine this terrain when the small highway ran through it. And I can now clearly understand why the autos got stuck. My hike is all uphill, from almost the first footstep.

"The walk on the west from Russlan Coulee Road is a nice walk," James had told me before I visited the forest. "You can see old U.S. Forest Service conifer plantings in the ravine and some recent timber harvesting farther in. There are white pine that are only forty years old, but they are huge!" he promises.

Since James had previously told me that the last planting of trees on the forest happened in the early 1990s, I ask him how, then, could the forest be sustainable if active timber harvests are continuing today. James answers:

We're thinning the pine plantations that were established in the 1970s and 1980s. Plantations are usually thinned every ten or twelve years. But for several years, we didn't have markets for the smaller-diameter trees that grow in plantations. As the markets improved, however, we were able to sell the timber and get the plantations thinned. But hardwoods, such as oaks and walnuts, have been cut as part of the management program ever since the forest was started. Usually, one or two timber sales are set up every year, so cutting has been pretty regular.

According to James, though, if native hardwoods are harvested properly, a younger stand of trees will be regenerated naturally.

Part of a forester's work is to organize and place a harvest in the right spot and at the right time of year. Perhaps we wait for a good acorn year, for example. Then we'll cut the big trees so that the little acorns have overhead sunlight during the next year to grow. That's all part of managing a forest. So while we've had some incidental plantings where someone, for instance, may have wanted to try planting oak trees after a harvest, we haven't had to plant any big, several-acre plantations.

Despite a lack of permanent water, the Coulee Experimental State Forest plays host to diverse creatures, great and small.
John T. Andrews

My hike on the abandoned Russlan Coulee Road is indeed "nice," as James said it would be — peaceful and full of the smells, sights, and sounds of deep woodlands. I keep walking up and up, and although I can't see through the vegetation to an overlook, my calf muscles tell me I must be hiking straight up a ridgeline. There is no one else on this side of the property for miles, I'm sure. It is strikingly quiet, even on this Saturday afternoon. Other than the songs of birds that tell me they are here, too, I feel totally alone. I know, however, that that is only an illusion.

Because the Coulee Experimental State Forest contains virtually no permanent water other than a small number of spring seeps, is much smaller, and supports a less complex mosaic of vegetation types than most other Wisconsin state forests, that doesn't mean that there is not still plenty of wildlife. In fact, hunters are the main recreational users on the forest. The primary game species are white-tailed deer, ruffed grouse, squirrels, wild turkeys, and rabbits.

But the wildlife is not limited to game animals. "Two migratory birds, Acadian flycatchers and cerulean warblers, which are threatened in the state, have been found here for several successive years now," says James. "In an area where land is constantly being fragmented into smaller and smaller pieces, having a place like the Coulee forest is important for bird and animal species that need large areas of woods in order to survive. And not only are there threatened birds and animals on the Coulee, but we have some rare plants, such as yellow gentian, growing here."

And humans aren't the only hunters who find this forest enticing. "I've seen a lot of coyotes," says James. "There's a place called Billy Goat Ridge on the northeast corner of the Coulee. Sometimes I climb up there in the course of my work, and I see a coyote run past me, so intent on hunting that he doesn't necessarily know I'm there. And there's a marsh hawk, also called a northern

STORIES UNDER THE WHITE PINE

THE ONEIDA HAVE A STORY ABOUT A TREE OF peace. Six different tribes who were fighting buried their weapons under a giant white pine. Their armaments, they believed, would be sent off on the path of the tree's roots and carried away by underground waters. After that, the tribes no longer fought, and they formed the Iroquois League of Nations. And according to the front cover of a 1922 book published by the Red River Lumber Company, the "marvelous exploits" of the mighty Paul Bunyan were told in the camps of white pine lumbermen. It seems Wisconsin's white pine inspire great things in people.

A Wisconsin native, the eastern white pine (*Pinus strobus*) is the state's largest conifer. Standing seventy to a hundred feet high, white pine once dominated our northern forests, with central Wisconsin being the southern part of their range. They were the backbone on which our timber industry was built. Having lost many of them to the logging era — and because they are susceptible to air pollution and thus environmental indicators of poor air quality — many state foresters would like to see them brought back.

A white pine has a single, tall trunk with evenly spaced whorls of horizontal branching. The soft, flexible, three- to five-inch-long needles are clustered, with five bluish-green needles per cluster. The resin-coated, curved cones are green, but turn brown when mature. Cones are four to eight inches long, with a pointed, white tip on each scale.

The bark of a white pine is gray to brown and smooth when young, breaking with age into large, broad scales that are separated by deep furrows. This thick, insulating bark protects the cambium from a forest fire's heat. Moreover, in dense stands, mature white pine usually have no branches on the lower half of the

These Wisconsin natives can live more than two hundred years.
Thomas A. Meyer, Wisconsin DNR

(continued on next page)

STORIES UNDER THE WHITE PINE

(continued from page 103)
trunk, concentrating them near the top in an irregular pattern — remote from the tinder of the forest floor and immune to practically anything but intense crown fires.

White pine was not only prized by Wisconsin loggers for its smooth-grained lumber but for the fact that it could still be processed in a lumber mill a year or more after being cut down. Most hardwoods, such as oaks, maples, and ashes, had to be cut into boards soon after felling or large cracks would develop in the trunk, damaging the value of the timber. And in old-growth pines, huge, knot-free boards were the rule rather than the exception.

If its life is not cut short by loggers, disease, or weather, a white pine tree can survive to be 200 to 250 years old. Some, however, live for more than 400 years. On December 29, 1937, a 426-year-old white pine "monarch" was felled in Lincoln County by the Forest Products Laboratory. When it was born in 1511, not a single European was living in North or South America. When brave and hearty Jean Nicolet first visited the land that is now Wisconsin, it was already 123 years old.

harrier, who resides up on the ridge in a field. Every time I go up there at this time of year, I see him hunting," reports James.

While James believes there are no black bears currently on the Coulee Experimental State Forest, he is quick to point out that "it would probably be a good place for one, if it wanted to move in."

Berg Prairie: Left Unexplored and Unresearched

Although I tried, sore calf muscles and all, I never did make it to the top. I walked for a few hours up the old Russlan Coulee Road, but I never felt a plateau under my boot heels; never had the sensation of going down. I can see now that it's like that in this forest, on both ends. Every place is just "up."

Is there anyplace here that a person can walk to that isn't in the skyward direction? James tells me there truly is a spot that you can hike *out* to and then look *down* at. It's called Berg Prairie.

"Berg Prairie is in the southeast corner of the property off of Antony Road," says James. "You walk out to the end of a big point in the woods, and the view is just incredible. The prairie is on the south- and west-facing slopes straight down below you, flowing down to the bottom of the valley at a 60- to

The access point to Berg Prairie is somewhere out there in the Driftless Area landscape, but it remained hidden to me.
John T. Andrews

90-percent grade. It's a ten-acre prairie; the largest one in the area that's a native, natural prairie. It's quite a vista," he assures me.

Every two out of three or four years, Berg Prairie is managed by a prescribed burn to encourage the growth of native flowers and plants. Because it's August, the prairie promises to still be in beautiful bloom.

The access point to Berg Prairie is supposed to be off County Highway II. However, again I can find no board signs and no signs of any paths or footsteps in. I don't even see a reasonable place to leave a car. Sadly, I head back toward I-90 and Madison, a bit dejected and disappointed.

When I get home, I call James and tell him that I couldn't find Berg

QUIET IN THE AIR: WHEN OWLS TAKE FLIGHT

SYMBOLS OF WISDOM AND PRUDENCE, OWLS are also often thought to portend death and hardship. For centuries, many cultures around the globe have tried to decipher the mysterious owl. From the ancient Greeks to today's young Harry Potter, owls play an important part in humanity's folklore. And one of the characteristics that captivate us most about owls is their capacity for silent flight.

Three kinds of owls are found on the Coulee Experimental State Forest: barred, great horned, and screech owls. The forest's dense trees make it the perfect owl habitat. And because this forest is an extremely quiet place, the great birds fit the forest's personality like a glove.

From dusk to just before dawn, owls hunt, waiting in a tree snag or high branch for an unsuspecting snake, frog, mouse, or bird. With large eyes that bring in lots of light to see in the darkness, they are able to quickly spot prey, swoop down on stealth wings, and capture their food with

Three types of owls frequent the Coulee Experimental State Forest: barred, screech, and great horned, pictured here. *Bob Leggett*

their sharp talons before even being heard. Owls then fly back to their lairs for dinner, using their knifelike beaks to rip meat apart.

For most birds, flight is a noisy business. Air rushing over feathered wings produces turbulence that most prey animals can hear as a swishing sound. But nocturnal owls are able to make their silent forays for three physiological reasons: first, the primary feathers on the leading edge of an owl's wings are serrated like a comb. This design breaks down turbulence into smaller currents called micro-turbulences, allowing air to pass through and eliminating sound. Some have suggested that these feathers may also shift sound energy to a higher frequency than prey can hear.

Second, the feathers on the back end of the wings are tattered like a scarf's fringe. As an owl flies and air flows over the wings, these trailing, tattered feathers break the sound waves.

Prairie, that there were no signs of it, no markers, no way to know where it was. "Nobody mows the entrance," says James. "To get there, you have to wade through the tall grass to find the cable across the trail that leads out to the prairie bluff."

I realize now that I couldn't find the entrance because there *wasn't* an entrance. I probably should have done a little more research before I went to the Coulee Experimental State Forest.

But perhaps it is best for now that I didn't disturb Berg Prairie; that I left it alone, in the quiet. I'm very sure that James was okay with that.

QUIET IN THE AIR: WHEN OWLS TAKE FLIGHT

Third, the owl's legs and the rest of the wings are covered in velvety, down feathers that absorb any remaining noise created in flight. And the fact that owls have broad wings with large surface areas that allow them to float through the air without flapping contributes to noise reduction.

While the silent flight of owls has long fascinated us and especially ornithologists, aircraft engineers are starting to take notice. In an effort to make planes as quiet as possible, they are looking at the unique design of owl feathers for potential applications in the aeronautics industry. Since major

An owl's wings are perfectly engineered for silent flight. *Bob Leggett*

airports have restrictions on how much noise they can generate per day, what is learned from studying owl feathers could someday increase where and how often airplanes take off and land. Researchers have postulated several ideas, including a retractable, brushlike fringe to mimic an owl's trailing wing feathers and a coating of soft material on aircraft landing gear to simulate downy legs.

One day, you might be traveling in a plane that is wisely designed in the image of an owl.

Coulee Experimental State Forest

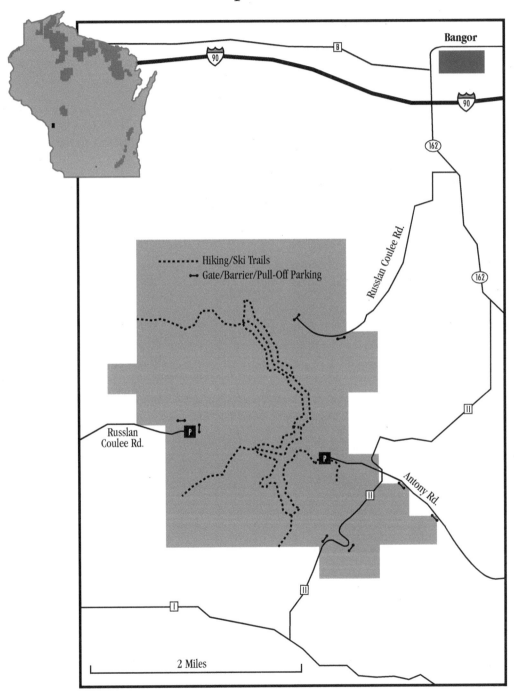

Hiking/Ski Trails
Gate/Barrier/Pull-Off Parking

Bangor

Russlan Coulee Rd.

Russlan
Coulee Rd.

Antony Rd.

2 Miles

Travel can be done only by foot — whether human or horse — in the Coulee Experimental State Forest. *John T. Andrews*

Almost every car in the forest's boundaries during June has a canoe strapped to its roof rack. For centuries, the Flambeau River has been a highway for Native Americans, fur traders, and loggers. *John T. Andrews*

6 Flambeau River State Forest

ROCKS, RIVER RUNNERS, AND RUFFLED FEATHERS

The Mighty Flambeau River: Nice, It's Not

"I think you could call the North Fork of the Flambeau River the nicest river in northern Wisconsin," says Jason Gillis, who was born just south of the Flambeau River State Forest and still lives there. "There are barely any houses on this stretch of it," he says about his favorite waterway. Jason has been a Chippewa River and Flambeau River guide for seven years as the owner of Flambeau Adventures, a canoeing outfitter and guide service located on Big Falls Flowage, three miles below Beaver Dam Rapids.

But I'm not so sure "nice" is the word I'd use to describe the character of this river and the forest that protects it. "Ruggedly beautiful"? Yes. An "engaging nature"? Yes. But "nice"? I'm not convinced.

From my quick view of it late yesterday when I arrived, the Flambeau River looked like a very rocky and treacherous place for a canoeist of my nascent skills. In fact, instead of taking a white-knuckle ride on the river, I'm opting to explore this forest — largely composed of rapids and riverbanks — during the next few days by foot.

That itself could prove to be a risky endeavor. Presently, there are only two maintained, established trails in this whole forest. The Oxbo Trail is eight miles long, and the Flambeau Hills Trail is a fourteen-mile trek. Although there are numerous smaller footpaths used by hunters and some hikers, the rest of the forest is largely undeveloped.

At Cedar Rapids, the Flambeau River is wide and deep. *John T. Andrews*

My decision to walk this forest is beginning to make me feel a little bit like a "fish out of water," or, more precisely, a "canoeist out of the river." Because on this Saturday in June, at 6:42 a.m., every other car I see coming into the forest has a boat strapped onto its roof rack.

River of Rocks

My drive getting to the forest from southern Wisconsin was filled with other quick views and visual cues, as well. On Highways 51 and 39 North, between Westfield and Coloma, one hand-painted road sign read: "Fresh Peas Ahead." And above The Roadhouse tavern in Hazelhurst, a banner proclaimed that just inside the doors "Blues, Booze, and BBQs" waited. In a few days, when my adventure in the Flambeau River State Forest would be over, I wondered what sign I'd paint on it, then, if I could; what its signature character — in a few pithy words — will be.

The Flambeau River — along with the Chippewa, Black, Mississippi, Fox, and Wisconsin — once acted as a highway for transporting timber. *WHi Image ID 62818*

Yesterday afternoon, my first forest stop was at Little Falls/Slough Gundy. Here, in the late afternoon sun, the wet rocks in the middle of the river glistened in the rushing, churning whitewater of the South Fork of the Flambeau River. Only the most advanced canoeists tackle the South Fork during high water, and I could see why. The rapids roared in my ears and surged around the huge boulders, a swirling contrast to the stately and staid pine forest in the background. This is one of the most extraordinarily beautiful and challenging rivers I have ever seen.

The Flambeau flows from north to south, from the Turtle-Flambeau Flowage in Iron County near Mercer down for approximately 150 miles to its confluence with the Chippewa River in Rusk County. More than seventy-five of those miles lie within the Flambeau River State Forest. Like the Wisconsin, Mississippi, and Brule Rivers, the Flambeau is one of the great rivers that played a major role in the making of our state and its history. For centuries, Native Americans fished and paddled down its winding course. Three hundred years ago, it became a highway for fur traders carrying pelts out of the forest. And in the nineteenth and twentieth centuries, the Flambeau River transported Wisconsin's great white pine logs downstream to mills, and from there to the nation's markets.

But today I see no floating logs. Just sturgeon in the shallows, a pair of wood ducks on the surface, and a great blue heron on the shore downstream.

Rapid Danger

Guide Jason says that where I had been standing, at Little Falls/Slough Gundy, is probably where the biggest rapids on the whole river system are found. "Springtime is about the only time you can run the South Fork," he says, "so I don't canoe it often. At other times, there's not enough water in it, unless there is a flood or a big rain. The North Fork is dam-controlled, so there's usually enough water to canoe it all summer long. The North Fork has about fifteen rapids; the South Fork about the same," he tells me.

It could be said that the pulsating rapids of the Flambeau River are the pulse of the forest. This river, at one spot or another, contains all five classes of rapids. The International Canoe Federation Whitewater Rating Definitions for classes of rapids are:

> **Class I — Easy**. Riffles; small, regular waves. Easy to find the course. Minor obstacles that are easily spotted. Beginner paddlers.
>
> **Class II — Medium**. Fairly frequent but unobstructed rapids; usually with regular waves and easy eddies and bends. Novice paddlers.
>
> **Class III — Difficult**. Characterized by numerous high, irregular waves covering the boat. The course is not easily recognizable; requires maneuvering in rapids. Intermediate paddlers. Solid whitewater paddling skills necessary.
>
> **Class IV — Very Difficult**. Long rapids with powerful, irregular waves. Dangerous rocks and boiling eddies. Powerful and precise maneuver-

ing is required. The course is difficult to determine without scouting from the bank. Holes will keep boats. Advanced paddlers.

Class V — Extremely Difficult. Long, violent rapids with difficult, irregular, unavoidable high waves and holes. Rescue is difficult. Fast eddies and vigorous crosscurrents. Frequent scouting is mandatory. Expert paddlers.

But even if you know the classification of a particular rapids, the Flambeau River can surprise you again with its temperamental nature. Water levels can and do fluctuate daily, if not hourly, and it is important for a canoeist to be aware of the river's current conditions on every trip out.

Here, at Slough Gundy, a Class II to Class III rapids, it is best to stop, scout, and plan your canoe route and portage if necessary. The rapids at Little Falls, the next set of rapids down, is so hazardous that it should not be paddled at all — there is a much-used portage there.

The dangers of the Flambeau's rapids are something Jason can tell me about firsthand.

"Once, a man and his son were canoeing in the spring when the water was still cold," says Jason. "The man tipped out of the boat at Beaver Dam Rapids and died. His son had to walk all the way down to Big Falls Flowage — about four miles — barefoot. He stood across the river, screaming toward our house. The boy was only about fourteen or fifteen years old. That was ten or twelve years ago. There have been a few other deaths, as well."

Attesting to the river's changing temperament, Jason adds, "I snorkel a lot in the rapids for gear that people lose when they tip over. But in summer, the water comes down pretty good, so you almost have to do something very wrong to hurt yourself."

A Singular History; Single-Tree Harvesting

At 90,147 acres, the Flambeau River State Forest is the second largest property owned by the State of Wisconsin (the Northern Highland-American Legion State Forest is the largest, at 223,283 acres). In fall, this forest of sugar maple, red maple, yellow birch, and white ash arrays itself in a spectacular range of colors. Established on November 29, 1930, the forest serves to protect most of the Flambeau River. The forest also functions as a timber supplier and

Lands that now make up the Flambeau River State Forest were logged during the first half of the twentieth century. They looked like the cutover country pictured here.
WHi Image ID 3990

an undeveloped recreation spot for canoeists, kayakers, campers, snowmobilers, ATVers, hunters, fishers, and hikers.

The idea for the forest was born in the 1920s, when Judge A. K. Owens of Phillips and a group of citizens, concerned over the swift destruction of the area's timber resources by fire and logging, began petitioning to preserve a large block of land on the Flambeau River. In 1929, the Wisconsin Conservation Commission (which became the Wisconsin Department of Natural Resources in 1967) purchased a 3,112-acre parcel.

In the following years, more land was purchased from lumber companies that had completed the cutover of their properties and were looking for a way to get rid of them. By 1946, the forest had more than sixty-five thousand acres.

In the early 1950s, the forest headquarters building was built from blown-down hemlocks. As more people began to use the forest, Lake of the Pines and Connors Lake Campgrounds were created.

Each year, there are fifteen to twenty active harvest contracts on about

Kids can enjoy an old-fashioned jump in the lake at the Connors Lake Campground. *John T. Andrews*

BIG FOREST TREES OF WISCONSIN

THERE ARE MORE THAN TWENTY THOUSAND different tree species in the world. One particular tree, in fact, is the world's largest known, living, single-stem organism in terms of volume: the "General Sherman" in Sequoia National Park, California. This giant is believed to be between 2,300 and 2,700 years old.

The Wisconsin Department of Natural Resources searches for our own state's largest trees. To encourage appreciation for some of Wisconsin's oldest beings, the WDNR invites you to register any large trees you know in a program called Champion Trees.

At the Web site at http://dnr.wi.gov/forestry/UF/champion, the Champion Tree register lists the top records for several species. Each tree's dimensions, location, and measurement date are recorded. Instructions on how to measure a tree you think qualifies for the designation of "champion tree" and a nomination form can be found on the Web site.

You can read more about Wisconsin's big, old trees in the books *Wisconsin's Champion Trees, Every Root an Anchor,* and *If Trees Could Talk* by arborist Bruce Allison.

fifteen hundred acres of the forest. The majority of these timber sales are conducted in the winter, when the frozen ground minimizes the disturbance to the soil. According to the Department of Natural Resources, an important management prescription for the Flambeau River State Forest "is to maintain and establish big trees within select forest types, such as northern hardwoods, white pine, red pine, red oak, and hemlock-hardwoods. Large-diameter trees are recognized for their aesthetic values." As a result, harvesting is primarily done by single-tree selection.

Where Emotions Run Like a River

The harvesting of trees in any forest can become an emotional issue, and it is certainly one for people who care deeply for the Flambeau River State Forest, such as Jason Gillis. The Flambeau seems to run through Jason's veins, and he'd like to keep its banks "natural" — in fact, he may be the youngest person to ever float the river during the spring run.

"My mother was pregnant in 1971 when my father took her out on the river in spring," Jason says after showing me a story his father wrote about the event. "For many local canoeists, being the first on the river in spring is a highlight of the year," he explains. "My father convinced my mother to go on the spring run in '71 to take photos, despite the fact that not only was she pregnant, but she was petrified of canoes." Luckily, Jason's mother was put ashore just before his father and a friend tackled Beaver Dam Rapids on the North Fork. They ended up with the canoe's open side down.

Today, as far as Jason is concerned, there is a lot of logging going on in the forest — sometimes, perhaps, too much. He says:

> From what I understand right now, the forest's management cannot cut a tree, plant a tree, or do anything within a quarter mile of the river. It's a natural buffer area. But a couple of years ago, a questionnaire from the Department of Natural Resources went out. It asked, "Do you think we should be able to manage within that shoreline buffer for scenic beauty?" So, that would mean cutting trees for the purpose of "scenic beauty." I think if you leave the big trees where they fall on their own and let them rot, you've got another nice habitat for all sorts of animals. When people ask, "Then, who's going to manage the forest?" I say, "Well, who managed it for ten thousand years? It doesn't need to be 'managed.'"

According to Jim Halvorson, superintendent of the Flambeau River State Forest, Jason is correct in stating that until recently, the Wisconsin Department of Natural Resources did not "manage" (remove invasive species from or cut trees on) the lands one-quarter mile back from the shores of the river, pursuant to the forest's master plan. Every twenty years, however, forest personnel are required to revise the plan. In preparation for the 2010 update, surveys — such as the one Jason mentioned — were sent out to frequent forest visitors and the river's users, and three to four public listening-sessions were held. States Jim:

> Most of the respondents to the questionnaire and the majority of those who came to the listening sessions were okay with now allowing us to manage within that quarter mile of the shore, but they wanted to be sure that we retain the backcountry atmosphere; they wanted to keep the forest natural and primitive. People didn't want road building or a lot of noise. While the directives in the new master plan will now *allow* us to cut trees within that quarter-mile buffer zone, the focus for the next twenty years will be on adhering to an "old-growth forest standard," meaning that we will be cognizant of preserving older, larger trees and retaining dead snags. In other words, we will strive for a natural, old-growth aesthetic.

Jason does admit that so far the forest still holds huge stands of pines, birches, hemlocks, and maples. "Certain areas haven't been cut much at all," he allows. "I've shot a deer that was standing 250 yards out into the woods. That's a long way to be able to see anything. The trees are so huge and tall that nothing is able to grow underneath them, and the forest floor is clear."

Logging, however, isn't the only force at work that deletes some of the trees that Jason cares so much about from the forest. Blowdowns take their share of the old giants, as evidenced in "the Big Block."

A Course in Nature

Controversy over cutting trees in the Flambeau River State Forest has been going on for a long time. In the 1950s, that concern was focused on an area in Sawyer County just two miles south of Connors Lake, east of the North Fork of the Flambeau River. It was filled with old-growth hardwoods (hardwoods are broad-leafed species with enclosed nuts or seeds, such as aspens, ashes, basswoods, cherries, elms, maples, oaks, and walnuts) and known as "the Big

KNOCK ON WOOD

YOU COULD SAY THAT IT WAS JUST PURE luck that saved a few large trees in the Flambeau River Hardwood Forest State Natural Area from the 1977 blowdown. And — knock on wood — let's hope that year's devastation won't be repeated any time soon.

Chances are that you know exactly what I mean by using the three-word expression above. The phrase "knock on wood" is typically spoken as a charm to keep bad things from happening or to avoid "tempting fate." But just where does the superstitious utterance come from?

Some think either pagan or early Christian beliefs are the source. Pagans thought that spirits lived in trees and that by knocking on bark while making a bold statement, you could prevent the spirit from hearing you and thus stop it from interfering. Another possible etymology is that pagans believed touching a tree showed respect for the wood spirit or indicated that you sought the spirit's protection.

An alternative origin for the phrase is the early Christian ritual of touching a wooden crucifix when taking an oath or praying for good fortune. The Christians may have believed they were actually touching part of the genuine cross used in the Crucifixion. Later it was thought that touching any piece of wood that once was part of a sacred tree would confer the same benefits.

Other experts think the expression came from a popular early-nineteenth-century children's game of tag called "Tiggy-Touch-Wood," where you achieved "safe" by touching — you guessed it — wood.

Block." Within the Big Block's borders, eastern hemlock, yellow birch, sugar maple, white ash, elms, basswoods, and some very large white pine stood. Well-known conservationists including Sigurd Olson, author of *The Singing Wilderness* (1956) and *The Hidden Forest* (1969), proposed that a one-mile buffer on each side of the Flambeau River be preserved with no cutting allowed. But before the Wisconsin Department of Natural Resources could come up with a plan to accommodate both the views of conservationists and the economic need for lumber, nature stepped in.

On July 4, 1977, a devastating windstorm and downburst flattened thousands of acres of timber on the Flambeau. The Big Block, which had been one of the last virgin forested areas left in Wisconsin, was the hardest hit. The storm felled the entire stand except for two small sections, leaving only a few large trees standing. The Wisconsin Natural Resources Board, which sets policy for the Department of Natural Resources, granted the state forest the right to apply salvage operations on 10,606 acres, which earned the state $1,426,998.

Today the Big Block encompasses three thousand acres of protected wilderness. It contains the 266-acre Flambeau River Hardwood Forest, one of eight State Natural Areas within the Flambeau River State Forest.

In 1976, the Flambeau River Hardwood Forest State Natural Area held a stand filled with eastern hemlock, yellow birch, and sugar maple with some American basswood, white ash, and white pine. Some of the trees were 220 years old. A small section of this State Natural Area was missed by the 1977 blowdown. Today, sugar maple, yellow birch, and American basswood are growing; the eastern hemlock are disappearing.

The Lake of the Pines Conifer-Hardwoods State Natural Area, situated on the east-central shore of Lake of the Pines, also preserves a band of eastern hemlock and yellow birch that was left standing after the 1977 storm. After the blowdown, some of this natural area was salvage cut, and today young sugar maple, yellow birch, and American basswood are the thriving species.

Although the 1977 storm has left its mark on the Big Block, positive results do grow here. The blowdown area is now an important site for education and research, especially for the study of how an old-growth forest regenerates following a natural disturbance. Human manipulation is kept to a minimum, and here nature is allowed once again to take its course.

A Forest Grandfather

This morning, I'm going to continue working my way north through the forest. Upon reaching its central section, I stop at the forest headquarters located on Highway W. On the premises is an open-sided shelter covering a huge piece of a cut log. Sadly, this log section comes from a tree known as the "Big White Pine," another "Big" in the list of "Big" names in this forest.

A sign says that the Big White Pine resided in the forest for more than three hundred years before the early winter of 2000, when it was felled. A "combination of lightning strikes, insect infestations, and disease" had ravaged it in its later years, and the tree had become hollow inside with mostly rotten wood. In August 2000, while the forest staff was assessing the safety of leaving the 130-foot giant standing, someone cut through the Big White Pine's four-foot, two-inch diameter and thirteen-foot, two-inch girth — and brought it down. Local people, with the help of the forest staff, salvaged a sixteen-foot-long log and transported it here. No one knows who cut the Big White Pine.

Walking around this remnant of the past, I think of a recent trip I took to New Zealand. There I had walked in the country's podocarp forests, where native Maori call the large, old trees — some up to 1,500 years old, of species that have survived since the days of the dinosaurs — their "grandfathers." They often go to the forest to sing to them. I begin to imagine what the Big White Pine must have looked like, standing proudly here in the Flambeau. I think of it having the stately comportment of my own grandfather, its trunk strong and straight, with limbs dressed in the color of evergreen. Henry David Thoreau once called the white pine "a great green feather stuck in the ground."

The Oxbo Incident

Images of the Big White Pine remain with me all day as I wander the forest. I keep bearing north, until I come to the Dix Dox Landing and the Oxbo Resort located on the North Fork of the Flambeau River. The resort consists of four cabins, a very small tavern, and about fifteen canoes lined up on the shore, which are available for rent. But just like with the section of the Big White Pine at the forest headquarters, what I see at the Oxbo Resort today is a ghost of another time in the forest.

Oxbo was once more than this small resort. In 1922, it was a bustling community with a resident population of about fifty and a post office, gas station, school, and zoo filled with adopted, orphaned black bears and other animals native to the Northwoods. Highway 70 once ran directly in front of the town hall (which is now the tavern). But in the 1960s, Highway 70 was rerouted, and Oxbo slipped into the quiet of the forest. Today, the post office, school, and zoo are gone. The gas station still survives.

With the sun now going down, I decide to spend the night at the Oxbo Resort. In my cabin, there is no telephone, radio, or television. But what my lodging does have aces out any of that. It has grandfather trees. Perhaps they are not quite as old as the Big White Pine had been, but they are getting there. They are towering creatures, with boughs high up. They shade out any vegetation below, and beneath them spent pine needles drape the ground in terra cotta. Above, the canopy is the color of fresh peas, and I realize the sign near Coloma was true. Orange-and-green is one of my favorite color combinations.

Before I turn in, Jan, the owner of the Oxbo, warns me to watch out for black bears if I venture out of the cabin at night.

Run, Wood Tick, Run

At the Oxbo, it seems you can run into the top of the forest's food chain as well as representatives from its lowest echelon. Unfortunately, I've arrived a month too late for the annual wood tick races in May. Secretly, I'm pleased. I've had my share of run-ins with the tiny beasts over the years.

According to local lore, almost thirty years ago, in the tavern of the Oxbo Resort, a man named Dick Kuhnert plucked a tick off of his arm, placed it on the bar, and watched as it sped around. That's where he got the idea for the yearly Wood Tick Race. Today, believe it or not, hundreds of contestants vie for the title of "Wood Tick Racing Champion."

To compete in the race, first you must find a wood tick by scouring the Flambeau River State Forest. Then you must win a series of heats. Two competing wood ticks are placed in a bull's-eye target. The first tick to emerge from the bulls-eye is the winner of that heat. The loser is smashed with the mayor of Oxbo's gavel. The elimination heats continue until only two ticks remain to contend for the World Champion Wood Tick title. The ultimate tick earns his or her "owner" a money prize, a champion's trophy, and bragging rights.

The literature about the race's rules imparts an interesting fact. Sometimes the most challenging aspect of participating in the race is keeping your tick contestant alive between heats. Some people have been known to place the ticks on parts of their body to keep the little fellows warm, while others have kept them in Ziploc bags, occasionally opening them long enough to allow fresh air to revitalize the critters.

Flowage on the Forest

The June sun is just about to rise on what promises to be a beautiful morning. Rather than watching wood ticks race, I've got something more picturesque in mind for today: I'll be going to one of the three "scenic areas" in the forest: the Sobieski Flowage (the other two scenic areas are Little Falls/Slough Gundy and Bass Lake Wilderness).

In 1941, the Ed Sobieski family had a dairy farm in the southeast corner of the forest, which they subsequently converted to a cranberry farm. In 1948, a flowage was built to provide a reliable source of water for the growing beds. The Sobieskis retired in 1973 and sold the land to the Flambeau River State Forest.

In 1989 the Flambeau River Chapter of the Ruffed Grouse Society and the Rusk County Wildlife Restoration Association began songbird, ruffed grouse, and woodcock habitat improvement on the former Sobieski land. Plaza Farms, a local cranberry grower, and the Wisconsin Department of Natural Resources lent their support for dike repair and additional upgrades.

DRUMS ALONG THE FLAMBEAU: RUFFED GROUSE

YOU'RE ALONE IN the forest, and suddenly you start hearing the beat of a drum that seems to increase in tempo with every step you take. But there's no need to worry — you're probably just hearing the sound of a ruffed grouse looking for love.

The Flambeau River State Forest is in the heart of ruffed grouse country. In fact, nearby Park Falls is known as the "Ruffed Grouse Capital of the World." Although sometimes referred to as "partridges," which thrive in hedgerows near farm fields, ruffed grouse are actually woodland birds. They are about the size of a small chicken and found from the Appalachian Mountains up through and across Canada to Alaska.

These mottled, brown to gray birds are ground-dwellers in deciduous and mixed forests. The Flambeau River State Forest Sobieski Flowage is perfect ruffed grouse habitat: they like to forage on the ground or in

Grouse and other game birds have long been a favorite quarry of Wisconsin hunters. *WHi Image ID 58411*

trees, and the former cranberry beds within the woods provide the berries, seeds, buds, and catkins that they like to eat.

In spring, a male attempts to attract a female by standing on a log and spreading his tail in a fan shape. He puffs up his black neck ruff for a very impressive look and begins a series of strong wing strokes — often continuing for hours at a time. As the wings compress the air, they create a vacuum, which pro-

Standing in front of the Sobieski Flowage on this summer day, I get another perspective on this forest, one that doesn't include trees or a river. From here, the Flambeau looks and sounds like an open field that is filled with birds and their songs. Narrow trails of blue water flow between small plains of tall, green grasses. Lily pads are in full bloom and add a touch of fragile beauty.

DRUMS ALONG THE FLAMBEAU: RUFFED GROUSE

duces a drumlike thumping noise. It begins slowly, but rapidly increases and can be heard for a quarter mile or more.

The female ruffed grouse lays nine to twelve buff-colored eggs in a leaf-lined scrape that is sheltered under a tree, stump, bush, rock, or log. The female

A drumming sound is often heard in the Flambeau River State Forest, which is in the heart of ruffed grouse country.
Candice Gaukel Andrews

incubates the eggs for approximately twenty-three days and keeps the chicks with her for about twelve weeks. A week after hatching, however, the chicks will be able to fly short distances.

While you might be surprised by grouse drumbeats in spring — or in the summer or fall if males are defending their territories — in winter, a ruffed grouse may startle you with a sudden exit from a snow bank. If conditions are right — seven or more inches of fluffy snow — grouse will "snow roost" by flying directly into a pile of snow, where temperatures may be twenty to thirty degrees warmer than in the exposed air. If snow is falling, it quickly obscures all evidence of the bird's entry point. When you walk by the following morning, a suddenly exiting bird can catch you off guard.

Ruffed grouse are well adapted for surviving our state's severe winters. Their toes grow bristly, comblike projections, which act like snowshoes, enabling them to walk easily on soft snow. The birds become vulnerable to predation, however, when the snow becomes ice crusted.

Along with canoeing, ruffed grouse hunting is one of the most popular activities in the Flambeau River State Forest. The season generally opens in mid-September and lasts until the end of January.

Ruffed grouse require significant tracts of forest, especially aspen stands, to maintain a stable population: places like the Flambeau River State Forest.

A sign at the flowage says that Ed Sobieski was proud to say his land was always open to everyone for hunting and fishing. I wonder if Ed, or his spirit, still comes here today to harvest what his land provides.

In the wild Flambeau River State Forest, black bears and deer walk through the understory looking for food.
John T. Andrews

It's a Wild Life

While hundreds of birds frequent the open Sobieski Flowage, numerous other beings float, fly, and forage beyond the trees. Muskies, sturgeon, walleye, bass, pan fish, mollusks, crustaceans, catfish, and insects ply the waters and wooded shores of the Flambeau River. Dragonflies, eagles, and ospreys flap wings amid and behind the branches. Black bears and deer walk the understory looking for food, and coyotes and barred owls call in the night. In the secret shallows and hollow trees, hooded mergansers hunt and nest, while mink, raccoons, and families of otters go about the business of making a living at the sheltered waterline.

Currently, several packs of wolves reside within the boundaries of the Flambeau River State Forest. As many as twenty or more wolves may live in the vicinity in winter. Wolf numbers increase in spring with the birth of pups.

According to Jason Gillis, another mysterious social animal once called the Flambeau River State Forest home ground. He was known by the name of Skunk Frank.

"Skunk Frank was an old guy that lived here probably just before the forest was made a forest in 1930," says Jason. "He used to live at the Beaver Dam Landing, the bottom rapids. People would come off the river and stop at his cabin to have pancakes. He had a guest book for the canoeists who went by. I think the Rusk County Community Library has some of those sign-in books. He was a real character, who was pretty well known down around the Beaver Dam Rapids area," laughs Jason.

When I inquire at the county library about Skunk Frank, librarian Betty Cowin tells me she just found a rare book there titled *Diary of Skunk Frank, Flambeau River Hermit.* She says there are several names and dates of visitors — from July 7, 1922, to March 11, 1934, along with the cities they were from. On the final page is a copy of a newspaper article, with a statement that reads, "Frank Strove, who lived on the Flambeau River for the past thirty-five years, was found dead on the shore of the river."

Legends Die Hard

Skunk Frank isn't the only "animal" legend of the North Fork. "Old Abe" the eagle predates the skunk-man by about seventy years and even has several books written about him.

In the summer of 1861, a twenty-five-year-old Ojibwe by the name of *A-ge-mah-we-go-zhig,* or "Chief of the Sky," captured an eaglet on one of the Flambeau's North Fork rapids. A few weeks later, while en route for the Chippewa Falls and Eau Claire area with furs, moccasins, and baskets, A-ge-mah-we-go-zhig sold his young eagle to a man named Daniel McCann for a bushel of corn. According to an article published on the Wisconsin Historical Society Web site, McCann, in turn, offered his eagle's services as a mascot to the Eighth Regiment Wisconsin Volunteer Infantry Company C, feeling that "someone from the family ought to serve."

Company C named the eagle Old Abe to honor President Abraham Lincoln. They swore Old Abe into the United States Army by putting red and blue ribbons around his neck and a rosette on his breast. The men designed a special perch for him and carried the bird into forty-two battles and skirmishes during the Civil War.

Old Abe conducted himself with valor during warfare. According to a contemporary: "At the sound of the regimental bugle, which he had learned to recognize, he would start suddenly, dart up his head, and then bend it gracefully,

The bald eagle known as Old Abe was the mascot of the Eighth Regiment Wisconsin Volunteer Infantry Company C.
WHi Image ID 7534

anticipating the coming shock. When the battle commenced, he would spring up, spread his wings uttering his startling scream, heard, and felt and gloried in by all the soldiers. The fiercer and louder the Storm, the fiercer, louder and wilder were his screams." Confederate troops called Old Abe the "Yankee buzzard" and tried to capture and kill him several times, but they never succeeded.

At the end of the Civil War, Company C presented Old Abe to the state of Wisconsin. He was given a home in the basement of the capitol building in Madison. He made appearances all over the United States, attending public events, such as the 1876 Centennial Exposition in Philadelphia and the 1880 National Encampment of the Grand Army of the Republic in Milwaukee.

The quiet waters of Le Tourneau Creek can be found at the north end of the forest.
John T. Andrews

But on a cold evening in the winter of 1881, a fire started in a stash of paints and oils stored in the basement of the capitol, near Old Abe's large cage. The eagle screeched, calling watchmen and attendants to the basement. They opened the door of his perch-room, and Abe swept out and away from the flames. The blaze was put out, but it had created an enormous volume of black smoke.

Following the incident, Abe never really seemed to recover. He remained in a half-comatose condition for a few days, and then on March 26, 1881, with a slight shake of his body and few feeble flaps of his wings, he died in the arms of his keeper, George Gillies.

A River, A Forest

Time is running out. I have one last afternoon to try to get a handle on describing the character of this forest. I know of the perfect spot to get the job done.

Bass Lake is about three miles off Highway W, but it might more aptly be placed in Canada. In 1983, the Wisconsin Department of Natural Resources designated it a "Wilderness Lake," where motorized vehicles, motorboats, mooring of boats overnight, and camping are prohibited. So loons glide peacefully on the clear lake surface, and largemouth bass and bluegills keep vigil below the blue-blue waters. It's a great location for contemplating just what it is that makes the Flambeau River unique among all of Wisconsin's state and national forests.

I watch one loon swim by, dunk his head under the water, and pop up with a bit of a disheveled look. I laugh, and it comes to me. Perhaps the character of this forest is in this forest's characters. It's in the stories about its bald eagles and racing wood ticks. It's in the Big Block, the Big White Pine, and the bare, dangerous rocks. It's in Skunk Frank and in a little town called Oxbo.

It's in its river guides, who care deeply for the trees here; and it's in the rapids of the river.

Flambeau River State Forest

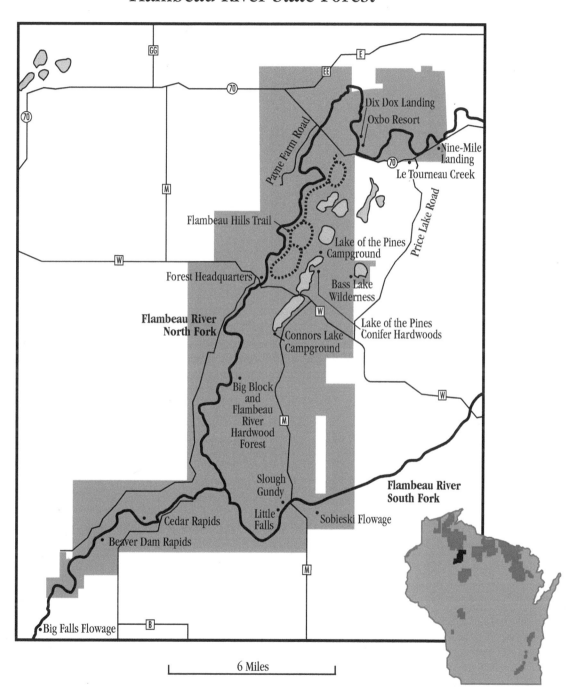

Payne Farm Road

Dix Dox Landing
Oxbo Resort

Nine-Mile
Landing
Le Tourneau Creek

Price Lake Road

Flambeau Hills Trail

Lake of the Pines
Campground

Forest Headquarters

Bass Lake
Wilderness

Lake of the Pines
Conifer Hardwoods

**Flambeau River
North Fork**

Connors Lake
Campground

Big Block
and
Flambeau
River
Hardwood
Forest

Slough
Gundy

**Flambeau River
South Fork**

Little
Falls

Sobieski Flowage

Cedar Rapids

Beaver Dam Rapids

Big Falls Flowage

6 Miles

The Sandrock Cliff Trail closely follows along the St. Croix River. Past the islands in the middle, you can see Minnesota on the opposite bank. *John T. Andrews*

7 Governor Knowles State Forest

LANDING IN THE COLD

Paper Thin

I visited the Governor Knowles State Forest in the dead of winter. I did so on purpose.

Gangly and thin, even spotty in areas, the forest lies on Wisconsin's northwest border with Minnesota, along the shores of the St. Croix River. It stretches from State Highway 77 near Danbury in the north to the community of Wolf Creek on County Highway G in the south. But at fifty-five miles long, the forest is never more than two miles wide, and I knew that to really see it, I'd have to look at it in winter, when it was laid bare. I wanted the landscape whittled down to snow and branches, for I knew I'd never be able to see something so slim beneath a full, rustling skirt of leaves.

I also chose to come in January because winter is the time when the furs of animals are at their thickest, longest, and shiniest; and I wanted to see the land of the St. Croix as the early fur trappers and the first fur traders that stepped into what is now Wisconsin did. I hoped to see the riverway at a time when I could picture them in the woods, working here.

Established in 1970 and originally named the St. Croix River State Forest, the Governor Knowles, it's often said, is one of Wisconsin's least developed and least treaded forests. Those who seek the woods for solitude like it that way. The forest was renamed in 1981 to honor Warren Knowles, who was elected governor of Wisconsin in 1964 and who had an energetic conservation agenda during his three terms in office. Governor Knowles, an avid outdoorsman, would be proud that the forest that bears his name now has five State

Natural Areas and a sixth in close proximity: Sterling Barrens in Polk County; Brandt Brook Pines, Kohler-Peet Barrens and Cedar Swamp, Norway Point Bottomlands, and St. Croix Ash Swamp in Burnett County; and St. Croix Seeps in Burnett County, technically owned by the National Park Service and within the St. Croix National Scenic Riverway.

This forest has had a job from Day One, and that is to act as a protection buffer zone for the St. Croix River. Although the river itself is part of the St. Croix National Scenic Riverway (established in 1968) under the management of the National Park Service, you can't speak of the forest without telling of the river.

Like all rivers, the 164-mile-long St. Croix has a unique personality, running a range of moods from swift and rocky whitewater to placid and calm flowages. From its spruce-and-tamarack-wetland beginnings near Upper St. Croix Lake in Douglas County, the river and its eleven or so streams sometimes rush and at other times quietly slip into the Mississippi River. The Namekagon River is its major tributary and joins the St. Croix in northern Burnett County. The lower 125 miles of the St. Croix act as the boundary line between Wisconsin and Minnesota, and a hydroelectric plant at St. Croix Falls supplies power to the Minneapolis–St. Paul metropolitan area.

Just as the forest works to protect the river, the river has worked hard most of its life. Not only does it supply our present-day urban areas with power and recreationists with one of the most scenic canoeing opportunities in the Midwest, but historically the St. Croix River system was a major trade route between Lake Superior and the Mississippi for Native Americans, voyageurs, fur traders, fur trappers, and loggers.

So while I will be looking for the foundations of this forest in the snow, I'll also be searching for the tracks of these forest — and river — employers.

Sioux Camp

My explorations of the forest start at the northern reaches of its 19,753 acres at the Sioux Portage Group Campground. No one is camping here on this January day, and the camp, the river, and the surrounding trees are quiet. But this was once a busy and noisy place. Today's campground is located at one end of a shortcut between the St. Croix and Yellow Rivers that was used by Native Americans for hundreds of years.

Prior to European arrival, the Santee Sioux and Ojibwe fought for control of the region's abundant fish, game, and wild rice.
WHi Image ID 9023

Along with the St. Croix River's important location, the river valley's natural resources were also always highly prized. The Santee (Dakota) Sioux and Ojibwe tribes often battled over the valley's lakes and the fish and wild rice they produced. In fact, in the Ojibwe language, the headwaters of the St. Croix River is called *Manoominikeshiinyag-ziibi*, or "Rice-Bird River"; while at the other end of the forest, below the confluence with the Trade River, the St. Croix is called the *Jiibayaatig-ziibi*, or "Grave-Marker River." Eventually, the Sioux were driven West onto the plains of southern Minnesota, but skirmishes over the region went on into the nineteenth century.

Trade in the Forest

Following the Sioux and Ojibwe lead, the French started making use of the St. Croix's waters and well-worn routes in the 1600s. They traded their goods to the Indians for beaver pelts, which were becoming popular in Europe for clothing, particularly hats. Then during the 1700s and 1800s, British and American fur traders began establishing outposts along the river, all hoping to control an exploding fur market. White people soon began trapping beavers to meet the insatiable demand.

It was mostly young men who took on the job of beaver trapping: those who were self-reliant in the woods; who could endure backbreaking work in the wilderness; and who could find beavers wherever they were located on a stream, despite the perils of other trappers, Native Americans, and frigid weather conditions. Competition for getting traps in the best beaver streams was keen.

When autumn came, a fur trapper would travel by canoe to a location thick with beaver. He'd set out his trap lines and build a shelter out of which he could sleep and work for two or three weeks, until the beaver became scarce. If the fast-flowing streams remained unfrozen, he could move again by canoe, carrying his possessions overland around the rapids. During heavy snow, he made a toboggan-type sled and pulled his supplies from one location to another.

A trapper spent much of his time in the water. During evening twilight he traveled the streams, searching for beaver houses and runs where he could set his traps. Placing the scent of castoreum (a secretion from a beaver's castor sac mixed with a beaver's urine, used to mark territory) on nearby twigs and branches to entice beaver, the trapper would place his traps under the icy water, anchoring the chain in such a manner that when the animal was caught, it was unable to surface for air and soon drowned.

Early the next morning, the trapper would walk his trap line, either reaching or wading into the stream to retrieve the beaver. He then skinned it on the spot and backpacked the hide to his temporary camp. There, the trapper would spend the day removing the remaining flesh from the hides — called "graining" — over a sloping wooden block and then stretching the hides over wood frames to dry. Snowstorms often interfered with the trapping routine.

At the trading posts, beaver pelts became the basis for monetary exchange. At the Hudson's Bay Company's posts, one beaver pelt would buy a pound of tobacco; four, a woolen blanket; twelve, a muzzle-loading musket.

By the 1830s, however, the area's beaver population had been depleted. Then in 1837, a treaty was signed at Fort Snelling with the Ojibwe, which

BUILDING WETLANDS: BEAVERS IN WISCONSIN

With their considerable building skills, beavers create beneficial habitats for themselves and other wildlife, such as otters and waterfowl. *WHi Image ID 35065*

THE FRENCH WERE THE FIRST IN A PARADE of white people who came to Wisconsin's Northwoods. What they came for was the beaver, the animal on whose back was built the gigantic fur industry and who probably made the most significant contribution to the settlement of Wisconsin.

Native Americans had long killed beaver for their fur, but they killed conservatively; beavers in Wisconsin remained in abundance. When white people arrived, however, things radically changed. By the 1900s, beavers had been trapped almost to the point of extinction. Legal protection, restocking, and a serendipitous whim of fashion helped to save them: French stylists invented the silk hat, replacing those made of beaver fur. Quickly, the demand for beaver pelts hit rock bottom.

Today, eighty-seven thousand beavers are estimated to live in Wisconsin. While they are found throughout the state, their numbers are especially high in the northern half. Only in eastern and southeastern Wisconsin, where agricultural lands lack suitable aquatic habitat, are beaver densities low. Beaver adaptability, a lack of natural predation, restocking, low pelt prices, and the regrowth of aspen forests have all played a part in the beavers' recovery. Beavers prefer aspen,

(continued on next page)

BUILDING WETLANDS: BEAVERS IN WISCONSIN

(continued from page 137)
alder, and willow branches to build their dams and lodges.

At forty-five to sixty pounds, beavers are North America's largest rodent. Their fur is long and coarse and ranges from a light, pale yellow to black in color. Adults measure thirty-five to forty-six inches long, which includes their wide, flat tails. Round, covered with leathery scales and sparse hair, a beaver tail can be used like a boat rudder for swimming and a balancing platform for gnawing sticks on land. A tail slapped on water makes a sound that echoes throughout the forest, a warning signal to others that danger is near.

When in the forests, you'll know you're in beaver territory when you see an aspen or white birch toppled toward the water, bark stripped off of tree branches near the ground, or sharp incison marks — "beaver chews" — on trees. Beavers are the only wildlife in Wisconsin who excel at "remodeling" their environment to suit their needs. They dam up small streams with branches, logs, and mud to create new ponds, where they then build a lodge. These homes, which can be fifteen feet wide and five feet high, and dams are an engineering feat that cause flooding of woodlands and farmlands, benefiting other wildlife such as otters, muskrats, bears, deer, mink, waterfowl, and grouse.

According to recent research from the University of Alberta, beavers have an overwhelming influence on creating wetlands. They can increase the amount of open water in a habitat ninefold by manipulating local hydrological systems with deep channels and dams. During the 2002 drought in Alberta, in fact, the area's worst on record, almost all beaver ponds held their water, while other ponds (without beavers) dried up. At a time when global climate models are predicting more frequent and severe droughts, beavers may be providing another considerable contribution to Wisconsinites.

ceded all lands in the triangle between the St. Croix and Mississippi Rivers up to the forty-sixth parallel to the U.S. government. This opened the region up to logging, and the St. Croix was again pressed into service as an important means of transportation for getting the lumber downstream. In 1890, a peak year, the St. Croix River valley produced 450 million board feet of lumber and logs. By the time of the last major log drive in 1912, the rich white pine forests of the area were gone.

It was along the banks of the St. Croix River, in the mill town of Stillwater on the Minnesota side, that our neighboring state was first proposed in 1848.

Over here, on our side of the water, there were other mills. One of those sawmills belonged to the family of Jake Lysdahl. Through him, I was able to track down some loggers of old.

Log drivers like these (circa 1905) ran massive pines down the St. Croix.
WHi Image ID 37826

Safe Landings

Seventy-six-year-old Jake Lysdahl used to be the postmaster for Grantsburg, Wisconsin, a little town situated on the Wood River and just four and a half miles east of the central portion of the forest along Highway 70. Today, Jake and his son own 110 acres of land in the Governor Knowles State Forest, where Jake currently lives.

"From 1905 to 1938," says Jake, "my grandfather had a sawmill on the St. Croix River. If you look at a map of the Governor Knowles State Forest, you'll see an area at the northern end marked 'Nelson's Landing.' That's my grandfather," he proudly tells me.

During the late 1800s and early 1900s, loggers were cutting the big pines along the St. Croix River and running them down the waterway to that town of Stillwater, where Minnesota was conceived.

"My father and his brothers knew that there were lots of 'deadheads' in the river — logs that got stuck on islands or underneath the water on sandy bottoms," says Jake. "So they would go out in their boats and pull the deadheads loose and float them down to the landing. Then they'd pull them up on shore by horse. That way, they had a lot of big, wonderful logs to saw for years," he says.

Jake's family eventually moved from the site surrounding the landing area, which was leased from the Northern States Power Company. Now, because the land along the riverbanks and the strip of forest next to it are protected, modern explorers can visit this logging landing — and five others — on the scenic St. Croix.

Coming Off the Croix

Since their reintroduction to Wisconsin in the 1970s, wild turkeys have made a strong comeback. Their range has expanded into the Badger State's northern reaches, including Governor Knowles State Forest.
John H. Gaukel

Looking out across the St. Croix River from Nelson's Landing on this January day, I imagine the loggers who pulled countless timbers out of these waters spread out before me. What's pulled out here today in any of the other three seasons of the year would be the lightweight and swift, fiberglass and Kevlar canoes and kayaks of the visitors to Governor Knowles State Forest. In fact, some of the fastest water along the entire St. Croix is found along the five-mile stretch below Nelson's Landing; during high water, a few of these rapids can run a Class II (see pages 114–115 for an explanation of the classes of rapids). Those who seek the watery thrills can set out from here. A couple of hundred years ago, it was the thrill of the marketplace that brought much heavier, bigger, birchbark canoes ashore, filled with iron kettles, axes, cloth, and beaver, fox, and otter pelts.

Walking the road back up from the landing to my car, I spot several wild turkeys crossing the path ahead. Seven of them are lined up, following each other in neat, single-file fashion. It's probably the way the fur traders walked up from the river, I think, having to jointly haul their canoes and hundreds of pounds of gear.

Just a bit north of Nelson's Landing is the Norway Point Landing. I stop the car there to watch the setting sun glint off the glassy surface of the St. Croix, where the ice is sliver-thin and the water is open. I stare straight across to the wooded Minnesota shore, not far beyond. I picture the crisp, thin, black lines that denote a state boundary on a map, but standing on this spot outdoors, no such lines are apparent. That side of the shore looks just like the one over here. The river winds around a bend up to my left and disappears around the corner, further blurring any borders made of ink.

The Cedar Interpretive Trail starts at the Norway Point Landing. At half a mile, it goes through the 330-acre Norway Point Bottomlands State Natural Area. Snow-dusted boardwalk sections take me through a stand of elderly eastern white cedar and a floodplain forest, a landscape that hits the northern limit of its range in Wisconsin. It seems like this floodplain forest stretched and worked to get here, wanting so badly to push its envelope and reach the wild St. Croix. The white-encrusted planks pass over thick mats of sphagnum moss, beaver sign, and several springs and seeps that feed Iron Creek. For a cedar to reach one foot in diameter, it may take more than two hundred years of growth. It is expected that some of these cedars will live for four hundred years.

As I walk out of the Norway Point Bottomlands State Natural Area, a yellow road sign with a simple, black-block representation of an Amish-looking, horse-drawn buggy stands posted, and it makes me smile. Here, at least, is one attempt at a crisp, black line on the map of nature.

During the walk down to Fox Landing, the third landing I visit in the northern part of this forest, I pass a small stream that is running and bubbling even on this January day, through a snow-bordered channel. Mid-stream, elaborate ice crystals clutch embedded twigs and leaves. The rocks in the riverbed are snow-topped, as if they are wearing hats made of thick, white fur; clear ice makes a delicate covering over selected sections of the flowing water.

The old, dead snags at Fox Landing have many bored holes, evidence of the animals working to make their livings here. As if to make this point emphatic and crystal clear, as I hike out of Fox Landing, a woodpecker starts to hammer on a branch above me.

The shanties of "hard-water" fisher folk harbor some of the most dedicated anglers, who seek community — but at a bit of a distance.
John T. Andrews

Hard-Water Fishing

Located on the forest's northeastern edge, on the side of the forest opposite from the St. Croix River, is the 359-acre Clam River Flowage. Red pine was planted here in 1964, and today the trees stand tall around the flowage's shores. A sign asks boaters to use care around the rice beds and warns, "Wild rice is important to wildlife and human harvesters, and is protected by state law. Rice is easily uprooted, especially during the 'floating-leaf' stage from May to June."

I am reminded of the tales of the Santee Sioux and Ojibwe, who fought so strongly over the gifts of the forest, such as this wild rice. Jake Lysdahl had told me another story about other benefits that come from settling near the forest's waters.

"They used to clam on my grandfather's land on the St. Croix," Jake told me. "The fishermen would go out in their skiffs, come ashore, retrieve the clam meat, search for a pearl, then throw the shell in a pile. There were so many clamshells in huge piles that they would take them to Grantsburg, load them on railroad cars, and ship them to Iowa, where they made buttons from the shells. That was in 1920," he said.

Looking out at the Clam River Flowage today, I see another kind of fisherman, "hard-water" types with their fish shanties. The Clam River Flowage is well-known for its catches of largemouth and smallmouth bass, northern pike, and walleye, and the Clam River's tributaries feature brook and brown trout. These streams and the main river can also produce pan fish, a favorite with these colder variety fisher folk. Although within sight of each other, the shanties are widely spaced apart on the frozen flowage, as if the inhabitants of the small dwellings seek company, but only at "arm's length" — or much farther away. These are some of the most dedicated anglers.

Perhaps no one, though, had the passion for fishing as deep as the man for whom this forest is named.

Hunting and Fishing with Wisconsin's Top Man

Warren Knowles may have been Wisconsin's governor for three terms, but he was an outdoorsman for life, something Jake Lysdahl can testify to from first-hand experience.

"When I was young, I hunted with Governor Knowles sometimes," says Jake. "I was a 'deer driver,' a guy who walked through the woods, driving the deer out from cover. That's how I got to know Governor Knowles. When he died, his son gave me his father's hunting guns and most of his fishing equipment — his tackle boxes and fishing rods. Governor Knowles knew that, like him, I was a hunter and a fisherman," says Jake.

Warren Knowles was elected to the Wisconsin State Senate in 1940 and served until 1954, when he was elected lieutenant governor. His passion for the outdoors and Wisconsin's natural resources was apparent during his administration and shone throughout his professional career. He was a major force behind then-governor Gaylord Nelson's 1961 Outdoor Recreation Act Program, which authorized state expenditures of $50 million — over ten years — for the acquisition of land for recreational and conservation purposes.

In 1964, Knowles was elected to the first of his three terms as Wisconsin governor. By 1965, he had founded the Governor's Fishing Opener, an annual

Governor Warren Knowles was an avid angler and conservationist. He was the founder of Wisconsin's Governor's Fishing Opener. *WHi Image ID 74818*

event to focus attention on all that Wisconsin offers anglers. In the fall of 1966, he chartered a committee to examine how effective Gaylord Nelson's 1961 Outdoor Recreation Act Program had been and charged the committee to also recommend ways that the program could be expanded. Knowles even initiated the efforts to reduce water pollution in the state.

"I think of Governor Knowles as the father of the conservation movement in Wisconsin," says Jake. "Hunting, fishing, and preserving the forests were his 'thing.' On the roadside next to my property, right when you enter the state forest, there's a monument to Governor Warren Knowles."

Jake, it seems, has taken a cue from the governor and made conservation his personal mandate as well. At one time, Jake served as the chair of the committee that raised money for the wildlife education and visitor center at Crex Meadows, a thirty-thousand-acre, state-owned wildlife management area adjacent to the Governor Knowles State Forest. Crex Meadows is the largest wildlife area in Wisconsin.

"We held an auction and raised about $1.7 million for the center," says Jake. "The money I received from the Knowles estate I donated to Crex Meadows. One of Governor Knowles's shotguns brought in $1,700. But don't get me wrong, a lot of other people around Wisconsin and from Minnesota worked hard and gave much to make the center possible," he is quick to point out.

One of Governor Knowles's favorite trout fishing spots lies in the forest; it's near the mouth of Iron Creek, located in the northern section close to the Norway Point Landing. Warren Knowles participated in his Governor's Fishing Opener for many years after he left public service. He died from a heart attack during a break from fishing on opening day in 1993.

Right: This trail is part
of Crex Meadows, a
state-owned wildlife
management area
adjacent to the Governor
Knowles State Forest.
At thirty thousand
acres, Crex Meadows
is the largest wildlife
area in Wisconsin.
Candice Gaukel Andrews

Below: One of Governor
Warren Knowles's favorite
fishing spots lies near
Norway Point Landing,
located on a river bend.
John T. Andrews

Tracking the Trails

So far, I've been able to follow in the footsteps of the Native Americans, the voyageurs, the fur traders, the fur trappers, the loggers, and the hunters and fishermen in this forest. But trying to find my way along present-day trails

TURNING THE CORNER ON HUNTING

LIKE LEAVES OF TREES IN THE FORESTS, many Wisconsinites in fall turn orange — blaze orange. As a child growing up in the southern part of the state, seeing the inevitable procession every year used to make me cringe. How could *anyone*, I questioned, willingly go out into the woods with the intention of killing an innocent animal? But today as an adult, with a little more experience in listening to and understanding viewpoints different from my own, I believe I've made a 180-degree-turn.

Most hunters will tell you that for them, hunting is a connection to the natural world not attainable in any other way. It's a quest, really, for a primal, physical, and direct engagement with a wild animal; a mixing of flesh and blood and mind and soul.

Hunting not only gives these intangible and tangible (meat and hides) benefits to the hunters, it also helps all of us who live in Wisconsin, whether we hunt or not. Deer hunters in the state alone spend $900 million per year on goods and services such as lodging, food, transportation, and equipment. Those purchases generate nearly $133 million in state and local taxes. The total economic impact on the state from deer hunting is estimated to be $1.4 billion, providing sixteen thousand jobs. Deer license fees by themselves bring almost $22 million annually to the state of Wisconsin, money that is used to cover the cost of deer management as well as fund other wildlife, fish, and endangered species programs.

However, fewer people hunt today than in the previous two decades. More and more land is being closed to hunting as it passes into private ownership. And in an increasingly urban society, people tend to take a negative view of anything to do with guns. With less exposure to hunting and its responsible use of firearms, society wrongly associates hunters with any tragedy that involves weapons.

In recent years, however, I've talked with hunters in Wisconsin forests and across the country. And I've noticed that many of them have a familiarity with nature that I don't — and probably won't ever — possess. I've heard a hunter identify a type of bird under dark skies by the way it moves its wings. I've seen a hunter wait for hours for an animal to show itself, exhibiting a patience I have not yet met. I've never known a hunter to be afraid of going outside and getting lost. Hunters make great wildlife spotters when I'm trying to take photos. But most of all, they appreciate and know where the food they eat comes from, while the rest of us tend to think that meat comes from a grocery store freezer, neatly wrapped and labeled with no expenditure of blood or death involved.

I may never get to feel what hunters feel; that inexpressible "rush" and profound gratefulness of actually experiencing the hunt. But I do now feel that hunters live more honestly than I do. And every fall, I feel myself changing, too.

today is proving to be challenging. It could be that because I'm here in winter, they are difficult to uncover; or maybe it's because the Governor Knowles State Forest is still a wild and undeveloped place, so locating a cut-and-dried course to hike is difficult.

I ask Mike Giles, a former superintendent of the forest, just where the designated trails in the forest are.

"That's a tough one," says Mike. "In the conception stages, a hiking trail that ran from one end of the forest to the other was visualized. It sounded like

On a small stream near Fox Landing, elaborate ice crystals clutch embedded twigs and leaves. The rocks are snow-topped, as if they are wearing hats of white fur.
John T. Andrews

a good plan. A crew was sent out to walk through the woods and hack a little trail out. It was really pretty primitive," he explains.

The forest is relatively new, having been established in 1970. And Mike admits that it's easy to get lost in the woods in Governor Knowles; in fact, sometimes even he has marveled at how the trail just seems to disappear. "During my time there, we undertook to improve segments of the long trail to the point where it was pretty nice, developed, level, and viable. And we further developed portions to function as interpretive trails," he says.

As of today, in addition to three interpretive trails (the Cedar, Brandt Pines, and Wood River) and some horse and snowmobile trails, this stretched-out, squiggly-line forest has two long hiking trails totaling thirty-eight miles, which parallel the St. Croix River. They run along a craggy, high ridge that sometimes drops to the water's edge. The North Trail system is twenty-two miles long, and the South Trail system is sixteen miles long. The North Trail consists of the Sioux Portage, Kohler-Peet, and Fox Landing Hiking Trails. The South Trail is made up of the Benson Brook and Lagoo Creek Hiking Trails. Like all good trails, these two systems surprise users with steep climbs and descents, short bridges, stairways, and slippery spots in between stretches of level going. But unlike most trails in Wisconsin forests, these routes have full-length views along a National Scenic River (one of two in Wisconsin; the other is the Wolf River that rises in Forest County and flows south through Langlade, Menominee, Shawano, Waupaca, Outagamie, and Winnebago Counties) that are awe inspiring.

Cliff Walk

But it's neither the North nor South Trail that I'll hike today. Instead, I've chosen to walk the five-mile Sandrock Cliff Trail, a hiking and cross-country ski trail maintained by the National Park Service. The looped route follows the ridge on the St. Croix's edge very closely on the way out from the trailhead, and then circles back inside the forest on the way in.

"It's funny," says Mike Giles, "but we don't manage what goes on in the river. It's a little odd when people hear it, but the water frontage proper is under the jurisdiction of the National Park Service. They manage from the high-water mark inland 412 feet, the buffer between the river itself and the Governor Knowles State Forest," he explains.

The St. Croix National Scenic Riverway was established in the late 1960s as one of the original eight rivers under the National Wild and Scenic Rivers Act. The riverway includes one hundred miles of the St. Croix River from Gordon, Wisconsin, to St. Croix Falls, Wisconsin, and the total ninety-eight miles of its major tributary, the Namekagon River. (The Lower St. Croix National Scenic Riverway was added to the system in 1972.) The Northern States Power Company once owned much of the land along the river, but through a cooperative agreement, NSP agreed to donate its land to the National Park Service and the states of Minnesota and Wisconsin. This donation was the nucleus of the Governor Knowles State Forest.

The Sandrock Cliff Trail gets its name from a story that began six hundred million years ago, when an ancient sea retreated, leaving sediments that later transformed into sandstone. Then, glacial meltwaters sculpted the sandstone into cliffs.

Walking out along the trail, I pass three islands in the middle of the St. Croix River, and I can see the Minnesota state park on the other side of its banks. Below me, I know these clean and unpolluted waters harbor a rich array of freshwater mussels and the clams Jake talked about. At the midpoint of the trail, just before it turns back into the forest, is a cliff-top overlook on the St. Croix. There's not another human being around; just the eagles, patrolling the open stretches of water on this January day. I watch the quiet settle over the river and sparkle in the fading light of the winter sun.

A Philosopher Fisherman among the Fishers

When Jake Lysdahl goes into the woods these days, it's not for the eagles, for the deer, or for the fish — it's for the fishers.

"I just like to go out into the forest, sit down, and watch the wildlife," says Jake when I ask him how the forest plays a part in his life today. "Sometimes a fisher will come. It's marvelous to watch how quick they are, what great hunters they are. If I'm lucky enough, once during a fall I get to see a fisher. But I also like to see the beavers. I don't let anybody trap them on my land. The beavers might take a few trees, but then they move on," he says rather philosophically, and I can't help but think there's some lesson in there for us humans.

And rather philosophical, too, is the fact that trees, even when dying or

Hammering on a branch above me is a woodpecker, just one representative of the three hundred kinds of birds found in the Governor Knowles State Forest.
John T. Andrews

dead — whether the cause is beavers or other natural phenomena — still play a pivotal role in the forest. Not all of them should be removed by the logger's saw. More than fifty of the three hundred species of birds that frequent the Governor Knowles State Forest require standing dying or dead trees to survive.

The Forest As Dance

Trying to balance the demand for lumber against the need for leaving enough dead, rotting, and living trees standing to preserve the forest and the birds and animals dependent on it takes a lot of skill — and hard work.

Says Mike Giles: "Managing the Governor Knowles State forest means maintaining a natural area along the river so that the St. Croix's users feel like they are in an undeveloped and wild place of solitude. Along with that, timber sales need to be set up and trees need to be planted. It was a real dance half the time. But with the help of some local citizens and some people at the Wisconsin Department of Natural Resources, we came up with a good compromise, I think."

After exploring the Governor Knowles State Forest, I believe Mike is right. Even during the winter, I feel as if the forest is full of trees and hidden trails, despite the fact that during my visit, timber harvests were going on to stop oak wilt, an aggressive disease caused by a fungal pathogen that kills thousands of oaks every year.

Sustainable forestry practices are in place here and seem to be functioning well. Over the past twenty-five years, more than 2.5 million trees have been planted on the Governor Knowles State Forest. Most of them were pine species — such as red pine, jack pine, and white pine — and white spruce. Northern pin oak, which makes up most of the forest's hardwood stands, regenerates itself after being cut (its stumps sprout new growth).

Like the St. Croix River itself, then, the Governor Knowles State Forest works on many levels.

A WARMING IN THE WOODS

FORESTS ARE FLUID; ALWAYS IN A STATE OF flux. Over time, trees live and die, creating avenues whereby new species of plants can slip in and test out. Over hundreds of years, animals, too, migrate in and out and sample new territories, creating change. But

storms. Tree blowdowns will certainly increase. With extreme heat more common in summer and a reduced snow pack in winter, seeing a snowmobile or cross-country ski trail may become rare in the forest.

A sustained change of even only a few degrees will

If global warming continues at its current pace, Wisconsin winters will be more like those now in Iowa, and the snow pack will be reduced. More dramatic storms will increase tree blowdowns. *John T. Andrews*

global warming is happening at a pace so fast that the normal, natural processes of plant and animal adaptation to new conditions may not be able to keep up. And if, as expected, global warming outpaces the speed at which southern trees can migrate north, our northern Wisconsin forests as we know them could disappear altogether.

Research suggests that by the end of the twenty-first century, Northwoods summers will feel much like those of current-day Arkansas, and the winters will be like those now in Iowa. Springs and falls will be wetter, with more driving downpours and intense, dramatic

create severe ecological dislocations. Among other changes, a rapidly warming forest will likely cause:

● **A major shift in forest composition and fewer forested lands.** White spruce, eastern hemlock, balsam fir, red pine, jack pine, and paper birch may be extirpated. The new, warmer conditions will probably favor oaks and other hardwoods, but they may be slow to migrate north. Mixed northern hardwood and oak forests would be transformed to oak savannas and grasslands within as little as thirty to sixty years.

(continued on next page)

Goodbye to the Cold

The first book I ever wrote was about winter in our state and how to enjoy it. Wild Wisconsin is an incredibly diverse place, full of native species that include 279 birds, 146 fish, 67 mammals, 35 reptiles, and 19 amphibians. I fear that rising temperatures, however, will alter this, forcing wildlife to adapt, flee, or succumb swiftly. While nothing stands still and change is inevitable, change that comes about too quickly can bring not a change in life, but an end to it.

Researchers say that forested areas in northern Wisconsin could decline by as much as 55 to 70 percent as a result of global warming, and the resulting drier weather conditions will thin and fragment the conifer forests left in southern Wisconsin. One day within ours or our children's lifetimes, it may not be possible to go to a forest thick with trees and covered in snow, as I did this January to see the Governor Knowles State Forest.

There may no longer be any safe, cold, and quiet landings for us, when we ache for a wild place.

A WARMING IN THE WOODS

(continued from page 151)

- **A loss of bird diversity.** Cardinals, chickadees, and other full-year resident birds might be able to breed earlier and raise more broods. But these bigger populations will reduce the food available for migratory songbirds, shorebirds, and waterfowl, making it difficult for them to survive.

- **A major change in local mammal populations.** Raccoons, skunks, and white-tailed deer may benefit from milder winters. And some mammals — such as bats, groundhogs, thirteen-lined ground squirrels, and jumping mice — are already breaking hibernation sooner. Their populations and the accompanying stresses on their environments could soar.

- **An increase in forest pests and tree diseases.** Insects influence ecological and biological systems in the forest, soil composition, nutrient cycling, and successional processes. Cold winter temperatures currently determine the northern limit of some devastating forest pests, such as the gypsy moth caterpillar. These insects will almost certainly become more widely established throughout Wisconsin's Northwoods in a warmer climate.

As a living, breathing entity, a forest will inevitably change over time. It's when the forest doesn't have time to meet the changing conditions that it becomes endangered of surviving. And northern Wisconsin without a Northwoods seems unthinkable. It's part of every Wisconsinite's mental and spiritual landscape.

Governor Knowles State Forest

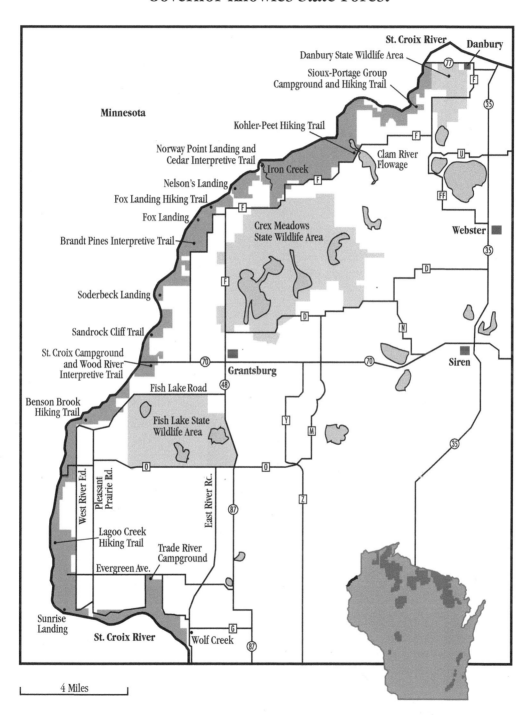

St. Croix River
Danbury
Danbury State Wildlife Area
Sioux-Portage Group
Campground and Hiking Trail
77
F
35
Minnesota
Kohler-Peet Hiking Trail
F
Norway Point Landing and
Cedar Interpretive Trail
Iron Creek
Clam River
Flowage
U
Nelson's Landing
Fox Landing Hiking Trail
F
FF
Fox Landing
F
Crex Meadows
State Wildlife Area
Webster
Brandt Pines Interpretive Trail
35
F
D
Soderbeck Landing
D
Sandrock Cliff Trail
N
St. Croix Campground
and Wood River
Interpretive Trail
70
70
Siren
Grantsburg
Fish Lake Road
48
Benson Brook
Hiking Trail
Fish Lake State
Wildlife Area
Y
M
35
O
O
West River Rd.
Pleasant Prairie Rd.
East River Rd.
Z
87
Lagoo Creek
Hiking Trail
Trade River
Campground
Evergreen Ave.
Sunrise
Landing
St. Croix River
Wolf Creek
G
87

4 Miles

On the back boundary line of Milwaukee's Havenwoods State Forest, Wisconsin and Southern Railroad cars roll through a prairielike setting. *John T. Andrews*

8 Havenwoods State Forest
EDUCATION AND RESTORATION

It's a Process

It would be easy to say that Havenwoods, a 237-acre green space in the center of the city of Milwaukee, is just that. A haven from the city; a woods — as if it were done, completed, finished. But Havenwoods isn't whole yet. Not by a long shot.

You can find Havenwoods State Forest north of I-94, between West Mill Road on the north and West Silver Spring Drive on the south, one block west of North 43rd Street. Sitting as it does smack-dab in the middle of Milwaukee, this land has seen a lot of people coming through, a lot of urbanization, and a lot of "progress." Getting back to being a forest, therefore, is going to take a lot of time and a lot of care.

Those two commodities — time and care — are what constitute healing. And healing the land, or restoration, is mostly what this forest is all about. It has just begun. But in that long process, there is much to be learned. Coincidentally, education can also never be considered fully accomplished, completed, or done.

It's a Preserve

Although technically a state forest, Havenwoods can more appropriately be thought of as a wildlife sanctuary and environmental awareness center. Within its confines, no hunting or logging is allowed.

The Milwaukee streets surrounding the forest are busy and noisy; cars buzz by, horns honk, trucks speed past. On the forest's back boundary line, Wisconsin and Southern Railroad cars roll down the tracks and whistle. Neat houses with small yards closc in around the forest property. Just inside the Havenwoods entrance, there's a nice-sized asphalt parking lot, the kind you'd find next to any grocery store or strip mall in the city.

But once you walk through the environmental center's doors, you won't feel like you're in Milwaukee anymore.

A Growing Awareness

The Havenwoods Environmental Awareness Center is a passive-solar building that nestles comfortably in its wide-open-spaces setting. It keeps a low profile, a nod to the need for long looks across grasslands and prairies. Immediately inside the ten-thousand-square-foot structure are spinning racks and table-top brochure stands filled with informational literature — everything from a one-page sheet by the University of Wisconsin–Extension on scab (a fungal disease of ornamental and fruit trees in the rose family) to a two-page newsletter about bees from Michigan State University. There's a multipage booklet about the Milwaukee River titled the *State of the Watershed* put out by the Water Quality Initiative and a *Forest Where We Live* publication funded by the U.S. Forest Service and the Wisconsin Department of Natural Resources.

The open fields of Havenwoods offer long looks across grasslands and habitat for elegant monarch butterflies.
John T. Andrews

One of the interior walls holds several glass tanks and cases, temporary homes for a rotating variety of native reptiles and amphibians. Today, I count a fox snake, a garter snake, an ornate box turtle, and a tiger salamander.

There is a resource library, an auditorium, and several meeting and classrooms for school, family, and public groups. A quick look at recent programs reveals events such as "Learn the Sky with Your Naked Eye," a stargazing party on one July evening, and a "Make Your Own Snowshoes Workshop" in September. A Saturday in August has a "Grasshoppers, Beetles, and Bugs . . . Oh, My!" drop-in class, and a "One Wild Saturday Morning Drop-In" in June features a "Wonderful Wetlands" activity, where children and their families can learn how to do cattail weaving — a craft I can't say I've ever heard of before.

But what sticks in my mind most about the center is the painting above the main door, a huge image of the Earth. The 1991 work was created by Reynaldo Hernandez, a Milwaukee artist who has painted more than 125 murals across the state, including more than fifty in Milwaukee itself. Next to the painting are the words "Good planets are hard to find."

A Prairie Place

Maybe that's why Havenwoods is trying to save this little piece of it, so that even those in the city will have a nearby place to experience a natural vista. Few vast prairies are left in Wisconsin, but restoration projects such as those on Havenwoods will teach upcoming generations what they were like. Natural plant communities and open grasslands are slowly reclaiming a land once covered by buildings and concrete.

I find it strange, though, that what is supposed to be a state "forest" is actively being turned into a "prairie." In all my travels these past two years through Wisconsin's national and state forests, I have never been to one that is more treeless and unforestlike. It probably should be called "Havenwoods State Prairie."

I ask Havenwoods Superintendent Judy Klippel where the "forest" comes in. "We conduct a lot of resource management on the property," says Judy,

but this isn't a "managed forest" in the traditional sense because of the site's history, the past soil disturbance, the cultivated trees left from landscaping efforts of the 1920s and 1930s, the weeds that have a stronghold, and the highly engineered creek. So stated briefly, our efforts are focused on restoring and maintaining native vegetation, controlling invasive species, managing a flood control site, and providing diverse wildlife habitat. But there are areas in Havenwoods that are forested; however, you are correct in saying that there are more grasslands here than forest. In the beginning, the planners envisioned a site where people could see wide open spaces. If you live in a city and look out a window, usually there's a building in front of you. There was also a strong interest in having a variety of "edge" habitats — places between water and woods, or water and grasslands, or grasslands and woods. That increases the diversity of wildlife.

"There are more grasslands here than forest," says Havenwoods Superintendent Judy Klippel.
John T. Andrews

It makes sense, then, that as a wildlife sanctuary, Havenwoods would be designed to encourage the widest range of animal and plant species that it can. That means that it should be a place not only of trees but also of meadows and prairies.

Just before exiting the Environmental Awareness Center, I pick up a brochure titled *People and the Land* at the front desk. It's a numbered guide to a 1.4-mile interpretive trail. It's also a peek into Havenwoods's past.

Correcting Past Mistakes

During the late 1800s, family homesteads once stood on the land that is now Havenwoods. By the early 1900s, Milwaukee County had acquired the site and constructed a jailhouse, which opened in 1917. My interpretive trail brochure says stop number 1 is the former location of this County House of Correction, which remained in operation until 1945.

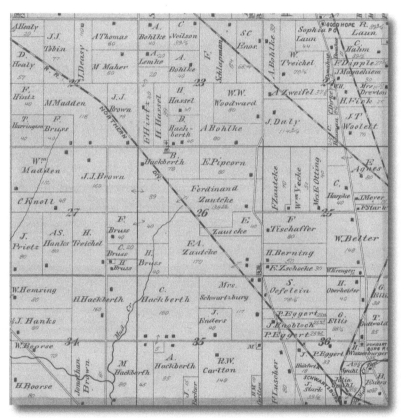

This 1896 plat map shows the names of families that farmed what is now Havenwoods State Forest. *Courtesy Wisconsin Department of Natural Resources*

It wasn't the only time that Havenwoods would be used as a site for "correcting" behavior, however. From 1945 until sometime in the 1950s, Havenwoods was put to use as an army prison, otherwise known as a United States Disciplinary Barracks (U.S.D.B.).

Although army history on Havenwoods is hard to track down, I did find several old photos showing that barracks buildings were situated on about a quarter of the land that is now part of the state forest. One of the few accessible documents is a cover from the *Northern Star,* a barracks newsletter. It seems that even as far back as the 1940s, education was a mission on the land that is now Havenwoods: on an August 1949 issue is printed the statement that "The *Northern Star* is published monthly by and for the inmates of the Branch U.S.D.B., Milwaukee, Wisconsin, with permission of the Commandant, under the supervision of the Director of Education. Its purpose is to furnish inmates with self-expression and a medium for discussion of public and personal problems."

From 1950 until 1967, the army reserves were also on the Havenwoods site. According to city of Milwaukee demolition records, thirty-nine buildings were demolished in 1974.

Bird Haven

Just before the brochure's third stop, I enter a shaded space, one of the few here. In among the trees, I can feel that the temperature has dropped at least ten degrees from the high of ninety-seven on this July day. I have come into what is Havenwoods's woods.

Beth Mittermaier, the state forest's conservation biologist, tells me that most of these trees are only about twenty-five years old.

"Havenwoods was officially established in 1980," she says, "and about three years later, schoolchildren on field trips began the planting of more than forty-five thousand trees and shrubs that were grown at state nurseries. Although rabbits and deer ate quite a few of them, some of the trees survived and have reached a nice size now. Staff, volunteers, and contractors have also planted a variety of trees on the property, that were either donated, obtained through grants, or purchased as part of restoration projects."

My woodsy respite from the heat doesn't last long. By stop number 8, I am out in the open sun again, at a pond, a wetland that was constructed in 1983 to collect rainfall and runoff from the surrounding land. This is one of those edge habitats that Judy Klippel talked about, between grassland and wetland. It is favored by Canada geese, great blue herons, painted turtles, leopard frogs, and sunfish.

Says Beth, "There are about eighteen species of mammals here, all of the ones that you would expect to see in an urban landscape — such as squirrels and skunks — plus more, such as coyotes, foxes, muskrats, and raccoons. There is a good variety of frogs and toads, as well as snapping turtles and Butler's garter snakes, which are on the state's threatened species list."

But the number of different kinds of birds spotted at Havenwoods tops them all: bobolink, great egret, sandhill crane, American woodcock, olive-sided flycatcher, tree swallow, blue-gray gnatcatcher, veery, Swainson's thrush, gray catbird, brown thrasher, northern parula, yellow warbler, Wilson's warbler, black-and-white warbler, sedge wren, scarlet tanager, white-crowned sparrow, indigo bunting, orchard oriole, and Baltimore oriole, to name just a few.

Says Judy Klippel, "We've recorded more than 160 species of birds. A lot of them are migrants, but some, like red-tailed hawks and wild turkeys, are year-round residents. We've seen long-eared and great horned owls. Several

LONG-LIVED ROAD WARRIORS: WISCONSIN'S SNAPPING TURTLES

LONGEVITY **COULD BE THE WORD THAT MOST** describes a turtle. This reptile has probably been on Earth for two hundred million years — and has changed little throughout that time. Turtles are also among the longest-living creatures on the planet, with some individuals easily making it past their hundredth birthdays.

Wisconsin has eleven turtle species: seven box and water turtles, two softshell turtles, one musk and mud turtle, and one snapping turtle.

The common snapping turtle (*Chelydra serpentina*) is Wisconsin's largest turtle, weighing up to eighty-five pounds and measuring about eighteen inches long. Its shell varies in color from light brown to black. The shell, or carapace, is oval-shaped and widens toward the back, where it is strongly serrated. The turtle's tail has saw-toothed scales and is almost as long as the carapace.

Snapping turtles get their name from their large, powerful jaws — but they have no teeth. In self-defense, they are very aggressive and will snap or strike at anything. When approached or threatened, they will hiss and emit a musky odor and may rotate their cara-paces to face the danger. They can strike straight out or to the sides, but most amazingly (and dangerously), they can strike across their carapaces toward their shells' rear with their heads upside down.

Omnivorous snapping turtles will eat anything they can catch, including frogs, snakes, and insects. Contrary to popular opinion, they are not adept at catching ducklings. They often feed on aquatic plants and slow-swimming fish or fresh dead fish, providing an important service in aquatic food chains.

Snapping turtles mate from May to November but nest almost exclusively between mid-May and mid-June. Most eggs — typically twenty to forty — are laid within a few feet of the water's edge, but some females travel as far as a quarter-mile inland. Mothers leave the eggs to hatch on their own; that is, if they escape being un-covered and eaten by foxes, raccoons, or skunks.

In Wisconsin, eggs incu-bate from sixty to ninety days. During a cool summer, it might take longer. Some eggs laid late in the season may not hatch until the following spring. Those that hatch in early fall will overwinter in the nest, protected by a glycol-like substance that acts as antifreeze. But, if the winter is very dry or cold with little snow cover, many of the eggs and hatchlings will die. The incubation temperature of the eggs determines the sex: at high incubation temperatures, more females are produced; at lower temperatures, more males.

The life span of a snapping turtle is up to forty years. Currently, they are common in Wisconsin, but their numbers are declining. Many are killed on roads. Most turtles will stop moving when they feel or see a vehicle coming, so it's easy to drive around them. Despite their armor, turtles are no match for a three-thousand-pound automobile.

It's not important *why* the turtle is crossing the road, just that he gets to the other side.

Turtles live long and — we hope — prosper in Wis-consin's woods. *John T. Andrews* expert birders have visited Havenwoods and returned many times, pleased with the diversity and the surprise of seeing birds they never thought they'd find here."

WILD TURKEYS, BIRDS OF COURAGE

IN THEATRICAL CIRCLES, A "TURKEY" IS A failure or a flop, but nothing could be further from the truth in the natural world. In fact, wild turkeys (*Meleagris gallopavo*) are North America's largest game birds and were considered by one of our nation's forefathers, Benjamin Franklin, to be superior to the country's national emblem, the bald eagle.

Wild turkeys are large, plump birds, thirty-seven to forty-six inches long. Unlike their heads, which are colored blue and red and are featherless, a turkey's body is iridescent brown and glossy bronze with five thousand to six thousand feathers. They have a fan-shaped tail and a long, straight, black beard in the center of the chest. Females, however, usually lack the breast beard. The legs of both genders are long and reddish-orange to gray-blue in color.

Wild turkeys, ancestors of the domesticated farm-

In spring, male turkeys strut with tail feathers spread in a glorious fan. *Bob Leggett*

yard birds, inhabit open forests, such as those in Havenwoods. Although they feed on the ground, turkeys are strong fliers, able to approach sixty miles per hour. They roost in trees at night and do not migrate. Their eyesight is three times better than that of a human's, and they can hear competing males gobble as far as a mile away.

In spring, each male will strut in his own small clearing in the forest or in an adjacent field, with his tail feathers spread in a glorious fan. With his head held back and his wings dragging, he'll give out a mating call. A dominant male will hold up to twenty females in his "harem."

After mating, the females will depart to lay eight to sixteen buff-colored, spotted eggs in a shallow, grass-and-leaf-lined depression in the woods, often at the base of a tree or against a fallen log. Females incubate the eggs for about a month. The fluffy chicks leave the nest soon after hatching and are able to make short flights within a few weeks. They will stay with the mother until the following spring.

While they were extirpated from Wisconsin in the late nineteenth century due to loss of habitat and overhunting, wild turkeys have made a strong recovery since their first successful reintroduction in 1976. So strong is their comeback that they can be seen on the edges of and sometimes — as is the case at Havenwoods — right in Wisconsin's largest cities.

A year and a half after the Great Seal was adopted by Congress on June 20, 1782, with the bald eagle as its centerpiece — a process that took Congress six years — Benjamin Franklin wrote a letter to his daughter with his thoughts about this new, bird-emblem of America:

I am on this account not displeased that the Figure is not known as a Bald Eagle, but looks more like a Turkey. For the Truth the Turkey is in Comparison a much more respectable Bird, and withal a true original Native of America.... He is besides, though a little vain & silly, a Bird of Courage, and would not hesitate to attack a Grenadier of the British Guards who should presume to invade his Farm Yard with a red Coat on.

Preserving the Peace

The last numbered stop on the interpretive trail, number 15, leads to a gravel path behind and to the left of the Environmental Awareness Center. From 1956 to 1963, this was a U.S. Army Nike missile site.

Project Nike, named after the Greek goddess of victory, was first proposed in May 1945 by Bell Labs. In 1953, the project delivered the nation's first operational, line-of-sight, anti-aircraft missile system, the Nike Ajax. This missile's first-stage, solid rocket booster would later become the basis for NASA's Nike Smoke rocket, used in upper-atmosphere research.

By the early to mid-1960s, however, the Nike Ajax was surpassed by the Nike Hercules, a missile with greater range and destructive power. Ajax sites were either upgraded to the Hercules system or decommissioned. In 1963, the Havenwoods missiles were declared obsolete and abandoned.

In 1996, the Nike missile silos at Havenwoods were finally obliterated. The magazine holes were filled in, and prairie grasses were planted on top. Only two berms, a sidewalk, the foundation of a small building, and post holes from the security fence remain to indicate it was ever such a spot. Luckily, the active missiles that once lay inside the silos never had to be fired.

A Land Filled and Unfulfilled

Overlapping the U.S. Army's occupation of Havenwoods, a municipal landfill sat on the site from 1958 to 1970. In 1974, the army no longer needed the grounds and decided to turn them over to the city of Milwaukee. Judy Klippel explains what happened next:

> A number of plans were drawn up for possible uses of the land, involving housing, public buildings, a technical college, and others. When the city determined to restore the land for an environmental park, the National Park Service administered the transfer of the land from federal to local ownership. As the city pursued and analyzed plans for the park development, officials determined that the city would not be able to fund it. So Milwaukee sought other government agencies that might be able to develop and manage the park, and that's how the Wisconsin Department of Natural Resources got involved.

In 1978, a mutual agreement was reached between the Natural Resources Board, the decision-making body for the Wisconsin Department of Natural Resources, and the city of Milwaukee. The next year, the site officially became a property of the WDNR. In 1981, restoration began. Says Beth Mittermaier,

> Some of the initial work the WDNR had to do was to continue to clean up years of accumulated garbage, a process that had been started by the city of Milwaukee. But that was a minor pickup of little pieces compared to the big chunks of asphalt and concrete that needed to be dealt with. There were still some roadways and parking lots here in the early 1980s. In 1983, many of those concrete slabs and blocks were removed, and those areas were seeded with prairie plants.

Urban Green

My circular tour through Havenwoods's history on the interpretive trail brings me back to the Environmental Awareness Center. Across a small road from the center's front doors is a fenced-in acre of organic gardens.

The University of Wisconsin-Extension partners with Havenwoods in administering these gardens. This is a true educational program, with several

Several garden plots at Havenwoods have ethnic themes, such as the Native American, Asian American, and Latin American beds.
John T. Andrews

separate plots demonstrating native gardening and composting techniques, herb growing practices, and even a sunflower maze for children. Also intriguing are the ethnic plots. In the African American garden, Egyptian onions grow; the Asian American tract features Siam Queen Thai basil and Chinese parsley; the European American soil is filled with eggplant and broccoli; while the Latin American beds produce Mexican black sweet corn and tomatillos. On the outside edges of the gardens, I can investigate various types of composting bins and gather printed information on how to set up a composting station in my own backyard. Before I visited Havenwoods, Superintendent Judy Klippel had told me that today the state forest is about "nurturing the land back to health, providing education that results in increased personal responsibility towards the environment, and demonstrating the value of urban green spaces."

In the children's maze, I walk up to the sunflowers that are as tall as I am and look into their big, yellow faces. The fact that such small, urban spaces can be made so "green" hits home.

Utilitarian Beauty

Where different types of habitats meet is not the only kind of "edge" I find at Havenwoods. There is an edge where form meets function.

A trail behind the environmental center that heads west takes me down to the rebuilt Lincoln Creek, a flood control area. On this summer day in the grasslands alongside the creek, prairie flowers are in full bloom, and the field is ablaze in orange butterfly weed, yellow coneflowers, purple prairie clover, and white Queen Anne's lace.

I sit down on a bench that overlooks three ponds. Although in reality these ponds are water retention basins for urban runoff — put here so the basements of Milwaukee residents won't flood — the scene of

Big yellow faces of sunflowers greet children in a maze created just for them.
John T. Andrews

the tall, green grasses dripping with orange, yellow, purple, and white flowers and backed up by a stand of trees is breathtaking.

"For years, we worked with the sewerage district on what the flood control area was going to look like," Judy Klippel tells me. "What its shape would be; what could be planted there; how we could ensure that the wildlife habitats would be restored. Together we developed a functional area that still included native vegetation, trails, and space for wildlife. To our delight, many

Yellow coneflowers set fields ablaze with color alongside the creek.
John T. Andrews

of the species we saw here before it was redone are still there now, and some new species have even showed up," she says, smiling.

A Lesson Plan for Small Spaces

While I'm relaxing by the ponds, I hear the happy chatter of children coming down the trail, and I decide to move on in order to give them the chance to gaze across this prairie from the perfect vantage point. From planting trees to sowing gardens, children have always been important at Havenwoods — not only for what they can learn here, but for what they can teach.

"Back around 1990 in the early years of the forest," says Judy Klippel, "I once had a group of kindergarteners visit Havenwoods on a field trip. They hadn't been here before. Their school was located by one of the viaducts in Milwaukee, so open, natural places were not familiar to them. At one point during the program, the children started running ahead of the teacher and me to a little area where the grasses were almost as tall as the kids themselves. They started jumping around in it and waving their arms through it. The teacher and I both looked at each other, and she said, 'They've never seen anything like this before.' They were so excited and giggly and happy.

"On the flip side, though," Judy relates, "over the years there have been numerous kids who were afraid to sit down in the tall grass; they worried about rats or snakes or spiders. Some have even thought there could be tigers or lions or bears lurking there. We help them to feel comfortable in the state forest and to get a better idea about what critters really live here."

Seeing how the children react to and learn from nature is just one of the ways Judy is continuing her education here. But there's one big lesson she's already learned, the hard way. Says Judy:

In school, I imagined myself working at a pristine natural area with magnificent wild animals and rare wildflowers. But coming to Havenwoods has taught me that we don't always have to be looking so much on the grand scale as on the small scale. Finding and enjoying nature in the city has opened my eyes to the intricacies of flowers, the clues that animals leave behind, and the songs of birds. Havenwoods is a heavily used piece of land. I've been amazed at nature's ability to heal the scars caused by human use, but healing the land is a long, slow process. This land will never look like it did two hundred years ago. I hope that the story of Havenwoods will help people realize that it is easier to protect beautiful natural areas than to try to restore them.

I walk through the Environmental Awareness Center one last time on my way out to the parking lot. I can't resist tempting fate and randomly picking up one last brochure, with my eyes closed. Opening them, I find I've selected a piece on how to build a worm-composting bin. The brochure says that the worms will eat household scraps and — thankfully — stay in the box. Feeling like the kindergartners in the tall grass, I was excited and happy to hear that.

The brochure also said that worm composting can be done in apartment buildings or other small urban places: a process of nature that can happen smack-dab in the middle of a city landscape, just like Havenwoods itself.

FOREST TREES OF WISCONSIN: HOW TO KNOW THEM

PUBLISHED BY THE WISCONSIN DEPARTMENT of Natural Resources Division of Forestry, the little green booklet called *Forest Trees of Wisconsin: How to Know Them* has been around since 1928. Chances are that you've picked one up somewhere during your Wisconsin travels and have stashed it in the glove compartment of your car.

A friend of mine, Dorothy Klinefelter, a University of Wisconsin associate dean emeritus, even told me that when she was cleaning out her recently deceased mother's bookcase, she found a copy nestled between other, thicker field guides. "Finding the booklet certainly brought back lots of memories of my family's shared interest in nature," says Dorothy.

The booklet, still in print today, was written by Fred G. Wilson, one of eleven original forest rangers hired by the state in 1911. According to the brochure's foreword, Fred "was the first to use seedlings to replant forest stands and was instrumental in developing the state forest nurseries for this purpose." In 1979, the year of his death, he planted his one-billionth tree through the State Nursery Program that is still in operation and that has now produced 1.5 billion seedlings for public and private use.

The title *Forest Trees of Wisconsin* may have been borrowed from an essay of the same name written by Increase Lapham in 1858. Considered to be "The Father of the U.S. Weather Bureau" (see pages 214–215) and "The Father of Wisconsin Forest Conservation," Lapham advocated for tree preservation long before anyone else. In the essay, he writes:

> The dense forests have a marked effect upon the climate of the country in several ways. They protect our houses and our cattle from the rigors of the north winds of winter, and from the fierceness of the burning sun in summer. They preserve the moisture of the ground, and of the air; and render permanent and uniform the flow of water in springs, brooks, and rivers. By the fall of their leaves, branches, and trunks, they restore to the soil those elements of vegetable life and growth, that would without this natural process, soon become exhausted, leaving the soil barren and unproductive. Their leaves absorb the carbonic acid from the atmosphere and restore it to the oxygen; thus rendering it more pure and better suited for respiration by man and animals. Without this restorative agency, all animal life would long since have ceased to exist.

But the thing I appreciate most about Lapham's regard for trees is his "unscientific" reasons for championing them:

> Trees, besides being useful, are ornamental — they enter largely into the material of the landscape gardener. Desolate indeed would be our dwellings were their environs entirely treeless. They are associated with our early recollections — they become in a great degree companions of our lives; and we unconsciously form strong attachments for such as grow near our homes — thus increasing our love of home, and improving our hearts.

The next time you stop into a WDNR office, be sure to pick up a new copy of *Forest Trees of Wisconsin: How to Know Them.* Chances are your old one is dog-eared and well loved.

Havenwoods State Forest

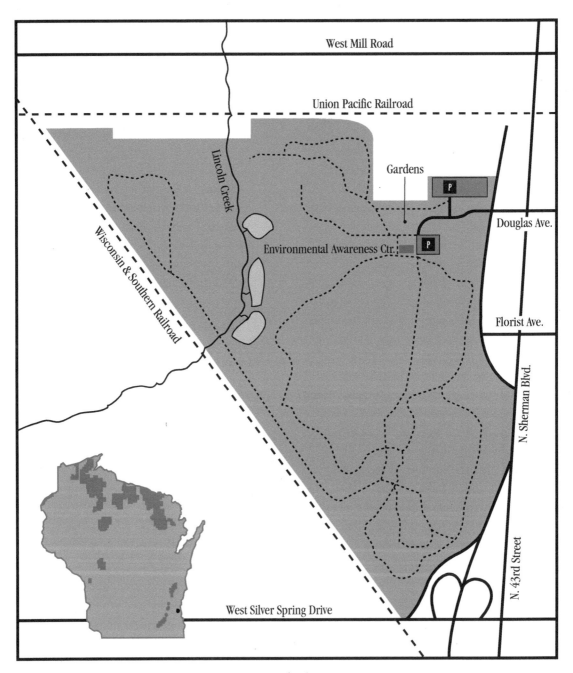

West Mill Road

Union Pacific Railroad

Lincoln Creek

Gardens

Douglas Ave.

Environmental Awareness Ctr.

Florist Ave.

Wisconsin & Southern Railroad

N. Sherman Blvd.

N. 43rd Street

West Silver Spring Drive

1/4 Mile

Children are intrigued by the tall grasses at Havenwoods, often giggling and waving their arms through it — and sometimes believing large animals could be hidden within. *John T. Andrews*

The Parnell Observation Tower is located on the Northern Unit's highest point.
On top of the tower, you are more than 1,300 hundred feet above sea level
with a panoramic view of the glacial hills to the southwest. *John T. Andrews*

9 Kettle Moraine State Forest–Northern Unit/ Pike Lake Unit/ Loew Lake Unit

TOOLING AROUND THE TOPOGRAPHY

Tops at Topography

She's probably the first topophiliac I've ever run into.

In a quick online search, I found *topophilia* in *Webster's New International Dictionary of the English Language*. It's a relatively new word, coined in 1974, and means "love of place." I think Deb Coblenz's co-workers at the Northern Unit of the Kettle Moraine State Forest had to invent the "-iliac" offshoot to describe Deb, because no other word in current usage would do.

"People here call me a 'topophiliac' because I just love topography," says Deb, who works part-time for the Henry S. Reuss Ice Age Visitor Center within the Northern Unit's boundaries. "I'm someone who loves to talk about drumlins and kettles and kames; I love discussing the hills and why they're made that way," she explains. "We have some of the finest glacial formations in the entire world here in the Northern Unit of the Kettle Moraine. Every little hill here means *something*; every little dip means *something*. And when someone comes in to the Ice Age Visitor Center and asks, "What's an esker?" Oh, well. I get pretty excited about that."

The Episode Begins

I'm starting my explorations of the 29,268-acre Kettle Moraine State Forest–Northern Unit with a stop at the visitor center, located a half mile west of Dundee on Highway 67. The building sits high on the moraine edge left by the Green Bay Lobe of the Wisconsin Glacial Episode, and from the back deck, you can gaze out at a heck of a lot of the geologic features that get Deb so fired up. Spread out before me, from left to right, is Dundee Mountain, the largest "kame" in the forest; White Kame; the Jersey Flats "outwash plain";

As the largest kame in the Northern Unit, Dundee Mountain is the "King of the Forest."
John T. Andrews

the jumbled "end moraine" of the Lake Michigan Lobe of the same glacial event; and the East Branch of the Milwaukee River. I can understand why Deb is so enthusiastic about the forest she's been associated with for the past eighteen years — the first fifteen of which she spent as its law enforcement ranger. The variety and unusual shapes in the landscape are visually stunning.

"Before I was a ranger, I was a firefighter and an emergency medical technician," says Deb. "I drove an ambulance in Milwaukee and Sheboygan, but I got burned out on EMT work. Growing up in the Black River Falls area, where it's woody and wild, I learned to love the outdoors. I wanted the rest of my career to be a part of that. I saw that the Civil Service Exam was coming up, and I knew that I would need to take that to get a full-time job with the state government," she says.

Still glued to the view off the back deck of the visitor center, I begin to pick out some of the more subtle features of the terrain. The convolutions and rhythm of the ridges and depressions mesmerizes me. It is frequently acknowledged in geological literature that this dense concentration of glacial landforms is unequalled anywhere else in the world, and being able to stand before so many of them at one time is astonishing.

Deb can identify with my sense of wonder. "What a fantastic career I've had!" she says, referring to her experience as a forest law enforcement ranger, which means she's also a certified police officer. "Every day, out and about in the forest, I could watch the hills, the trees, and the land change. I could observe what was going on at almost any moment."

Inside the Henry S. Reuss Ice Age Visitor Center are educational exhibits on how this region was formed; a big, world map and a glacier timeline; and a theater that showcases a National Park Service film on glaciers narrated by actor Eli Wallach. In front of the big screen in the dark, I watch the twenty-minute movie and learn how glaciers shaped the face of Wisconsin. When the film ends, I step outside into a bright, hot summer day and grope inside my backpack for my sunglasses. The Age of Ice seems like a long, long way away.

A sign that points to a short nature trail that winds from the building catches my attention. It invites me to take a self-guided hike back into the Ice Age.

Between the Lobes

The Wisconsin Glacial Episode, the last major advance of continental glaciers in North America, was made up of three "glacial maxima" (sometimes called "ice ages") separated by interglacial periods, such as the one we are experiencing now. The oldest of the three maxima reached its farthest extent about seventy thousand years ago. The youngest, and third, of these ice ages was the least severe and began about thirty thousand years ago. Its greatest advance was about twenty thousand years ago, and it ended approximately ten thousand years ago.

A sheet of ice more than a mile thick called the Laurentide Ice Sheet, ground its way over and covered the Upper Midwest and much of the northern United States from the Atlantic Coast to the Rocky Mountains. At the site of the Kettle Moraine State Forest, two gigantic, fingerlike extensions of ice — the Green Bay Lobe on the west, which carved out Green Bay and left Door County hanging, and the Lake Michigan Lobe on the east, which created Lake Michigan — merged, except near the front, where a V-shaped trough was created. As the lobes retreated, the trough continued to move north. Vast meltwaters from the two lobes ran into this trough and left fan-shaped outwash deposits. Billions of tons of gravel, sand, and rock were squeezed, deposited, and then piled up on stagnant masses of glacial ice. When that ice melted, knobby "collapse topography" formed. Deb Coblenz explains why this makes the Kettle Moraine State Forest so unique: "The reason we're so loaded with glacial features is that we are the *only* 'interlobate moraine,' where two massive lobes met and made a moraine. The Ice Age Visitor Center rides the Green Bay Lobe moraine; out on the deck, you can look across the valley and see the Lake Michigan Lobe moraine. We weren't the farthest extent of the ice, but we have the most illustrative evidence of it because of the way the two lobes bumped up here," she says.

While both the twenty-five-mile-long Northern Unit and the thirty-mile-long Southern Unit of the forest are situated on the Kettle Moraine, the Southern Unit is closer to the terminus of the Green Bay Lobe, or on an "end moraine," a large glacial deposit formed at the end of the moving ice. And that's the reason for the different looks to the two units, according to Deb. "The Northern Unit and the Southern Unit appear dissimilar," she states. "But we're just two different critters of the same ice age; it just depends where on the glacier you happened to be. In the Wisconsin Glacial Episode, the glacier stretched down into Illinois, and it had a total of six lobes."

The Kettle Interlobate Moraine, as it is sometimes called, runs for 110 miles from north to south, from southern Manitowoc County down to Waukesha County. It is one to ten miles wide and rises one hundred to three hundred feet above its surrounding landscape. And while both the Green Bay Lobe and the Lake Michigan Lobe created the features we see today, most of them were subsequently reworked by gravity and running water.

As the glacier retreated and ice started to melt, streams gushed over its surface. At weak points, the streams bored holes in the ice, washing tons of debris through the funnel-shaped openings. As the water landed beneath the ice, the debris was deposited, forming conical heaps of material that today remain as kames. Long, winding ridges called eskers were formed when stream channels flowing beneath stagnant glaciers filled up with sand and gravel.

Kettles, or depressions in the ground, were created when sand and gravel settled over and buried huge, melting ice blocks. Many of these kettles then filled with water and formed our lakes and ponds. Others, on high land, remained open and are as deep as two hundred feet.

Potholes were worn into rocks by swirling sand, stones, and gravel ferried by powerful currents of meltwater rivers. The melting ice also caused huge glacial lakes to form, which eventually drained into flat, broad lakebeds that now are fertile agricultural fields.

Compared to the onset of the ice, humans are latecomers to what is now the Kettle Moraine State Forest. The first native people arrived about ten thousand years ago.

THE LANGUAGE OF GLACIERS

MORE SO THAN ANY OTHER PHYSICAL FEATURES on Earth, glaciers seem to demand that we learn a special language when describing them and the things they leave behind. The prominent glacial features in the Kettle Moraine are erratics, eskers, kames, kettles, and outwash plains. Their definitions, and those of other glacier terms, are below.

Ablation — refers to melting, erosion, and evaporation, which reduce the area of glacial ice.

Ablation area or **ablation zone** — the region of a glacier where more mass is lost by evaporation or melting than is gained.

Alluvium — sediment (clay, silt, sand, gravel, or similar detrital material) eroded from adjacent areas and deposited by running water in and along rivers and streams.

Crevasse — an elongated open crack in glacial ice, usually nearly vertical, and subject to change at any moment.

Crustal rebound — when the Earth's crust slowly expands after the removal of intense pressure from the mass of a glacier. Some rebound movements may cause earthquakes.

Drumlin — a long, whale-shaped hill made of glacial debris. Its tapered end points in the direction of the glacier's advance.

Erratic — a rock or boulder carried and deposited by glacial ice from its place of origin to an area with a different type of bedrock.

Esker — a narrow, long, wormlike ridge of sands and gravels formed by debris-laden meltwater. Eskers probably mark the channels of subglacial streams.

(continued on next page)

THE LANGUAGE OF GLACIERS

(continued from page 177)

Esker fan — a small plain of sand and gravel built at the mouth of a subglacial stream and associated with an esker that was simultaneously formed.

Glacial drift — general term for all material transported and deposited directly by the ice or by water running off a glacier.

Glacial ice — consolidated, relatively impermeable ice crystal aggregates with a density greater than 0.84.

Kame — a low but steep-sided, conical hill of glacial debris, deposited by melting ice.

Kettle — a depression (which usually becomes a lake or marsh) in a deposit of glacial debris that formed when a block of ice melted after separating from a glacier.

Moraine — unsorted till deposited either along the sides (lateral moraine) or the ends (end or terminal moraine) of a retreating glacier; or the material below a retreating glacier (ground moraine).

Moulin — a narrow, tubular crevasse or chute through which water enters a glacier from the surface. Water flowing down moulins often makes loud, roaring sounds. The lower end of a moulin may be exposed in the face of a glacier or at the edge of a stagnant block of ice.

Outwash — deposited, stratified sands and gravels washed out from glaciers by meltwater streams.

Outwash plain — a broad, alluvial plain with a low slope composed of glacially eroded, sorted sediment (termed "outwash") that has been transported by meltwater. The alluvial plain begins at the foot of a glacier and may extend for miles, becoming finer in grain with increasing distance from the glacier's terminus.

Sublimation — an endothermic physical process whereby ice passes directly into the vapor state.

Forever Apart

But there is certainly no shortage of people today. The Kettle Moraine State Forest is located almost in the heart of Wisconsin's most heavily populated area, and it gets a lot of recreational use.

The idea for having a large parkland in the southeastern portion of the state was first planted by a natural disaster. In August 1924, the Milwaukee River flooded and caused major damage to the city. Milwaukee leaders realized that protecting the river's headwaters (in Watercress Creek in what is now the Northern Unit) by placing it in public ownership could help prevent future floods — and provide an ideal location for a park.

In 1926, the Milwaukee Chapter of the Izaak Walton League, an environmental organization dedicated to protecting fishing opportunities, bought 842 acres around Mauthe (then called Moon) Lake. Eleven years later, when a small group of southeastern Wisconsinites began to lobby for forestry and outdoor recreation facilities, the Wisconsin Legislature passed a bill appropriating funds to acquire and develop forestlands in specific locations. Those locations included counties in the southeastern portion of the state.

In early plans, a protected, continuous 120-mile forest stretching across the whole Kettle Moraine was envisioned. But the state never approved enough monies to purchase all the land parcels. Today, there is still a forty-mile gap between the Northern and Southern Units, and there is already so much development there that we will probably never have an intact preserve.

A Popular Place

Precisely because the Kettle Moraine State Forest–Northern Unit is in the middle of so much development is what makes it so popular — and heavily used by urban dwellers.

Says Deb Coblentz, "Our visitors, especially our camping and recreational hikers, are Chicago, Madison, Oshkosh, Sheboygan, Green Bay, and Milwaukee metropolitan residents. Our Northern Unit makes remoteness and wilderness very accessible to an urban population. Even though we get such heavy use, we are still big enough that people can get away from it all and not see anybody."

Riding out into that wilderness by horseback is just one of the favorite activities city residents come to the Northern Unit to do.

"We've got a great bunch of horseback riders and forty-two miles of trails for them," says Deb. "We had to expand our New Prospect Horseriders Campground recently because the old one just couldn't handle the amount of visitors. And our six backpack shelters on the Ice Age Trail are booked solid every weekend. You could probably do a walk-in Monday through Thursday — *possibly*. They're very, *very* popular."

A Way to Walk across Wisconsin

In fact, the famed Ice Age National Scenic Trail is a gigantic draw to the Northern Unit of the Kettle Moraine State Forest. Like the seven other National Scenic Trails (Appalachian, Continental Divide, Florida, Natchez Trace, North Country, Pacific Crest, and Potomac Heritage National Scenic

Trails), the Ice Age National Scenic Trail is like a siren song to outdoor enthusiasts for both its scale and its scenery.

The 1,200-mile Ice Age National Scenic Trail roughly follows the outline of the third glacial maxima of the Wisconsin Glacial Episode. In a course that begins on the shores of Lake Michigan in Potawatomi State Park in Door County, the trail heads south through the Kettle Moraine and almost to Illinois, then sweeps north to Langlade County before turning west. It ends in a steep bluff high above the St. Croix River in Polk County in Interstate State Park. A thirty-two-mile segment of this geologically rich route runs the length of the Northern Unit and hooks up with most of the other trails in the forest.

Another impressive aspect to this trail is that it has always been a citizen-driven endeavor. Raymond Zillmer of Milwaukee, a lawyer who was a mountaineer, avid walker, and student of natural history, first proposed the idea for an "Ice Age Glacier National Forest Park" on the site of the Kettle Moraine in the 1950s. In his vision, he pictured that an extensive footpath would be the central feature of the park. In 1958, Zillmer founded the Ice Age Park & Trail Foundation to begin efforts to establish the park and the footpath.

Ray Zillmer never lived to see his idea of an "Ice Age Glacier National Forest Park" fulfilled. But in 1980, the Ice Age Trail became a National Scenic Trail; in 1987 it was designated Wisconsin's *only* State Scenic Trail. *Courtesy of the Ice Age Trail Alliance*

Zillmer died in 1961, and the idea for the grand forest nearly died with him. Later that year, the National Park Service decided that while many of the unique glacial features of Wisconsin did deserve national attention, a park more than a hundred miles in length would be too difficult to administer. However, the land making up today's Northern Unit was identified as having the "significance of a national monument administered by the NPS."

Grassroots supporters and Wisconsin leaders went back to the drawing board. They developed the idea of having an "Ice Age National Scientific Reserve" — an affiliated area of the National Park System (a collection of physical properties owned or administered by the National Park Service) composed of nine separate units throughout Wisconsin. In 1964, thanks to the efforts of U.S. Representative Henry S. Reuss, the Ice Age National Scientific Reserve Act was passed by Congress and signed by President Lyndon Johnson.

In the early 1970s, the Ice Age Trail Council was formed to carry out Raymond Zillmer's dream of a long-distance hiking trail. Older trails, such as the Glacial Hiking Trail in the Kettle Moraine State Forest–Northern Unit, became building blocks for the Ice Age National Scenic Trail. But much of the remaining route was developed in a true grassroots fashion: volunteers got access to private lands by talking to owners, securing handshake agreements, and constructing the footpaths themselves. The Ice Age Trail Council merged with the Ice Age Park & Trail Foundation in 1990. In 2009, the organization's name was changed to the Ice Age Trail Alliance.

Under the sponsorship of Congressman Henry S. Reuss and with the signature of President Jimmy Carter, the Ice Age Trail was named a National Scenic Trail on October 3, 1980. In 1987, it was designated Wisconsin's *only* State Scenic Trail.

Today, with the sections of the trail that are complete and temporary connecting routes, it's possible to hike — or participate in other silent sports — on the entire 1,200 miles. The National Park Service, the Wisconsin Department of Natural Resources, the Ice Age Trail Alliance, and many county park and forest departments maintain the existing portions of the trail. But individuals, outing clubs, youth groups, and local civic organizations are integral to keeping the trail's development moving forward.

Unlike on most forest trails, there is no "looping back" on the Ice Age National Scenic Trail. If you keep going, you'll walk clear across Wisconsin. I decide to hike it a mile or two, just to experience the state's most famous of trails. Seeing land formations born eons ago — yet still existing today — is phenomenal. We are fortunate in Wisconsin to have had the most recent glacial episode. That's why so many of our glacial features have not yet completely eroded. In other words, like a colossal cookie cutter, the great glacier's imprint is impressed on our state landscape more sharply and harder than anywhere else in the nation.

Perhaps due to her police training, Deb has a way of putting things succinctly. "What's wonderful is that we're *preserving* these features," she says. "A lot of other glacier formations around the world were lost as gravel pits. They can't dismantle this one! Just think: instead of the visitor center we now have here, there could have been someone's McMansion — with one incredible view."

It's Not All Hard Rocks

As much as the boulders, potholes, kames, and eskers astound me with their longevity and their rocky beginnings, the forest is not all hard surfaces. There are many beating hearts and breathing beings.

CONFERRING A PECULIAR DISTINCTION: SANDHILL CRANES

The head of a sandhill crane emerges through a break in the foliage. Its ancestors have been in the Kettle Moraine far longer than ours. *John T. Andrews*

MUCH AS THE KETTLE MORAINE STATE FOREST is about geology "older than the hills," there is a bird here that dates back 2.5 million years, making it the oldest known surviving avian species.

While the earliest, unequivocal fossil of a sandhill crane places it at least at the 2.5-million-year marker, the bird may go back as far as ten million years. But even at 2.5 million years of age, sandhill cranes are nearly half again as old as the earliest remains of modern bird species, which date back only to the Pliocene/Pleistocene boundary, 1.6 million years ago.

Sandhill cranes hold another impressive record: they are among the tallest birds in the world. They stand on their stately, long legs at heights of three to five feet. The gray-colored cranes also stretch out when flying, extending their long necks and using an upstroke that is quicker than the downstroke.

You can recognize an adult by its bushy tuft of feathers over the rump and red skin on the forehead and crown. During spring and summer, its back and chest feathers are sometimes stained rusty-brown, due to self-painting with iron-rich mud.

CONFERRING A PECULIAR DISTINCTION: SANDHILL CRANES

The Kettle Moraine State Forest, with its open areas, provides excellent habitat for these birds. Usually seen in large fields near water or in wetlands adjacent to short vegetation, pairs will return to the same nesting territories year after year. Young cranes learn migratory routes from their parents; without this modeling, they do not migrate.

But you'll probably notice their voices first, long before you see them. Many say that their distinctive, rattling call is the anthem of spring. Mates engage in "unison calling," a complex series of coordinated calls delivered with heads thrown back and beaks skyward. The female will initiate the display and utter two, higher-pitched calls for each male call.

Singing isn't the only artistic talent these birds possess. All cranes engage in dancing, but sandhill choreography is spectacular. Two birds face each other, then bow and jump, flapping wings and making loud, cackling sounds. They often toss sticks and grass into the air. Though usually associated with courtship, dancing occurs at any age and season and is believed to be a normal part of motor development — a way to thwart aggression, relieve tension, and strengthen the pair bond.

In his 1949 book *A Sand County Almanac*, wildlife biologist and naturalist Aldo Leopold wrote:

> *Our appreciation of the crane grows with the slow unraveling of earthly history. . . . The other members of the fauna in which he originated are long since entombed within the hills. When we hear his call we hear no mere bird. We hear the trumpet in the orchestra of evolution. . . . Their annual return is the ticking of the geologic clock. Upon the place of their return they confer a peculiar distinction. Amid the endless mediocrity of the commonplace, a crane marsh holds a paleontological patent of nobility, won in the march of aeons.*

In fact, the Kettle Moraine contains half of Wisconsin's thirty different plant communities. The Northern Unit alone holds twelve State Natural Areas — pretty impressive for a forest surrounded by urban expansion.

The Northern and Southern Units of the Kettle Moraine State Forest, along with the Point Beach State Forest (see chapter 14), are known as Wisconsin's "southern forests." But unlike the Southern Unit's predominance of oaks and red and white pine in its forested acres, the Northern Unit is filled with red and white oak, shagbark hickory, sugar maple, and basswoods on the uplands, with American elm, silver maple, white cedar, ashes, and tamaracks on the lowlands.

Back at the Henry S. Reuss Ice Age Visitor Center, my wanderings around the grounds are soon pleasantly interrupted. A sound rises from within the tall grasses bordering one of the center's paths. I could swear someone is crouched in the foliage, shaking an old, wooden rattle. But then the tall head of a sand-

Barred owls still find shelter in the Kettle Moraine, as they have for hundreds of years.
Ben Branch

hill crane emerges through a break. From his otherworldly noise alone, I would guess his ancestors have been in the Kettle Moraine far longer than mine.

Chances are that if you didn't come to the Northern Unit to see the topography, you probably came to watch the birds. Nearly 250 species have been documented, and because the forest lies along an ecological "tension zone," there are both northern and southern types present. In the two-hundred-acre Jersey Flats, a prairie restoration within the forest, bobolinks, northern harriers, eastern meadowlarks, and grasshopper sparrows nest. Common loons and ducks flap over the lakes every spring, and ospreys, green herons, black terns, horned grebes, and sandpipers have been discovered here.

Against this backdrop of landforms with strange names such as moulins and erratics, birds with titles like colors fly. Red-shouldered hawks, red-bellied woodpeckers, black-billed cuckoos, blue-gray gnatcatchers, red-eyed vireos, indigo buntings, and scarlet tanagers all go about their business here. And below their outstretched wings, nearly forty mammal species walk the forest's floor.

"As far as animals, we've got everything," says Deb. "White-tailed deer, badgers, foxes, coyotes, beavers, otters, and mink. We've even got the threatened Butler's garter snake," she says proudly.

"Do you have black bears?" I ask, wondering if Wisconsin's bruins would care to live so close to our urban centers.

"No black bears," Deb answers. "But never say never. They like to travel. I know in 1972 a black bear was sighted here at Shelter Two, but he was never again seen."

King of the Forest

As beautiful as the panoramic vista of the moraine off the back deck, the nature trail walk, and my wanderings around the Ice Age Visitor Center have been, it's time to venture out once more into the forest and see some of the glacier's gifts and remains up close. By traveling on the Kettle Moraine Scenic Drive, a 115-mile route marked with green acorn signs that runs through the heart of the Northern and Southern Units, I can get to some of the most impressive and much-photographed landmarks. I ask Deb to suggest some places I should visit.

"You bet I have some favorite spots!" she says. "Because I've worked for fifteen years as a ranger, I've probably bushwhacked almost every part and parcel of this entire forest."

"I could go on for a long time," she continues. "But we're really well-known for the kames here. At Garrity Hill, a road was built and the kame was cut in half. Geology students can come here now and see how this kame actually developed — how the rocks piled up in that manner. And, of course, Dundee Mountain is the 'King of the Forest.' It's just incredible."

I head north up to the top of the forest on the Kettle Moraine Scenic Drive, up to the Greenbush Trails, about two and a half miles north of Highway 67. The oldest and best established in the forest, the four trails in the Greenbush Loop System, totaling nine miles, mostly follow along old logging roads. Not far off the roadway is the Greenbush Kettle; a more perfect example of that glacial landform does not exist.

I stand at the overlook above the Greenbush Kettle off the Kettle Moraine Scenic Drive and look down into what seems to be an overflowing pot of thick, green, living liquid. Here, at this exact spot, a big block of ice separated from the main body of a massive continental glacier. Here, that block was left, stranded. Here, it became buried in outwash and lay hidden for thousands of years.

What looks like a living, green liquid fills the perfectly formed Greenbush Kettle, a glacial remnant.
John T. Andrews

A wooden stairway invites me down to get closer to the nearly circular, steep-sided cauldron below. Seen from rim level, the green glaze looks dense enough to walk on, but I know it's an illusion. On my way back up the stairway, I find a cracked and bleeding bird's egg lying in the gravel between the wooden braces of the steps. The force of nature is palpable here — where something as immense as a glacier can live and die, and something as fragile as a baby bird.

This little bird will never fly, never sail over this topography and get the "big picture." I think back to what Deb Coblenz said about her view on high of the forest.

"In the early years, I used to do drug interdiction for plants with the sheriff's department. We used the National Guard's helicopter," explained Deb. "We flew at treetop level, looking for marijuana. Of course, I got to see the forest from a bird's-eye view. Oh, it is just *so* amazing!"

Since access to a helicopter is out of the question for me, I continue south down the Kettle Moraine Scenic Drive by car. My next stop is the Parnell Tower Trail and its observation tower. Situated on top of the Northern Unit's highest point, the sixty-foot Parnell Observation Tower lifts me to more than thirteen hundred feet above sea level and 450 feet above the surrounding forest. Below, I can see the oaks, maples, and tamaracks standing and swaying in the light breeze. The glacial hills to the southwest are clearly visible.

Slithering southward away from the Parnell Observation Tower is the Parnell Esker. This meandering gravel ridge stretches out for more than five miles through the forest's midsection and is from five to thirty-five feet tall. At Butler Lake, the Butler Lake Trail shares the Ice Age National Scenic Trail's path along the esker before branching off and completing a 3.1-mile loop. I take the time to walk on top of the wooded esker and along the trail that unfolds over it. It seems as if I'm walking on the spine of some mythical, giant, reptilian creature.

I'm close to Deb's "King of the Forest," the 250-foot moulin kame known as Dundee Mountain. (Dundee Mountain is 1,201 feet above sea level; the mean elevation of the state of Wisconsin is 1,050 feet.) This unmistakable icon of the forest looks foreign and exotic, like a wooded cone. I'm not surprised that the nearby town of Dundee calls itself the "UFO Capital of the World," and Dundee Mountain itself is an annual gathering place for believers and nonbelievers alike. Local lore says that Native Americans once called Dundee Mountain "Spirit Hill"; and over the years, several UFOs have been reportedly sighted on nearby Highway 67. Early Irish settlers claimed the Dundee area was inhabited by "little people" — otherwise known as leprechauns — and Long Lake was said to have a forty-five-foot monster. Now, every July during the UFO Daze festival, some Dundee residents can be spotted wearing headgear that is Hershey's Kiss shaped and made of tin foil to prevent aliens from reading their minds.

Coincidentally, Deb Coblenz had described the perfect kame as appearing like a "weathered Hershey's Kiss," and White Kame, just south of Dundee Mountain fits the bill. It's the kame I realize I've seen many times during my elementary school years; it's a favorite image for geology textbooks.

Motoring down through the forest, I'm now past the Henry S. Reuss Ice Age Visitor Center again, which is about at the unit's midsection. On Highway GGG, I come to my favorite place in the whole Northern Unit of the

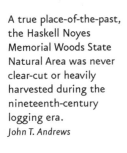

A true place-of-the-past, the Haskell Noyes Memorial Woods State Natural Area was never clear-cut or heavily harvested during the nineteenth-century logging era.
John T. Andrews

Kettle Moraine State Forest so far. The Haskell Noyes Memorial Woods State Natural Area is sixty-seven acres of never-cut, old-growth forest. Luckily, the stand was purchased in 1947 to prevent it from ever being logged. This is what a Wisconsin forest looks like when it has been left to its own devices.

What's even more unusual about this very natural area is that you don't have to bushwhack for hours into the backcountry to get to it. It's right next to Kettle Moraine Drive — *right* next to it. Just pull your car over to the side of the road, open the door, walk a few paces, and step under a thick, dense canopy of beech, hickory, and maple trees. Until a great tree falls here and creates an opening to the sky, even a seedling won't be able to make a start on the dark forest floor.

White-tailed deer, coyotes, beavers, woodchucks, muskrats, badgers, cottontail rabbits, raccoons, and mink live under the same trees as generations of their kind have before; while crested flycatchers, red-shouldered hawks,

A FONDNESS FOR FERNS

ONE OF THE REASONS I LOVE FORESTS IS because they harbor ferns, the feathery-light, almost-spiritual beings that populate the floor. Among the types of ferns that grow here are maidenhair, fragile, cinnamon, and lady ferns. Every spring, they seem to distinguish themselves from the forest's other lower-level inhabitants by the way they choose to appear — instead of pushing up, they seem to elegantly unfurl.

In summer, a grouping of lacey ferns that happens to catch a sunray glows for a moment, like a warm fire. And much of the interesting life of the forest is found at fern-level: does hide their newborn fawns among the ferns, while oven-birds and blue-spotted and red-backed salamanders make their homes in this herbaceous layer.

During the Paleozoic era's Carboniferous period (350 to 290 million years ago), feathery-light ferns were the dominant form of vegetation on Earth. *John T. Andrews*

Ferns are among the oldest kinds of plants that live on land; more than 350 million years ago, their ancestors flourished. Today, botanists know of approximately ten thousand species of ferns worldwide, more than three hundred of which grow in North America.

The best places to look for ferns in the woods are along streams and in the cracks and overhangs of rock cliffs. In the Kettle Moraine State Forest–Northern Unit, you can find them in Sheboygan County's Kettle Moraine Red Oaks State Natural Area and in Fond du Lac County's Haskell Noyes Memorial Woods State Natural Area.

Located just to the south of the Northern Unit's midpoint and decorated with kames, kettles, and ridges, the sixty-seven-acre Haskell Noyes Memorial Woods is a true Wisconsin place-of-the-past. The forest here was never clear-cut or heavily harvested during the nineteenth-century logging era. For the past several hundred years, no fire has burned its moist soils. The open understory is rich in a diversity of ferns, including maiden-hair, fragile, cinnamon, and lady ferns.

About one mile south of the intersection of Highways T and A in Greenbush is the Kettle Moraine Red Oaks State Natural Area. It is a mature, 316-acre, second-growth, southern dry-mesic forest that originated in 1889. It is one of the richest oak forests in the region and has more than one hundred species of trees, shrubs, and herbs. Bedstraw, sedges, American squawroot, large-flowered trillium, sweet cicely, Canada mayflower, and maidenhair fern seem to flow up from the ground.

Ferns have some of the most varied and beautiful leaves in the plant world, and maidenhair ferns

(continued on next page)

yellow-throated and red-eyed vireos, pileated woodpeckers, hooded warblers, wild turkeys, barred owls, scarlet tanagers, and rose-breasted grosbeaks find shelter in the same branches that have harbored their kind for hundreds of years.

Two for the Road

The nice thing about starting at the north end and heading south out of the Kettle Moraine State Forest is that when you leave the boundaries of the Northern Unit, you're not really leaving the forest quite yet — there are four more parts, and two of them are coming right up.

Between the Northern and Southern Units are three smaller parcels of forest known as the Pike Lake Unit, the Loew Lake Unit, and the Lapham Peak Unit (covered in chapter 10).

The 678-acre Pike Lake Unit of the Kettle Moraine State Forest is in the middle of the Kettle Moraine. The lake itself is a 446-acre kettle, which forms the western border of the property. Most visitors, I'm told, come to the Pike Lake Unit for Pike Lake — the fishing, boating, and swimming opportunities.

As you can guess, Pike Lake was named for its reputation as a fine northern pike fishing spot. But on warm days like today, the number of those on the beach soaking up the sun and cool breezes rivals the count of those out on the lake.

Two roads, Kettle Moraine Drive and Powder Hill Road, divide this forest

---

A FONDNESS FOR FERNS

(continued from page 189)
(*Adiantum*) have taken it upon themselves to exemplify that statement to a tee. Delicate and dainty, common maidenhair ferns have wiry, purple-brown leaf-stems and feathery, circular fronds that grow outward in a flat, fanlike position.

The name *Adiantum* is derived from the Greek *adiantos*, which means "unmoistened." The Greek botanist Theophrastus (371 BC–287 BC) said it is in vain to plunge the *Adiantum* in water, for it always remains dry. This property was attributed to the hair of Venus, when she rose from the sea; and thus black maidenhair fern was given the name *Adiantum capillus-veneris*. In the Catholic Church, the maidenhair fern was known as the "Virgin's hair."

That may partly explain that spiritual feeling a fern forest holds.

Water activities, including fishing, swimming, and boating, draw urban dwellers — and, apparently, Canada geese — to the forest's lakes and streams.
John T. Andrews

unit into three distinct ecological sections. Along Pike Lake, the wetlands, scattered prairie remnants, and spring-fed ponds are level and open; the middle section is characterized by glacial hills sprinkled with woods; and the eastern portion is a mix of forest and field. A segment of the Ice Age National Scenic Trail passes diagonally through the unit, looping from the northeast corner across to the southwest corner.

In the middle ecological section is a glacial formation known as Powder Hill. This steep kame rising above Pike Lake is the second highest point in southeast Wisconsin at 1,330 feet above sea level. A sixty-foot observation tower perched atop the grassy summit offers a broad view of this glacier-formed country. You can see Washington County's highest point, Holy Hill (1,332 feet above sea level), from the top of Powder Hill. The 1931 church that now sits on the summit of Holy Hill replaced several other churches that have stood there since an oak cross made from a tree growing on the hill was first erected at the spot in 1858.

Back in the car and pointed south again on my way home, I had hoped to savor one last piece of the forest on this adventure at the Loew Lake Unit. But when I traveled through the property, the forest remained hidden from me. I could see nothing past the trees lining the blacktop; no trail markers or obvious roads into the heart of the unit itself. The Ice Age National Scenic Trail does wind through this picturesque valley around the twenty-three-acre Loew Lake, but this time, literally, I could not see the forest for the trees.

When I ask Deb about the Loew Lake Unit later, she says, "Loew Lake hasn't been developed yet. That's what's so cool about it. You have to get in your canoe to see it; you have to work hard to know it."

Forest Secrets

Because Deb does know the forest so well, from bushwhacking at ground level to marijuana-hunting from helicopter-heights, I phone her when I get back home and tell her I'm curious: just what is her favorite formation in the forest?

"I do have a little, magic place," she confesses, "at the northern end of the forest, up by the Greenbush area. At the bottom of a huge moraine, there's a spring. Where the water comes up, it makes the sand bubble. The grains just jump and dance. It's gorgeous! I could sit there and watch it all day — it's one of those Zen things, I think."

"Where is it?" I ask her.

"You wouldn't find it," she states quickly. "You'd need a guide to show you. Northern end of the forest — that's all I'll tell you. It's a very spiritual place."

But while Deb is keeping one, small bit of the forest to herself, she strongly believes that the Kettle Moraine is a resource that should be taken advantage of by all those Wisconsinites who live near it. "You know," she tells me, "kids today are really in nature deficit. They say our goal in education is 'No child left behind.' I think it should be 'No child left indoors.'"

Spoken like a true topophiliac.

The Vista Trail Overlook behind the Henry S. Reuss Ice Age Visitor Center is a favorite path of "topophiliacs." *Candice Gaukel Andrews*

Kettle Moraine State Forest–Northern Unit

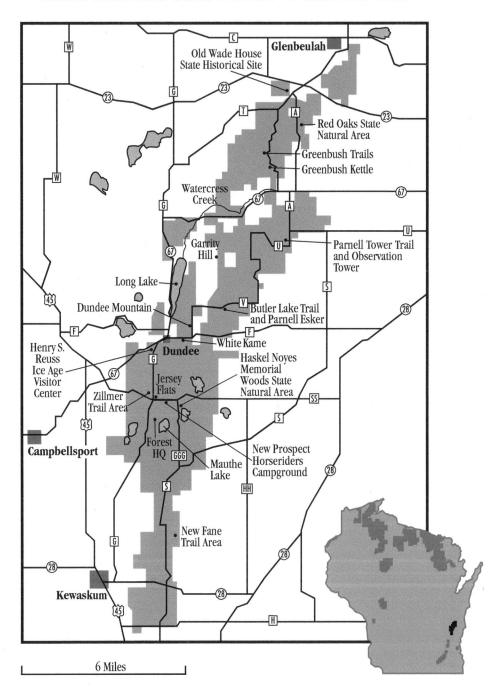

6 Miles

Kettle Moraine State Forest–
Pike Lake Unit/Loew Lake Unit

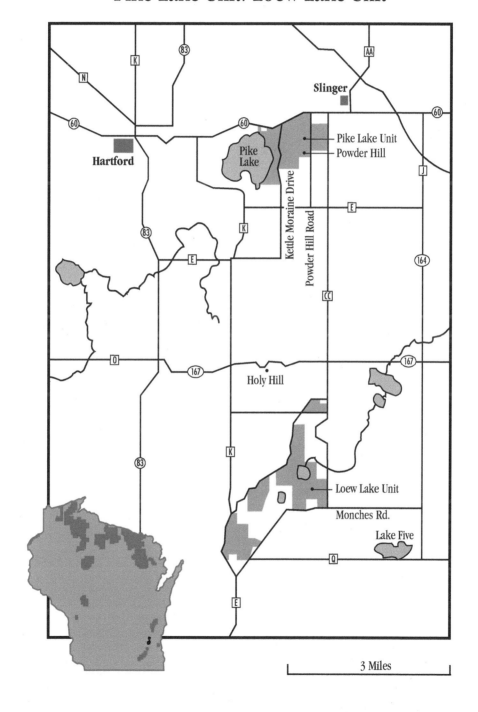

3 Miles

From the Big Hill, you can see the silhouettes of
civilization: Oconomowoc, Dousman, and Holy Hill,
about thirty miles away. *John T. Andrews*

10 Kettle Moraine State Forest–Southern Unit/ Lapham Peak Unit

A Very Civilized Forest

Settling Down in the Kettle Moraine

Sunday on the Big Hill. That's how I'm spending it. Sunday is supposed to be the day of rest, and I'm thinking there's no more restful place than here. Even the simplicity of the name is peaceful.

Sitting at 1,050 feet up on this grassy knob of earth on this morning in May, I've got an impressive view. Below me, outstretched are rolling, ivy-green fields. If I look straight out across the horizon, I can see Holy Hill about thirty miles away and the highest point in the whole Kettle Moraine at 1,332 feet. I can also see in the distance the silhouettes of the cities of Oconomowoc and Dousman. It's fitting; for as alone as I am on the Big Hill, the Kettle Moraine State Forest–Southern Unit is pressed by civilization on all sides, on all plains, on all fronts. People are the standout natural feature of this forest, it seems, since the time when there first were people here.

Homesteading the Forest

I'm not the first to go to the Big Hill on Sundays. This is the old Stute Homestead, and when friends and family members came to visit the Stutes — three generations of them — from the 1850s through the early 1940s, the Stutes would take them to the top of Big Hill, too. For more than a hundred years,

Sauk warrior and leader Black Hawk is said to have twice escaped U.S. Army forces in the hills of the Kettle Moraine.
WHi Image ID 11706

then, people like me have been coming here to reflect on this forest that is so full of the ghosts of Wisconsin Indians, immigrants, farmers, soldiers, and hikers. Families and homes are part of the soil of this forest, ingrained in the very leaves of its trees.

When white European settlers first arrived in this section of the Kettle Moraine, the Potawatomi were the dominant group in the area. It is reported that the Sauk leader and warrior Black Hawk, or Black Sparrow Hawk (*Makataimeshekiakiak* in the Algonquin language of the Sauk), twice eluded the U.S. Army in the hills of the Southern Unit as he was pursued across Wisconsin in 1832. Interestingly, the Black Hawk War, as it was called, gave young Abraham Lincoln his one experience in the military.

Even Ray Hajewski, the trails coordinator for the Kettle Moraine State Forest–Southern Unit from 1974 to 2005 and a man who personally knows almost every piece of soil on this forest, typically refers to portions of it by their "human" names:

We always identified locations in the forest by the old family farms. For instance, we'd give directions by saying something like, "It's by the old Hamilton farm" or "by the old Armstrong farm." Or we'd say on the radio, "There's a fire by the old Peacock farm." Even though those places had long been totally knocked down, that's how we'd get our bearings in the forest. Only recently did we start having to steer clear of that kind of terminology, and that's because of the young folks who started working for the forest. Those of us who'd been in the Kettle Moraine for a while would say, "There's the old so-and-so farm," and the younger people would look at us and say, "I don't see a farm." Then I would come back with, "Well, look over there. There are some old tulips coming up. That was the front of the farmhouse."

Locations in the forest were long identified by the names of former farm families. The stone fence and building here are part of the old Stute Homestead in the forest's Southern Unit.
John T. Andrews

Ray's verbiage points up the good and bad news about this part of the Kettle Moraine State Forest. The Southern Unit, given its proximity to Milwaukee and Madison, is unquestionably one of the most trodden forests in Wisconsin and racks up more annual visits than its northern counterpart. It receives 1.2 million visits per year to the Northern Unit's one million. At 22,300 acres, smaller than the Kettle Moraine State Forest–Northern Unit's 29,268-acres, the Southern Unit is packed, especially on weekends.

And that fact does weigh heavily on Ray Hajewski's mind these days.

Scars on Her Skin

"I probably wasn't the typical forest employee," states Ray. "I tend to romanticize the Kettle Moraine. For me, it's not just a place; its soil is a living, breathing entity. I've spent a lot of time on the back of that moraine. I've seen her in all different types of weather, all seasons, and all times of the day from the wee hours of the morning until twelve o'clock noon. When I look at a map of the forest, it's not just a matter for me of black lines on a piece of paper, denoting trails and roads. I see every tree, every flower in spring, every snowfall in winter, and every curve going over that hill. And I am concerned," he says.

I ask Ray to explain what troubles him. He replies:

The last couple of years I worked there, I was always adamant that if we developed a new trail in favor of an already-established trail, we *must* put the landscape back to the way it was on the old trail before it even existed. A former forest superintendent was really into cross-country skiing. He wanted all the trails developed so that they ran straight up a hill and straight down a hill — the way ski trails were typically designed in the 1970s and 1980s. We took out every little curve. Well, what happens when you do that? The soil is composed of limestone with beach sand. So if you scuff up even a little of the moraine's skin, you've got an open sore there of rock and sand. Then once a little bit of rain falls, all the soil washes down the hill and leaves a scar.

Ray makes clear that he's not against making new trails in the forest to replace severely eroded trails or ones that could be better designed for their type of use — as long as they are being planned with erosion issues in mind and the former trails are not slighted and forgotten.

If you want to move a straight-up-and-down trail to wind around the sides of a hill in order to get water to shed more appropriately, that's okay with me. But now, go back to that original trail and remediate it. In other words, make that hill the way the glacier left it ten thousand years ago. You should never, ever leave a scar like that on the moraine.

Unfortunately, however, "remediation" means different things to different people. For Ray, just abandoning a trail and letting invasive species and, eventually, trees fill it in is not the correct definition of the word. "Underneath the growth you'll still have this ugly scar on this beautiful, green gem of ours," says Ray. "This is what bothers me the most."

Putting right the landscape where the older, straighter trails once cut through the forest is imperative if the soil on the Kettle Moraine is to be preserved. According to Ray, the "newer" trails that are designed to curve around the sides of hills are actually throwbacks to the first trail types in the state forest. He explains:

> People used to just park their cars along the side of the road and get out to walk in the forest As more and more people did this in the popular spots, we started marking the trees with colors so they could find their way back to their cars. That's how hiking and horse trails originated; often these trail users would coil up a hill in a circular pattern like people and horses naturally tend to walk. In fact, that's how the Scuppernong Trails and Palmyra Trails began. Of course, then the popularity of cross-country skiing changed everything. Trails had to be straightened and widened out. That allowed more snow to reach the trail tread instead of sitting up in the trees.

But the popularity of cross-country skiing hasn't been the only moraine marker in the forest. There is no single "villain" in this. All of our human activities and sports, of course, have made their presence felt. Says Ray:

> The combination of snowmobiles, horse hooves, cross-country skis, and even our hiking boots can contribute to making a severely eroded hill if there is a poorly designed trail. I've seen areas that were pristine and bursting with wild flowers and native grasses transform into gravel pits, all because of our not carefully considering the type of use on such a fragile soil.

Although I'm in no hurry to leave my pleasant perch on Big Hill, it is time to get to know personally some of the trails here that currently meander over the Kettle Moraine's soil and some of the places in the forest where human history has sunk in. I stand up, brush the grass off my shorts, and start my hike back down the Big Hill. I travel through an area that in winter becomes the McMiller Ski Trails, which are laid out along an 1850s wagon road. More than likely, Anton Stute, the family patriarch, arrived here from Germany on this route. And before him, generations of Potawatomi padded along this path. The

When cross-country skiing became popular, many forest trails were straightened and widened out to thirty or forty feet.
John T. Andrews

guidebook to the Stute Springs and Homestead Nature Trail says, "According to letters from pioneers, Potawatomi trails were narrow and several inches deep due to the constant use."

Apparently, some of the scars on the moraine that Ray worries about aren't modern inventions by any means, which come packaged only with new, shiny cross-country skis and sleek, speedy snowmobiles. Humans have been making their impact on the Kettle Moraine for a very long time.

In Paradise

I'm off to explore another nature trail in the Southern Unit where humans have left an indelible mark on the forest landscape and its history — some even long before the Kettle Moraine was officially designated a state forest in 1937. A unique feature about this trail, though, is that it is now designed with a diversity of people in mind, including those who are mobility handicapped.

The wooded, half-mile Paradise Springs Nature Trail is especially configured to accommodate forest visitors with physical disabilities. The level path has a guide cable along its route, and a tape-recorded version of its brochure is available at the visitor center.

You can see the grandeur of former days — as well as the Kettle Moraine forest — reflected in the waters of Paradise Springs.
Candice Gaukel Andrews

You can see and touch the grandeur of former days in the ceiling-less, field-stone springhouse that still stands over Paradise Spring. A large window separated into rectangular frames is reflected on the surface and creates a watery crystal through which to view the spring below. Multimillionaire Louis J. Petit built the springhouse in the early 1930s when he owned the place. Petit made his fortune in the salt mining business (and was dubbed the "Salt King"), and he had once placed a copper dome roof over his elaborate springhouse.

Every minute, five hundred gallons of water flow from the spring. Even on a warm May day, the fieldstones are cool to the touch. The structure seems to be a liquid part of this forest; not an intrusion but a beautiful enhancement, brought forth from the surrounding woods with care by loving hands.

From the springhouse, I can look across the trout pond to the spot where the Paradise Springs Resort Hotel once stood. Its construction started in 1937. The guide brochure says that a massive, two-story resort built of locally quarried Wisconsin dolomite contained a rather posh dining room, a cocktail bar, a roof garden with a sundeck, and deluxe bedrooms with private, steam-heated, tiled baths. Gordon Mertens, the owner of the property at the time, used the land's white oak for the hotel's inlaid flooring. Over the years, other stories have bubbled up about the springs — some of which are not in the guide booklet.

There's the story from Eleanor Larson, which was handed down to her from her grandmother, Sarah Fardy, who lived in a log cabin near Paradise Springs from 1883 to sometime in the 1920s. Grandma Fardy told Eleanor that on one night in the 1880s, she saw a large group of Native Americans camped on the far side of Paradise Springs Creek. The next day, as she watched from her cabin window, the Indians broke camp and departed, leaving one woman behind. Sarah thought the woman might be in trouble, so she walked over to the camp. The solitary woman was about to give birth, so Grandma Fardy assisted and washed the newborn in the creek. A short time later, the mother wrapped up her baby, mounted her horse, and left, following the others who had departed before her.

Sometime after the 1880s, it's rumored that the Paradise Springs area was purchased by a circus barker, a man named L. D. Nichols. He reportedly kept several exotic animals here, including peacocks, monkeys, and rare birds. After Louis J. Petit bought the place in 1927, he added the springhouse, horse track, a nine-hole golf course, an outdoor wading pool, and two fieldstone pillars at

Built in the 1850s, the Gotten Historic Log Cabin still sits on its original site.
Candice Gaukel Andrews

the entrance with a large stone eagle on top of each one. The Petits, apparently, were fond of holding elegant parties for their hunting friends.

It turns out that Louis J. Petit's grandson was August Pabst Jr. of the brewing dynasty. Whether August got involved with the spring-water bottling plant that was once on the site isn't quite clear. The plant, which sold Paradise water under the names of "Lullaby Baby Drinking Water" and "Natural Spring Water," closed in the 1960s.

Exotic animals, golf courses, and bottling plants. Are these more "scars" on the Kettle Moraine? While the water bottling plant is now gone, parts of its foundation are still visible in the undergrowth, a story on the forest not totally "remediated." And perhaps it shouldn't be. Human history is intrinsic to this forest, and the forest is now drinking it in and absorbing it.

Before leaving the Paradise Springs area, I walk across the street from the parking lot to the Gotten Historic Log Cabin, built by pioneer Henry L. Gotten, a Prussian immigrant, in the 1850s. The white-oak-and-chinking cabin is simple, an uncomplicated timber-and-mortar rectangle.

Although they never inhabited the same time frame, I wonder what Henry would have thought of his extravagant and exotic neighbors.

The Fabric of Flora

While the Northern and Southern Units of the Kettle Moraine share a glacial geology, part of what differentiates them is the abundance of prairie and savanna in the Southern Unit that is far less frequent up north. Currently, there are about five thousand acres of these rare habitats here, and, luckily, several State Natural Areas protect some of them.

The Clifford F. Messinger Dry Prairie and Savanna Preserve State Natural Area stretches more than twenty miles across the forest. Named for a former chair of The Nature Conservancy, it consists of sixteen separate sites, grouped into five units, containing prairie and oak-opening communities. Although each site has a unique flora, all of the prairies here tend to be interwoven with Indian grass, prairie dropseed, sideoats grama, pasqueflower, bird's-foot violet, purple prairie clover, old-field goldenrod, blazing star, and big and little bluestems.

One example of the oak openings sites is the Whitewater Oak Opening. While red oak claim the north-facing slopes and white oak make other grounds their own, it is the bur oak — the tree Ray Hajewski calls the "mastodon of the forest" — that dominates the ridge tops and south- and southwest-facing slopes. The bur oak were the only trees in the area during the prairie years (before European settlement) due to the fact that their rough, outer bark made them resistant to fire. Although shrubs and other woody growth such as honeysuckle, buckthorn, and prickly ash have invaded the Whitewater Oak Opening over the years, prescribed burns and cutting by Endangered Resources Program crews are helping to sustain the ecosystem.

The Bald Bluff State Natural Area in the south-central section of the Southern Unit is another one of those sixteen Clifford F. Messinger Dry Prairie and Savanna Preserve sites, and it is another place that has seen a parade of people.

Prairie Perspective

Originally blanketed with prairie grasses and flowers, Bald Bluff Scenic Overlook and State Natural Area, two miles south of Palmyra, is now covered by trees. At 1,050 feet, it is one of the highest points in Jefferson County. The high ground drops down to a deep kettle below, where, at times, strong winds gather.

On a summer day in 1832, on July 7 at the height of the Black Hawk War, General Henry Atkinson and 3,500 cavalry and infantry troops camped on the prairie just northwest of the bluff. One of the soldiers was young Abraham Lincoln. It was rumored by a settler, Earl Wilson, whose farm was located just

The Potawatomi used the summit of Bald Bluff as a signal hill and council grounds. Today on the top, you'll find wild-flowers and a panoramic view of Kettle Moraine country.
John T. Andrews

AT HOME IN THE IN-BETWEEN: THE BUR OAK

MUCH LIKE THE CITY PEOPLE WHO HELP define the nature of the Kettle Moraine's Southern Unit, the bur oak (*Quercus macrocarpa*), a pillar of the forest, has been described as an "urban tree." In fact, *City Trees* magazine, a journal of the Society of Municipal Arborists, once selected the bur oak as the Urban Tree of the Year. Resistant to air pollution and heat stress, the bur oak is also tolerant of a variety of moisture and soil conditions. It provides cool, dense shade for any who choose to seek protection under its full, impressive crown — which can attain an eighty-foot spread. Of notable strength, the bur oak often grows where other oaks fear to tread.

Another reason the bur oak, a member of the white oak family, flourishes in the Southern Unit is because it typically grows in the open, away from deep forest canopies. The Kettle Moraine Oak Opening State Natural Area in Jefferson and Walworth Counties is a mixture of oak opening and oak woodland dominated by open-grown bur oaks. Prescribed fires help manage and restore this natural area, and the fire-resistant bur oak thrives: its deeply furrowed, thick, medium-gray bark offers it better ground-fire protection than all but the cottonwood tree. Even its acorns are heavily insulated.

Bur oak acorns are favorite food for white-tailed deer, wood ducks, wild turkeys, blue jays, rabbits, squirrels, mice, and other rodents. Native Americans sometimes ate the large, sweet acorns raw or boiled. The acorn, which may reach a diameter of an inch or more and a length of 1.5 inches, is almost entirely enclosed in a shaggy, burr-like cap that is ovoid in shape. The "bur" in the tree's common name is in reference to its cap-covered acorn.

The bur oak's slow growth is compensated for by its longevity. There are bur oak trees that may exceed two hundred to three hundreds years of age and eighty feet in height. After its life in the forest, bur oak wood may serve us again in our cabinetry, barrels, hardwood flooring, or fence posts.

While exploring the Kettle Moraine, you can identify a bur oak by its distinctive leaf. Although it may be as small as four inches, at its largest the leaf is about a foot long and six inches wide, the biggest of all the oak leaves. The typical blade is thick, firm, and shaped like a fiddle; its lobed leaf has a pinched midsection formed by a pair of large, deep notches called sinuses. The leaves are glossy and dark green above, and pale and hairy below. In the fall, the leaves turn a muted yellow in color.

Like large portions of the Southern Unit, this long-lived, majestic oak has found its space between the pure prairie and pure forest — in the prairie savanna. And true to the Ice Age character of the Kettle Moraine, the bur oak is the tree Ray Hajewski was inspired to nickname the "mastodon of the forest."

---

outside of Palmyra, that General Atkinson buried a cannon nearby. In recent years, metal-detecting clubs and a University of Wisconsin–Milwaukee professor with special soil-technology equipment have come to the Kettle Moraine–Southern Unit to search for it, but so far, nothing has been found.

But long before a future U.S. president drank his morning coffee here, the Potawatomi had used the sacred bluff as a signal hill and council grounds. The spirituality of the spot can still be felt today on its summit — in the small, dry prairie's purple blazing stars, in its pale blue harebells, and in the wide-angle perspective it gives on this part of the world.

A Sweet-Scented Land

Today, I'm poking around in one of the oldest State Natural Areas in Wisconsin. The 185-acre Scuppernong Prairie State Natural Area and its adjacent

The Scuppernong River Habitat Area is now adorned by fens, tamarack swamps, cattail marshes, sedge meadows, oak trees, and bur oak openings. *John T. Andrews*

THE IMPORTANCE OF WETLANDS

STANDS OF TREES AREN'T THE ONLY BUILDING blocks in a forest landscape. Ephemeral ponds, fens, and bogs need to be added into the mix. Whichever exotic-sounding name and shape they take, these Wisconsin wetlands provide habitat for more species of animals and plants than any other landscape type in the state.

The Kettle Moraine State Forest–Southern Unit has several "ephemeral ponds" — depressions with impeded drainage that hold water for a period of time following snowmelt and spring rains. As the name suggests, ephemeral ponds typically dry out by midsummer. The ponds support common wetland plants such as yellow water-crowfoot, mermaid weed, smartweed, orange jewelweed, Canada blue-joint grass, spotted cowbane, and sedges. During their brief lives in the ponds, these plants provide food for many mammals and critical breeding habitat for amphibians, such as wood frogs and salamanders. They also supply songbirds with a place to rest, breed, and feed. The forest trees adjacent to ephemeral ponds benefit their neighbors by maintaining cool water temperatures, preventing premature drying, and adding to the detritus-based food web. The leaves that fall from trees surrounding the ponds sustain a variety of invertebrates. Without ephemeral ponds, much of the biodiversity in a woods would be lost.

A "fen" is a wet, springy grassland similar to a wet prairie or sedge meadow. This type of wetland has an internal flow of alkaline water, which comes from limestone and calcareous drift. Although fens are not common in Wisconsin, you can explore one and its flashy plants, grasses, and forbs at the Ottawa Lake Fen State Natural Area, north of Ottawa Lake in the Southern Unit. This unusual habitat features plants such as small fringed gentian, pitcher plant, southern sedge meadow, shrub-carr, grass of Parnassus, and nodding lady's tresses. Blanding's turtles, pickerel frogs, bullfrogs, lake chubsuckers, clams, and snails share the fen with green herons, blue-winged warblers, yellow warblers, and willow flycatchers.

A fen on a hillside is sometimes called a "perched bog." A bog is any area having a wet, spongy, acidic substrate composed chiefly of sphagnum moss and peat. Trees, such as tamaracks and black spruce, can grow in a bog. On the four-mile White Loop of the John Muir Trails, you can encounter three leatherleaf bogs. A member of the heath family, leatherleaf is a shrub with leathery, evergreen leaves and small, white, cylindrical flowers.

Unfortunately, Wisconsin's wetlands are declining. Only about half of the ten million acres of wetlands that were present in 1848 remain. Farm drainage and filling for development and roads have degraded and destroyed the majority of them. Invasive plants, such as purple loosestrife, have also taken their toll. The loss is not only ominous for the state's biologic diversity but for human safety as well. Wetlands store water to prevent floods, purify our water, and protect lake and stream shores from eroding.

Draining or filling a wetland without a permit is illegal. Before you decide whether to support the legal removal of a wetland or acquire the right to drain or fill one on your property, consider the forest piece — and peace — you will be giving up.

2,013-acre Scuppernong River Habitat Area are found one mile northwest of Eagle and just across from the Southern Unit's visitor center and forest headquarters on Highway 59.

A large portion of the river habitat's marsh was once drained for agriculture, and the suppression of natural fires, the pasturing of cows, and the introduction of nonnative plants almost obliterated the rest. Today, however, there is a major effort to restore this wetland to its presettlement condition; and fens, tamarack swamps, cattail marshes, wet-mesic prairies, sand prairies, sedge meadows, oak forests, and bur oak openings adorn the Scuppernong River Habitat Area site. In this large semiwilderness wetland, a former glacial lakebed, more than forty species of plants, insects, birds, and mammals that are either threatened, endangered, or "of special concern" live.

Scuppernong, a Ho-Chunk word meaning "sweet-scented land," probably originally referred to the strong, sweet aroma emanating from the wildflowers that were found in the low prairies bordering the Scuppernong River. Virginia mountain mint, bergamot, and sweet grass once perfumed the air here.

What I sniff in the air today around the Scuppernong Marsh is hope. With more than two thousand acres under restoration, this place is the largest wet prairie east of the Mississippi River and — it is said proudly — quite possibly the world.

As I walk back across the highway to the forest unit's headquarters and my parked car, I hear a sandhill crane call out from somewhere in the marsh grasses behind me. I think how sweet the sound is.

A Trail Called John Muir

This afternoon I'm headed toward the southern end of the Southern Unit, to a spot just north of the town of LaGrange, where the John Muir Hiking and Biking Trails lie. Organizations such as Wildernet and GORP have called these John Muir Trails "some of the best mountain biking and snowshoeing trails in the country." Consisting of five loops ranging from one and a half to ten miles, the John Muir Trails traverse terrain that goes from grass prairie to hardwood forest to pine plantation. On the intermediate-level White Loop, you can even look out over a large leatherleaf bog. But mountain bikers come here mostly for the hairpin turns, steep slopes, and a trail surface made with a range of materials, from natural limestone pack to plastic grid.

John Muir — naturalist and founder of the Sierra Club — spent his early boyhood on a Wisconsin farm. The John Muir Hiking Trail in the Southern Unit was named after him.
WHi Image ID 3948

It's a long way from the original plan for the trails named in honor of John Muir.

"The John Muir Trail was originally an idea that came from the Sierra Club," says Ray Hajewski. "The Sierra Club wanted a mostly undeveloped trail that people could hike. They wanted a walk through the wild woods. If a tree fell down across the trail, so be it. You'd walk over it or around it," he recalls. "So there was to be no tread work, no brushing, no human infringement other than posting yellow placards on the trees to help people avoid getting lost. That's the way the Sierra Club wanted it to be."

The plan, however, got away from them.

Says Ray, "When the decision was made that the forest needed more cross-country ski trails, we had to build all new trails and widen out others to four feet across — which is a joke now, because today's trails are widened out to thirty or forty feet to accommodate at least one traditional track and one skate-skiing lane."

According to Ray, the Sierra Club representative who made the original trail plans was aghast.

"We went in there with bulldozers," says Ray. "Cross-country skiers were going nuts; they were experiencing thirty-minute waits on some of the more aggressive hills. They needed more trails. Then, the all-terrain bikers came into the Southern Unit of the Kettle Moraine," states Ray ominously.

Not anticipating the surge of popularity in the sport of mountain biking, forest managers at first put no restriction on trail use by the bikers. "Within ten years," says Ray, "thousands of people were out there, pounding down on the forest, almost like they had power machines."

After a lot of trial and error, Ray discovered a way to minimize the impact the bicycles were making by implementing an improved trail design.

"I tried a million and one things to combat soil erosion," says Ray. "The only thing that worked was moving trails off to the side of the hill, making them serpentine, and creating a five-degree or less slope, which made better drainage and less erosion."

What goes into designing trails such as the John Muir Trails for biking is not always apparent when you're "dabbing" or going "endo" over the handlebars.

"Many, many hours and many, many days go into trying to get a trail from Point A to Point B," says Ray. "We found that you can sustain the soil on a mountain bike trail at five degrees or less. Once you have to go to even six or seven degrees, then you have to do something else to sustain that soil: harden it in some way or cover it with rocks or put erosion control devices down."

I think back to a quote from John Muir that I had read in college: "Keep close to Nature's heart, yourself; and break clear away, once in a while, and climb a mountain or spend a week in the woods."

Obviously, from the passion expressed in his voice, Ray Hajewski holds the John Muir Trails close to his heart. And, like Ray, it seems, the forest's subsequent trail coordinators are working hard to keep them close to natural.

The View from Twelve Hundred Feet

Just two miles south of the city of Delafield — and only a forty-minute drive away from downtown Milwaukee — lays the Lapham Peak Unit of the Kettle Moraine State Forest. This hilly moraine country is wooded in the eastern section of the unit and old-farm-field-with-restored-prairie-and-oak-opening in the western half.

At 1,230 feet, Lapham Peak is the highest point in Waukesha County. Even here, in this 1,006-acre unit, the footprint of human inhabitants falls deep. In the mid-1800s, Charles Hanson built a twenty-foot-tall observation tower on the top of the peak and charged people a fee to picnic here. A restaurant opened soon after. The foundation of the cobblestone Hanson home may still be discovered near the pond at the Homestead Hollow Picnic Area. A squeaky windmill spins in the wind, like an interactive monument to the social history of this place.

Today, a new observation tower on the peak stands forty-five feet tall. In 1940, the Works Projects Administration (formerly the Works Progress Administration) employed sixty men to construct it and the unit's benches and hiking trails.

The view from the top, as they say, is always good. In the spring and summer, you can see sixteen lakes sparkling like stars, pointing the way to high Holy Hill to the north. In the fall, the trees below turn from deep greens to

An engineer and self-educated naturalist from New York, Increase Lapham came to Wisconsin in 1836. The Lapham Peak Unit is named in his honor.
WHi Image ID 1944

scarlet and crimson and to yellow and gold. In the winter, the naked framework of the moraine is there for all to see, a skeleton shivering in the cold breezes.

Within the boundaries of the small Lapham Peak, life is abundant. The kinds of birds spotted here number somewhere around 135. Songbirds build nests in the spring and sing out loud and clear in the summer and fall. Cerulean, northern parula, pine, and prothonotary are a few of the nearly thirty species of warblers that flit through the forest during the spring migration. Belted kingfisher, bobolink, Cooper's hawk, eastern meadowlark, grasshopper sparrow, green-backed heron, scarlet tanager, wild turkey, and wood duck represent some of the eighty species that nest here. Deer, foxes, and coyotes are found along wooded and meadowed trails.

The peak has gone under several aliases over the years: Stoney Hill, Prospect Hill, and Government Hill (because it was used for government surveying purposes). Its final, 1916, name honors Increase Lapham, a prominent scientist and conservationist who founded the U.S. Weather Bureau. In 1870, Lapham had the Signal Corps of the U.S. Army establish one of the original National Weather Service signal stations on the peak. Weather data was received from Pikes' Peak, Colorado, and relayed to the U.S. Weather Service in Chicago. Lapham's weather forecasts were the first in an effort to warn ports on the Great Lakes of storms.

Originally a New Yorker, Lapham came to Wisconsin in 1836 as an engineer for the Milwaukee and Rock River Canal Company. The company hoped to link Milwaukee's deep-water port to the lead-mining region in southwestern Wisconsin by means of a canal. Since Lapham had previously worked on the Miami Canal and Ohio Canal, he was hired to oversee the new project's development. The canal was never built, but Lapham decided to stay in Wisconsin

The observation tower at the Lapham Peak Unit was built by the Works Projects Administration. From the top, you can see sixteen lakes sparkling like stars.
John T. Andrews

anyway. He later settled in the Oconomowoc area, where he resided until his death.

Lapham also mapped many places around the state, including what is now Milwaukee County and Waukesha County, and surveyed the state's Indian mounds. One of his best-known publications was *Wisconsin: Fauna and Flora, Grasses, Forests, Trees and Antiquities.* Those "antiquities" included glacial kettle ponds and outwash plains.

Acting Uncivilized

There is another man, perhaps not quite as famous as Increase Lapham, who has made a big impression on visitors to the Southern Unit of the Kettle Moraine State Forest. Ray Hajewski tells me about him:

There was one old guy, a big, heavyset man, who would never walk on the trails; he'd always go cross-country. He used to map the jungles of New Guinea for the U.S. government, so he preferred to walk around in the bush. He'd carry this huge knife with him to whack away at the foliage so he could get through. He scared the heck out of a lot of people! He'd get into prickly ash, and because he was on blood thinners, his arms would bleed excessively from getting scraped up. Then he'd walk out of the woods, all bloody and holding a huge machete. People coming out of the forest would come up to me in a panic. They'd say "THERE'S THIS GUY WITH A HUGE KNIFE IN THERE, AND HE'S ALL BLOODY!" But he was actually just the nicest, sweetest man.

This machete-bearing army veteran was Ray's extra set of eyes and ears in the forest. "He'd tell me when he thought someone was camping illegally or was stealing firewood or when he saw horses where they shouldn't be," recalls Ray. "We did have to tell him, though, that he couldn't be walking around with that big knife in the forest. When he passed away, we dedicated a kiosk at the Ice Age National Scenic Trail crossing on Highway 12 to him."

For Ray, the soil in the Kettle Moraine holds more than its nematodes, earthworms, fungi, and plant life. It holds its humanity. "For every place I go to in the forest today, there's a different story about the people and the things that went on," he says. "There are a lot of memories."

Before I leave the Southern Unit of the Kettle Moraine, I ask Ray for his outlook on the forest's future. He responds:

Viewing the Kettle Moraine as a living, breathing organism gives me a much different perspective when looking at the development and use of any one area. Different user groups put pressure on the forest for more and more trails. This is not necessarily a bad thing, since you cannot completely enjoy the moraine from the road. Trails are needed. But the travesty comes when we feel a need to develop trails over the need to preserve the moraine as it was left to us by the glaciers. When you look at a trail, you may see dirt. I see an area never again to host a myriad of flowers and fauna as it did before such a trail was built, never again to be the rolling hill or the soft, gentle slope that inspires us, but a gouge in the earth to always remind us of our irresponsibility toward caring for the moraine itself. It behooves us as caretakers of this green gem to prevent this from happening in the first place, and to repair the areas where we've already allowed it to happen.

Farmers and circus barkers. Skiers and mountain bikers. Scary, old army guys and current curious writers. We are all making our marks on the moraine. Maybe we're just following in the footsteps of a heck of a big glacier.

Maybe that's not such a bad thing.

OUR FORESTS' BIGGEST THREAT

YOU WOULDN'T KNOW IT BY THE USE THAT the Kettle Moraine State Forest–Southern Unit gets, but it appears that nature, worldwide, just isn't as attractive as it used to be.

According to a recent study sponsored by The Nature Conservancy, nature recreation around the globe — measured on at least two dozen variables such as national park and national forest visits, camping, hunting, and fishing — has declined sharply since the 1990s. An earlier Nature Conservancy study conducted by ecologist Oliver Pergams of the University of Illinois–Chicago and Patricia Zaradic, an ecologist with the Stroud Water Research Center in Pennsylvania, correlated a decline in visits to U.S. National Parks with an increase in television, video game, DVD, and Internet use. According to Pergams and Zaradic, per capita nature recreation peaked between 1981 and 1991. Since then, there has been a decline of about 1.2 percent per year, with a total decline of between 18 and 25 percent.

While the correlation doesn't necessarily mean that electronic recreation has *caused* the decrease in people having firsthand experiences in nature, indications are that that could be the case or that whatever is causing us to be so engaged in electronic recreation is also causing the decline. "Computers are great, but nothing beats the real-life experience of catching your first fish, feeling the mist from a waterfall, hearing a coyote howl, smelling a pine forest, or seeing fireflies light up the sky. These small moments are something no one should miss," says deputy director of The Nature Conservancy in Wisconsin Rebecca Smith, who oversees the state's conservation programs.

Such research should make all of us value the Kettle Moraine State Forest all the more. The Southern Unit, situated close to the state's most populated centers (Milwaukee and Madison), makes nature experiences, such as camping and hiking, readily accessible for a lot of Wisconsinites. Indeed, the good news is that stemming the tide against carpal-tunneled youngsters and adults, the Kettle Moraine State Forest–Southern Unit gets more use than its northern counterpart, roughly 1.2 million visits per year to the Northern Unit's one million. (The largest state forest property, the Northern Highland-American Legion State Forest — see chapter 12 — gets an estimated 2.25 million visits per year.)

Says Rebecca Smith, "Nature is not found just in some far-off exotic place. It's in our city and state parks and forests and even in our neighborhood open spaces. These places can inspire and teach."

Other research has shown that the time children spend in nature — camping, hiking, and visiting parks and forests — determines their environmental awareness as adults, an important missive for the future of the planet. If people stop being aware of what's going on in the environment, they stop caring about it. And even more so than global warming, apathy is the greatest environmental threat of all.

There are eighty-nine steps up to the top of Lone Tree Bluff, located in the southwest corner of the Southern Unit. The bluff is named after a bur oak that was believed to be one hundred years old when the first settlers arrived here in the 1830s. The tree died in the 1960s.
John T. Andrews

Kettle Moraine State Forest–
Southern Unit/Lapham Peak Unit

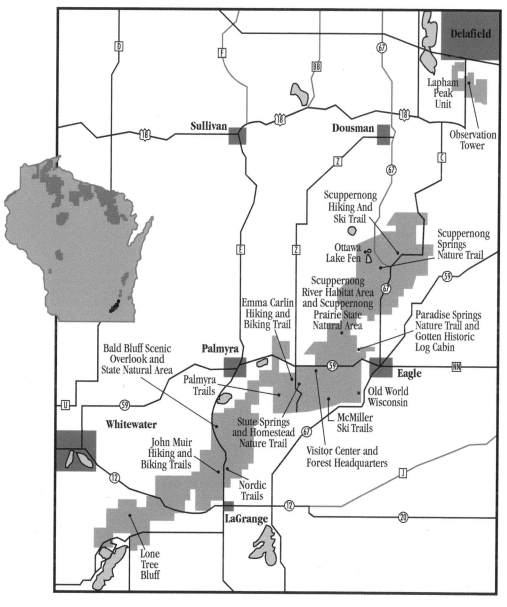

Delafield

Sullivan

Dousman

Lapham
Peak
Unit

Observation
Tower

Scuppernong
Hiking And
Ski Trail

Scuppernong
Springs
Nature Trail

Ottawa
Lake Fen

Scuppernong
River Habitat Area
and Scuppernong
Prairie State
Natural Area

Paradise Springs
Nature Trail and
Gotten Historic
Log Cabin

Emma Carlin
Hiking and
Biking Trail

Palmyra

Bald Bluff Scenic
Overlook and
State Natural Area

Palmyra
Trails

Eagle

Old World
Wisconsin

Whitewater

Stute Springs
and Homestead
Nature Trail

McMiller
Ski Trails

John Muir
Hiking and
Biking Trails

Visitor Center and
Forest Headquarters

Nordic
Trails

LaGrange

Lone
Tree
Bluff

6 Miles

21ft-9in. tall
LARRY
THE LOGROLLER
wabeno wis

It's hard to miss big Larry. He stands on Wabeno's town green, in the south-central section of the Nicolet. *John T. Andrews*

11 Chequamegon-Nicolet National Forest– Nicolet Land Base

RUGGED INDIVIDUALISM

Big Larry

The first thing you notice about Larry is that he's a darn big guy — twenty-one feet and nine inches tall. His full name is "Larry the Logroller," and he stands — rain, shine, or snowfall, four seasons of the year — in downtown Wabeno.

The small town of Wabeno, in Forest County, Wisconsin, is located in the south-central portion of the Nicolet Land Base of the Chequamegon-Nicolet National Forest. Its current population numbers 1,219.

Larry keeps good company on his small town green: an old-fashioned band shell, a Sherman tank from World War II, a logging museum, and a steam-powered Phoenix Log Hauler, one of the few remaining steam-powered log haulers in the nation that is still operational. The hauler is one of two hundred built in the early 1900s by the Phoenix Manufacturing Company and was used by the Jones Lumber Company at their mill in Wabeno from 1909 to 1935. The town purchased it in 1944. A small, nineteenth-century log cabin serves as the Wabeno Public Library.

The athletic teams at Wabeno's one high school sport the name "the Logrollers." Larry is their mascot. The town began when a brief lumber boom convinced the Chicago and Northwestern Railroad to push its line north through here in the closing years of the 1800s.

The community took its name from the June 2, 1880, tornado that swirled across upper Wisconsin, from Antigo all the way north to Lake Superior, and blew down timber in a strip one-half to one mile wide. The Potawatomi had called this area *Waubeno,* meaning "the coming of the winds" or "the opening."

By 1905, Wabeno had five sawmills along its railroad tracks, producing thirty-five million board feet of lumber per year. By 1936, however, all of the mills had closed.

Much has been "opened up" by the force of the winds and the brawn of the lumberjacks in the Nicolet since the time when both hit Wisconsin's Northwoods. And if the 1880 twister and Larry are any indication, whatever else the Nicolet National Forest is, it is a place made by and of singular, natural phenomena and rugged individuals.

A Different Argonne Forest

One of the best places to get a handle on the complex, controversial, and storied past — and present — of logging in Wisconsin is in the Argonne Experimental Forest in the Eagle River District of the Nicolet.

Today's 666,753-acre Nicolet National Forest got its start in 1933 by presidential proclamation. But by that time, Wisconsin's great Northwoods were almost nonexistent. For nearly one hundred years, northern Wisconsin's forests had been used to provide barns and home-building materials, fences and fuel, pallets and paper, ships and step ladders, railroad ties and roofs, whiskey barrels and window frames, and for thousands of other things. The fact that we have a Northwoods again today is a testament to one of the greatest conservation stories in the world. After surviving the eras of timber barons and immigrant farmers — after building much of our country — our state's forest cover has been largely restored.

The Nicolet was named after Jean Nicolet, a French explorer who came to the Great Lakes region in the 1600s to promote fur trading with Native Americans. During the seventeenth century, increasing numbers of Europeans and Indians made the Northwoods their home. Following close behind them were the lumbermen, who used the rivers to move pine logs to the sawmills. When the pinery finally dwindled, loggers used the railroads to move the heavier hardwood logs to the mills.

Then, when even the hardwood timber ran out, much of the cutover land was sold to immigrants for farms and homesteads. In the 1920s and 1930s, however, many farmers found the soils of the Northwoods more suited to trees than crops. Unable to afford the taxes on their lands, most forfeited or abandoned their holdings to county governments. Now with not much to stop them, raging fires burned the land.

Under the authority of the Weeks Law of 1911, the federal government, in 1928, began buying the abandoned and tax delinquent lands from the counties, with the idea of establishing a national forest. In 1929, a U.S. Forest Service office was set up in Park Falls to oversee land acquisitions in northern Wisconsin.

Workers in the Civilian Conservation Corps planted thousands of trees on the Nicolet.
John T. Andrews

In March 1933, shortly before he left office, President Herbert Hoover issued a proclamation establishing the Nicolet National Forest. Then a second U.S. Forest Service office was opened in Rhinelander to handle land acquisitions in the eastern part of the state. In November 1933, President Franklin Roosevelt set aside the Chequamegon as a separate national forest from the Nicolet's westernmost lands. The Park Falls office became the headquarters for the Chequamegon, and the Rhinelander station was named the headquarters for the Nicolet. Both national forests, then, were born from Wisconsin's cutover, farmed-out, and burned-through lands.

When the Great Depression rolled across the United States, thousands of young men joined the Civilian Conservation Corps. Corpsmen planted thousands of acres of jack pine and red pine, built fire lanes, and constructed recreational facilities across the Nicolet. Today, the CCC's pine plantations are seventy or more years old. It follows that a large portion of the forest, then, is even-aged, even though some trees appear much larger than others. The Nicolet today is still in need of some restoration, since a healthy forest is one that contains trees of different ages and different species.

I learn about all of this — what makes a healthy forest and how to restore one to well-being in the aftermath of a force as strong as logging — on the

Argonne Experimental Forest Trail. The trail is a three-quarter-mile loop, located off Forest Road 3905 near Argonne in the northwest portion of the Nicolet. Since 1946, the Argonne Experimental Forest has been managed by the North Central Forest Experiment Station of the U.S. Forest Service as a living laboratory to study methods for managing northern hardwoods and the effects of logging on tree growth, quality, and regeneration.

On a March day, more than seven decades after that other March when the Nicolet was established, I stand in the Argonne. I'm here to educate myself about logging and managing forests. Snow still covers the ground at this time in northern Wisconsin. The trees look spare, thin, and tall, what you might expect at the end of a long winter.

My studies begin right at the start of the trail, with a sign that identifies the six types of hardwood trees before me: red maple, sugar maple, northern red oak, paper birch, white ash, and yellow birch. At the station labeled "Commercial Clear-Cut," I learn that aspen was one of the first species to establish in the Nicolet after the logging and major wildfires of the early 1900s. Today, mixed aspen-hardwoods can be clear-cut to regenerate aspens or thinned to encourage shade-tolerant hardwoods like sugar maple. Aspens, like oaks, thrive in full sunlight.

I learn how foresters measure a tree's width at a point four and a half feet above ground, commonly referred to as "DBH" (diameter-at-breast-height). I discover that size can be deceiving — a large tree is not necessarily older than a smaller tree growing nearby. Tree growth varies with genetics and environmental conditions. For example, sugar maple and basswoods can survive with very slow growth rates for a long time beneath a forest canopy. Although the trees I see as I look at one particular stand have various shapes, forms, and heights, they are all nearly the same age.

My next lesson is in the different types of cutting foresters and harvesters use. Measurements have been taken on these trees since 1952, and those statistics have demonstrated how growth is affected by the management technique employed. Cutting all trees greater than a certain diameter is called "diameter limit cutting." At the next station I walk to, all of the trees greater than eight inches were cut in 1952 and in 1992. Research has shown that over time, this type of management reduces the quality of the forest. Future trees will get their start as seeds or sprouts from poor-quality stock because the most vigorous, fastest-growing trees have been removed.

I learn that a "light cut" is not always a good thing, as tree-huggers might suspect. Trees are constantly dying in forests from a variety of causes. One objective of selection cutting is to remove and use trees that are likely to die before the next scheduled harvest. A light cut produces high quality trees but may not salvage all the trees that are expiring.

"Heavy cuts," too, have their downside. Young trees grow larger, but when they mature, these trees have more low branches, reducing their lumber value.

A "medium cut" can, at times, work well on all counts. It balances the effects of heavy and light selection cutting, enhancing tree quality, providing adequate space for young trees, and salvaging most of the dying trees. It often gives a maximum, long-term, economic benefit by balancing growth and quality.

The Argonne teaches me that a knot-free hardwood log can be worth hundreds of dollars as veneer. Trees with fewer branches along the lower trunk have fewer knots. Trees shed lower branches that are shaded by other trees. And forest management methods can affect sunlight levels and branch development.

I learn that "thinning" removes poor-quality and diseased trees and increases growth of the remaining crop of trees. It may take a century or more for these "crop trees" to reach their greatest value for producing lumber. Some will live for over two centuries.

Leaving the Argonne Forest, I can't help but think of the other one, the Argonne Forest in eastern France. It was the site of the final offensive of World War I between September 26 and November 11, 1918. The objective was the capture of the railroad hub at Sedan, which would break the rail network supporting the German army in France and Flanders and force withdrawal from the occupied territories. The Battle of the Argonne Forest was arguably the bloodiest single battle in U.S. history (largest number of U.S. dead in a single battle) and the biggest operation and victory of the American Expeditionary Force in the war.

The town of Argonne, Wisconsin, got its current name in 1921, following the patriotic fervor after World War I. After what I had learned in our own Argonne Forest, I felt fortified to explore the Nicolet.

Today's Lumbermen and Lumberwomen

Denise Smith has lived in the Nicolet National Forest since 1972. She and her husband, Gary, own the Camp 20 Cabins in Laona, two vacation rental structures that Gary built with his own hands. From gathering the timber on his land to crafting the wooden lamps, Gary made the cabins and almost everything in them.

Visitors to the Camp 20 Cabins in the Nicolet forest often write about the stars here, as if noticing them for the first time.
John T. Andrews

"Right off my backyard is the Camp 20 Creek," says Denise when I ask her about the name of her cabins. "A lot of the places around here were lumber camps in the late nineteenth century. The Lumberjack Steam Train in Laona is located at Camp 5. Another area around here is Camp 6. Everybody knows these places where there was some kind of a camp, so owners pick up the name because it's woodsy and evocative of where we live," she explains.

And like these places in the forest, most of the people in the Nicolet are no strangers to the timber industry, Denise included.

"I was born in Milwaukee, and as a child, I lived about twenty miles south of it on a lake," says Denise. "When I was fourteen years old, my parents bought a tavern in the Northwoods. Moving to Main Street in Laona felt like moving to a city to me. I was moving from the shores of a lake to the middle of a town. I didn't feel like I was in a forest when I first came here.

"When I got married," she continues, "my husband told me he wanted to work in the woods — just like most of the other people around here at that time, thirty-two years ago — so I did, too. I ran a skidder, which is a short-wood forwarder [or log transporter] known as an 'Iron Mule.' It's like a tractor with a Caterpillar drive, enormous tires, and a claw on it," Denise explains. "Back then, guys like Gary cut the trees down, and people like me came through with skidders. Hardly anyone then had the big, automated processors, which clamp the tree off, lay it down, and strip the limbs," she says.

Denise and Gary's land has been in the family since Gary's grandfather homesteaded the place, when the ground contained nothing but stumps. Grandpa started a dairy farm, and when Gary's mother and father moved back to Wisconsin from Ohio, they helped run it. Eventually, they purchased it from their parents, and then it passed into Gary's hands. Retired from a logging career, Gary now operates his own sawmill. He builds cabins and furniture from the wood surrounding his home.

"But there are still lots of working loggers here," says Denise. "For example, a couple of guys have a garage north of here on U.S. Route 8. If you're a logger, it's good to live on a U.S. or state highway so that when spring breakup comes, you can still use your truck. Our county roads aren't made to the specifications that the state roads are. So load limits are on in spring. After winter, when everything starts to thaw, the roads get mushy, and everything underneath is very unstable. County roads are posted then, and big trucks aren't allowed on them. When the slush drains away — when the road stiffens up, dries, and hardens into a good foundation again — then you're good to go," she says.

Because most people who attempt to make their living in northern Wisconsin forests have to do a little bit of this and a little bit of that to get by, I ask Denise if it's possible to do any logging in the spring.

"Well, some loggers do have to stop for the season," answers Denise, "but most will hope for and try to get a logging project located on a big highway. If you're a logger and you don't, in the spring you're hoping that you worked hard enough during the previous year to put up some logs on a highway so you can haul during that time."

The Cathedral Pines are aptly named; a reflection on ice captures their spirituality.
John T. Andrews

Road Trip

I am here in the Nicolet during the spring breakup. I'm going to take to the back roads, but I have a compact car — no big logging truck to worry about.

The Lakewood Auto Tour is one of the most popular activities in the forest, the ranger at the Lakewood-Laona District office tells me. The sixty-five-mile route will take me in a loop-drive around the Lakewood and Mountain areas. It features seventeen numbered and signposted stops highlighting "wildlife, natural history, forest management practices, and historic sites," according to the brochure I picked up at the district office.

Tour stop number 1 is a direct contrast to all of the logging history I have been steeping myself in since I first arrived on the Nicolet. Cathedral Pines is an area that has miraculously managed to evade the logger's saw. Originally forty acres, Cathedral Pines was designated a State Natural Area in 2007 and now includes 1,874 acres.

The name is apt. The trees that climb into the sky here are venerable; spiritual. And down below, a pine needle floor makes my footsteps soft and hushed, as if I were walking down the aisle of a church.

The supercanopy, way up high above the quarter-mile hiking trail, like an arched ceiling of a basilica, is constructed of red and white pine. Aged eastern hemlock a hundred feet tall stand like the faithful around me.

A man named Devillo Holt, who founded the Holt Lumber Company, once owned this stand of trees. Devillo's son, William, who later took over the company, and his wife, Lucy, had a cabin near here. In the 1920s, Lucy and her children would nestle down with their backs against the trunks, and she would read Bible stories to them. She asked William not to cut the trees in what she called "Cathedral Woods" because she felt the place was truly special. When

FEAR AND LONGING IN THE WOODS

MAYBE IT WAS LITTLE RED RIDING HOOD. Or the neighborhood where the witch who tricked Hansel and Gretel lived. Perhaps it was because of Rapunzel or Snow White, who were supposed to have been hidden away from society in some remote, dark place. It could be from all those teen-slasher movies, set in a cabin somewhere, where tall, dense tree stands are obligatory props on the film set. Maybe it's just that chainsaws sound and look so menacing. Wherever it comes from, somewhere deep down inside of us there has been instilled a fear of the woods.

Of course, in some of us it is more pronounced than it is in others. Denise Smith, owner of the Camp 20 Cabins in Laona, Wisconsin, tells the story of a couple who checked in, took one look at their rental cabin, and immediately checked out. The reason, said the male half of the twosome, was that "my wife thinks you're too far out in the woods. There are too many trees here." This even though, says Denise, the cabin was located only two and a half miles from town, the lawn surrounding the cabin was mowed, and there was a neighbor just one backyard away.

Some who have pondered and tried to make sense of this fear say that it comes from our immigrant European ancestors, who viewed the woods as the "dark unknown" and brought their fairy tales with them. After all, in the fields they had cleared with

their own hands, everything was out in the open; the land had been controlled and their will asserted over it. But in the forest, they were not in control, enclosed and surrounded on untamed terrain.

The urge to quantify and exhibit some kind of mastery over the forest is still with us today. How many times do we try to define our forests by their commercial tree species composition, board feet, basal area, or number of white-tailed deer per acre? We may know how many rows of soybeans we've planted or bushels of corn we've harvested from a defined field, but who can count the number of orchids or ferns in all the recesses of a forest floor?

Adding to this puzzle is that just as woods call up feelings of the Dark in us, they also call up a closeness to the Light. The woods double as our sacred groves and spiritual places; lofty trees make us feel hushed and small, in the presence of something greater than ourselves. Even the light comes from above. How many weddings transpire in the woods; how many Bible stories did Lucy Holt read to her children in the Nicolet's Cathedral Pines?

While we fear things that we can never truly know and things that make us feel inferior, most of us still harbor a nostalgia for the woods in our hearts, a yearning for them because of their mystery. It is the great paradox of our forests.

she passed away in 1939, William honored her request not to cut here. In 1968, the family gave the land to the U.S. Forest Service.

Although I do not hear it today, in a few months a celestial choir will start singing high in the canopy. Baby great blue herons will cry out to their parents from about eighty treetop nests that will sway in the breeze. The Cathedral Pines harbor one of Wisconsin's largest active heron colonies.

But for now, the holy sanctuary is quiet. It's a good place to send up a little prayer of thanks for one of the only old-growth pine-hemlock stands left in the state.

Not Climbing the Mountain

The Cathedral Pines aren't the only hardy survivors on this auto tour. At stop number 9, near the town of Mountain in Oconto County, I meet another enduring individual.

During the winter of 1934–35, the men and boys of the CCC erected the Mountain Fire Lookout Tower under the direction of the U.S. Forest Service. This was at the height of the time when the cutover landscape was prone to fire, and drought conditions added to the infernos that were blazing across the land.

The one-hundred-foot-high Mountain tower — along with nineteen other steel compadres — stood guard over the Nicolet National Forest for almost thirty-five years. But at 10:30 a.m. on April 25, 1970, the fire lookout on duty in the tower radioed in to the Lakewood Ranger District's office the location of the last fire spotted from his lofty perch. He then closed the hatch and climbed down, the last fire lookout to do so.

In the 1970s, airplanes took over the surveillance job from those with their steely footings bolted into the forest floor. The Mountain Fire Lookout Tower is one of only two (the other is the Laona Fire Lookout Tower in Forest County) to survive dismantling out of the nineteen towers that once served the Nicolet National Forest — probably because it found other gainful employment. From 1977 to 1992, the Mountain Fire Lookout Tower functioned as a radio relay station for the U.S. Forest Service and the Oconto County Sheriff's Department.

The Mountain Fire Lookout Tower is one of four in Wisconsin recorded on the National Historic Lookout Register (Fifield in the Chequamegon

National Forest in Price County, Monahan in Price County, and Paust in Marinette County are the other three).

Usually, visitors can climb up to the top of the Mountain Fire Lookout Tower and take a look around above the treetops. On the day of my March visit, however, the tower was closed. The stairs were too icy, I imagine.

I'm okay with staying down here, below. As with the nests of the blue herons high in the top of the pines and hemlocks, I almost feel like the high homes of the defunct fire tower lookouts should be left alone, out of respect.

Back at Camp

By the time I reach one of the last stops on the auto tour, I have come full circle — in more ways than one.

Tour stop No. 14 is the site of a Holt and Balcom logging camp from the late 1800s. The remains of the stone walls in a cleared meadow are visible from the road. I park the car and walk into the old camp. The walls, at various heights, suggest that there was once an organized space cut out of the forest here — bunkhouses and a cookhouse; but the exact floor plans are now slowly being erased, eased back into the landscape.

At this time of year, the color of the brown stones is the dominant one. They are the deepest hued amid the subdued browns, soft blacks, and off-whites of a clearing in March. The dark green of the conifers ringing the camp is the only variation on the scheme. I stand in the middle of the camp and slowly turn in a 360-degree circle. I'm the only one here today. Do the stones wonder where all the voices have gone? Do they miss the tall tales of lumberjack bravado that certainly once split the air in these woods as surely as the axes?

The texture of these rough stones makes for some interesting photographic possibilities. On both sides of some of the walls that are two- and three-boulders thick, thin trees have grown up. One evergreen even grows on top of a crumbling partition. As the sun starts to go down, the skinny trees make long shadows across the stones.

I'm not sure which is happening faster: the trees growing up, or the stones falling down. More circles. The loggers take the trees; the trees take back from the loggers.

Tonight, I go back to my own logging camp to sleep, the Camp 20 Cabins.

Today, the exact floor plans of a logging camp ruins are being erased, eased back into the landscape.

John T. Andrews

The MacArthur Pine died in 2003. It had stood here for 420 years.
Courtesy Wisconsin Department of Natural Resources

Paying Final Respects

If a nod to World War I was given in the Argonne Experimental Forest, homage to the Second World War is in order. This morning it comes in the form of a big tree named after General Douglas MacArthur.

Before 2003, a white pine believed to be more than four hundred years old stood in the Nicolet, off Forest Road 2167. Known as the General Mac-Arthur White Pine, it was one of the largest of its kind at 148 feet in height and 68 inches in diameter. Its lumber volume was estimated at eight thousand board feet — enough to build an average-sized home. Unfortunately, over the years age, wind, lightning, and root disease took their toll on the giant. It burned to the ground in 2003. This MacArthur, like the general, was tough.

When the tree did finally die, there was a ceremony at the site. Pieces of the pine were given away to forest ranger stations, courthouses, and other places around the state where the public is welcome to come and admire what once was.

But today, in a quiet grove deep in the forest, I kneel before the charred remains of the MacArthur Pine that are still standing upright — shards pointing up to the sky — and a huge chunk of its trunk that is lying beside them. Only the surrounding birches, hemlocks, and spruces look on.

Ronald E. Scott, an Upper Peninsula native and retiree from the U.S. Forest Service, reported in a post on forestryforum.com that in 1988 cones from the MacArthur Pine were sent to several nurseries. The resultant seedlings were then given to other states and countries. Now, descendants of the MacArthur Pine can be found all over the world.

Extraterrestrial Explorations

This afternoon, I'm going out to explore another weathered, rough, and tough face of this forest. This one is in the Lakewood District area of McCaslin Mountain, a place long known for its quartz crystals.

As with so much else in Wisconsin, glaciers shaped this mountain land-form, which is a four-mile-long quartzite hill with a local relief of more than two hundred feet. The Quartz Hill Trail, which leads to the top of McCaslin, is short — a little more than half a mile. It starts off on a boardwalk and then gets progressively steeper over rockier terrain. As I climb, I try to take inven-tory of the beeches, red oak, and sugar maple that sprout from the ravines and slopes. I lose count.

Near the top, I pass a quartz crystal deposit. Quartz is frequently used today for manufacturing watches, glass, jewelry, radio equipment, sandpaper, and grindstones. A U.S. Forest Service sign warns, "No digging for quartz allowed."

Times have changed since the first century BC, when Native Americans were digging right here for quartz for use in making tools. Quartz fragments similar to those that result from breaking quartz to produce pieces for such a purpose have been found scattered around here. The ancient Indians proba-bly carried the quarried chunks back to their dwellings and finished the tools there. This went on until as late as the seventeenth century.

Although quartz is the most common rock-forming material — with the one exception of feldspar — in the Earth's continental crust, this fact does not make the walk up to the top of McCaslin Mountain anything less than uncom-mon. The ground is strewn with giant rocks and gargantuan boulders, and the rocky, gray cap of McCaslin is covered in spots with a rich, velvety-soft moss that works hard to cover up the roughness underneath, like an incomplete apology. Roots of trees grab onto the wild boulders for dear life, as if they are afraid of tumbling downslope. This is like a fairy tale forest out of the minds of the Brothers Grimm.

Another mineral that has been found here is specular hematite. Hematite is black, brown to reddish brown, or dark red — but it always has a rust-red streak. Red ocher, an earthy form of hematite, is used to color paint. The word *hematite* means "bloodlike," and any fresh scratch on a piece of hematite rock will make it look like it's bleeding. It is another facet to the fantasy character of McCaslin.

The Quartz Hill Trail, which leads to the top of McCaslin Mountain, is strewn with enormous boulders.
John T. Andrews

Hematite is found in the Lake Superior region of the United States and Canada; near the border of Labrador and Quebec; and in Alabama, Tennessee, South Africa, Brazil, and Australia. And just recently, it has been found on the planet Mars, near the Martian equator and at a site named Aram Chaos near the Valles Marineris.

Coincidentally, "chaos" is what it looks like on the rock-strewn Quartz Hill Trail.

Where the Wisconsin River Begins

My explorations of the Nicolet forest would not be complete without a visit to its farthest border — the top of Wisconsin — and the birthplace of our much-loved and great Wisconsin River.

About five miles northwest of Phelps, Wisconsin, is the sprawling 4,200-acre Lac Vieux Desert, the largest lake in the Nicolet and one of the largest lakes in northern Wisconsin. Here, on our border with Michigan, the Wisconsin River begins. From out of Lac Vieux Desert, the Wisconsin journeys for 430 miles to empty into the Mississippi River just below Prairie du Chien.

This cabin at Lac Vieux Desert, built in 1860, served as both a home and a trading post. The area had long been a trade hub prior to European arrival.
WHi Image ID 9816

Lac Vieux Desert, the birthplace of the Wisconsin River, is known for its muskie, walleye, bass, and northern pike fishing.
John T. Andrews

Because there are close to fifty power and storage dams along its route, the Wisconsin River has been dubbed "the hardest working river in America."

However, the river's place of origin has been no slacker, either. *Lac Vieux Desert* has often been translated as "Lake of the Desert." However, in Canadian French, it means an "old clearing" and probably refers to the cultivation of land by native peoples on the lake's islands. The Ojibwe have lived at Lac Vieux Desert for centuries, and it was the intersection for five trade routes. By moccasined feet, canoe paddles, horse hooves, logging rafts, or oxcarts, people for hundreds of years have traveled to this industrious hub of pioneer activity.

The nation's hardest working river and its busy birthplace deserve a spot in the Nicolet National Forest, this forest of rugged individuals, who go their own way.

The Forest Present

There are other individuals going their own way through the forest, but they travel by paw. Although less numerous than their human counterparts, black bears are certainly here — and their numbers have steadily increased over the last twenty-five years. Given that they inhabit some of the same territory — sometimes in very close quarters — that people do, most everyone who lives in or near the Nicolet has a bear story. Denise Smith is no exception.

"Bears often come up on my deck; they always want to eat from my bird-

(continued on page 240)

ONE HUNDRED YEARS AT THE MENOMINEE TIMBER MILL

by L. B. Kuppenheimer

The Menominee Indian Reservation lies along the southern border of the Nicolet National Forest. On the reservation is a healthy forest that holds ancient trees — even after a century of the tribe's use. It could be said that the Menominee were the first to practice what we know today as "sustainable forestry," and their forest is recognized as one of the best managed in the world. In August 2008, L. B. (Bud) Kuppenheimer attended the one-hundred-year anniversary of the Menominee Timber Mill. — C. G. A.

IT WAS 7:00 P.M., AND THE SUN WAS WANING, though you would hardly know it under a forest canopy so high and dense that the sky was barely visible. There were several hundred of us sitting in a natural amphitheater. The smell of fry bread and tacos was in the air; aging veteran flag-bearers stood waiting along with five drum-groups for the signal from the master of ceremonies to begin the Grand Entry that would formally open the annual Menominee Pow-Wow. But this year, the opening ceremonies would include a special celebration of the Menominee Timber Mill's first one hundred years.

Following the grand march and several rounds of inter-tribal dances, a small delegation of employees from the Menominee Tribal Enterprises led by Adrian "Dusty" Miller, Chief Executive Officer, was called to the center of the dance circle to be honored. Amid the happy noises of the crowd and dancers, the words of the soft-spoken CEO were nearly inaudible in the stands. But for me, they were the culmination of a very rewarding and illuminating day, as he articulated the mission and achievements of the Menominee Tribal Enterprises over the past century.

Early that morning my introduction to the great Menominee Forest began the instant I left the flat farmlands of Langlade County on Route 47 and entered "Menominee County and Reservation." Suddenly, I was in a 230,000-acre primordial forest with beautiful, healthy trees towering sixty to a hundred feet in the air. The sun was blocked out, and I was immediately reminded of our childhood fairy tales of "the forest deep and dark," but I found nothing frightening about this magnificent forest. To the casual observer, it looks untouched by human hands, yet nothing could be further from the truth, as I was to learn in my day of discovery.

"Start with the rising sun, and work toward the setting sun, but take only the mature trees, the sick trees, and the trees that have fallen. When you reach the end of the reservation, turn and cut from the setting sun to the rising sun, and the trees will last forever." With these words, spoken in 1854 by the visionary Chief Oshkosh, the saga of the Menominee forest and sustained-yield management was begun. By diversifying the species, taking the weaker first and allowing the strong, healthy trees to reseed, the Menominee have gradually developed one of the highest-quality sustainable forests in the world — which actually contains more board feet today than it did in 1908 when the mill was established.

Now after one hundred years, the rest of the world is finally awaking to the wisdom of the Menominee as the numerous awards decorating the corporate offices eloquently attest. Underlying this vision is an ancestral world-view that is based on a profound love and respect for nature in all of its forms. Adrian Miller put it best when he said, "We are not above nature; we are part of it."

GONE RICING

"For those of us who do it," says L. B. (Bud) Kuppenheimer, pictured here with his wife, Mary, "ricing is so much a passion, that here in northern Wisconsin the word is used both as a noun and a verb." *E. Dolf Pfefferkorn*

by L. B. Kuppenheimer

L. B. (Bud) Kuppenheimer and his wife, Mary, learned ricing many years ago in Rhinelander from a legendary forester and trapper by the name of Paul Munninghoff. Following a career in business, Bud went back to school to become a historian with a subspecialty in Native American history. In 2001, the Kuppenheimers retired to Vilas County, where they enjoy sharing their Nicolet National Forest adventures with seventeen grandchildren. — C. G. A.

IT IS A BEAUTIFUL MORNING FOR THE START of this year's rice season. And as white puffy clouds float by in a pristine blue sky, we are standing at the boat landing finishing the last of our morning coffee while waiting for the 10:00 hour, when we can legally begin the harvest. Depending on the lake, opening day is a variable determined by the U.S. Forest Service or the "rice chiefs" of the Ojibwe Nation and is based

(continued on next page)

GONE RICING

(continued from page 239)
upon the health and ripeness of the crop. For those of us who do it, ricing is so much a passion that here in northern Wisconsin the word *rice* is used both as a noun and a verb.

Today, the rice looks healthy and dense; we are optimistic for a bountiful harvest. In its mature stage, wild rice grows about four feet off the surface of the water, so the only way to harvest it efficiently is in two-person teams. One person stands in the back propelling the boat with a long pole fitted with a "duck bill" attachment on its bottom end, which offers a base to push against and at the same time prevents the pole from sticking in the mud. The other person sits in the middle facing the poler and holds two cedar wands, one of which is used to draw the rice stalks over the gunwale, while the other wand strokes the kernels into the canoe. "Stroking" ensures that only the ripe seeds are taken, leaving the rest as the basis for next year's crop. In fact, wild rice isn't really rice at all; it is a grass that grows anew each year from seeds that drop from the year before.

Again this season, our close friends with whom we share this passion join us, and as we launch into the lake, each boat heads for a different area of the rice beds. Standing, I am able to see over the entire lake, which is so thick with rice that all I can make out are water pathways. We are quite alone now, and the only sounds are those of the canoe brushing along the grasses and the song of our competing ricers, the red-winged blackbirds. The mood is so magical that we don't want to break the spell with conversation or unnecessary movement in the boat. It takes little effort to imagine how it must have appeared to Native American ricers hundreds of years ago. For me as a historian, the opportunity to engage in such an ancient activity each year never loses its thrill.

We listen now for the sweetest music a ricer can hear: that of grain falling so plentifully that it sounds like rain on the inside of the canoe. Indeed, it is falling well enough that we can afford to pause and watch a pair of bald eagles feeding their young, now old enough to be sitting on the edge of the nest. With the constant press of population, it is rare, even in the Northwoods, for one to find such a unique opportunity to interact with both nature and history on such an intimate level.

feeder," says Denise. "One day, two years ago, I heard a sound and went to check out my back window to see what was going on. When I looked out, a bear was standing on the other side of the window, looking back at me. Whoa! It scared me. I'm usually not afraid of things; I'm not a sissy. But if I had walked out my back door, I would have walked right into a bear. Literally."

I ask Denise if she's had other four-footed visitors. "We have a few chickens," she says. "And just this last fall, I spotted a coyote in the yard grabbing one of them in the middle of the day. My collie dog and I quickly went outside, and the coyote dropped the chicken and ran away. Luckily, the chicken was okay," she states.

While Denise is accumulating several wildlife stories due to her habitat inside the forest's boundaries, there are other "gifts" she is collecting from the Nicolet, as well. "I love the 'free stuff' the forest gives you," says Denise. "You can pick asparagus and buckets of blueberries. There are blackberries, wild onions, mushrooms, morels, leeks, and wild rice here. There are pinecones you can pick up for decorating. It's harder for a vacationer, of course, than a local person to find all of these things. But if you are hiking and you're adventurous, you'll see that they are there."

Some of the forest's presents are less tangible, but highly appreciated nonetheless.

"The other day, I was paging through the guest journals that I leave in our rental cabins," Denise begins. "I noticed that a lot of our visitors had written something like 'thank you for letting us relax.' The other thing that stood out was that people often mentioned the stars here, writing that 'we saw the stars as if for the first time.' It's the peace and quiet and dark of the Nicolet that I, too, enjoy the most," she tells me.

Strength in the Woods

On my way south out of the Nicolet National Forest and pointed toward home, I resolve to make one final stop.

In the town of Lakewood, adjacent to the McCauslin Brook Golf and Country Club, is the Holt and Balcom Logging Camp No. 1. The camp is the oldest standing lumber camp in Wisconsin. Listed on the National Register of Historic Places, it remains where it was built in 1880. The building was constructed by expert woodsmen, it is said, demonstrated by the skilled workmanship on the hewn corners, floors, and bunks. The trail alongside the McCaslin Brook was the path over which lumberjacks traveled on foot and on bobsleds to get into and out of the forest for more than half a century. Although some of the original logs in the historic camp building have rotted and have been replaced, all of the restoring timbers have also come from the Nicolet National Forest.

Forestry today has certainly come a long way since the clear-cutters of the late nineteenth century. Today, instead of losing forested lands, the practice of sustainable forestry is actually creating more of them. But while we may have changed our ideas about the best way to go about logging, we have never turned our backs on the rough-and-tumble men who were the loggers more

Holt and Balcom Logging Camp No. 1 is the oldest logging camp in the United States still situated on its original site. The building's walls are a testament to the expert craftsmanship of the woodsmen who constructed them.
John T. Andrews

than a hundred years ago. They will always be a part of Wisconsin lore; their spirits are always there, somewhere amid the forest trees.

There is one bit of history that I purposely missed going to see while in the Nicolet. The "Treaty Tree" is supposed to be "an out-of-the-way historic site" where Captain Thomas Jefferson Cram, an army engineer, negotiated a safe passage agreement with a band of Ojibwe in 1840. Cram was doing a land survey of the Wisconsin-Michigan border. Under a tamarack tree, they supposedly etched a treaty on birch bark.

Seeing a 1940s photograph of the treaty tamarack from the Wisconsin Historical Society's archives reminded me of the old expression "a real man's man." To go into almost-uncharted territory in a wild land, Captain Cram must have been made of the same stuff that the brawny, strong loggers of old were. The past few days, I have been impressed with the notion that the Nicolet seems to be "a real forest's forest." A place of rugged individuals, such as Larry the Logroller, the Mountain Fire Lookout Tower, and McCaslin Moun-tain. This is a forest about trees and logging, and for getting lost in the dark and quiet in. This is the kind of forest where individual trees can be so outstanding that the only way we humans are able to get our heads around them is to give them a familiar name, like an old friend.

I didn't go to see if the Treaty Tree is actually still standing in the Nicolet. I've read that it's not. I'm afraid I'll feel the same sadness I did when I found out the MacArthur Pine had fallen, just six years before my arrival.

I want to believe such trees are still there, standing tall.

Chequamegon-Nicolet National Forest – Nicolet Land Base

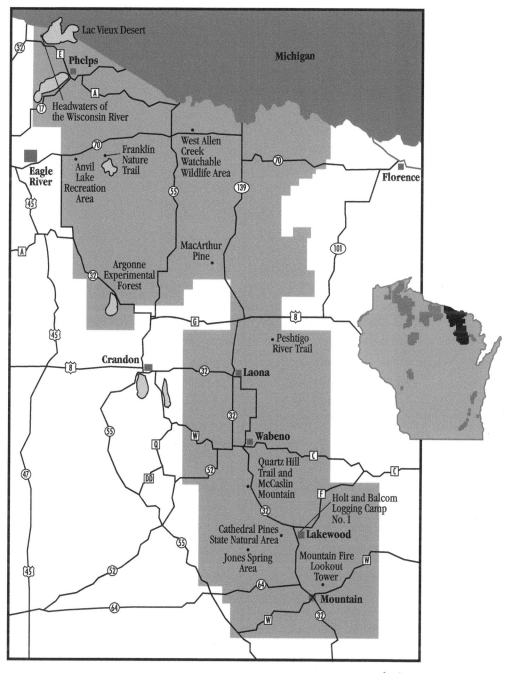

Lac Vieux Desert

E Phelps

Michigan

A

17 Headwaters of the Wisconsin River

70 Franklin Nature Trail

West Allen Creek Watchable Wildlife Area

70

Florence

Eagle River

Anvil Lake Recreation Area

45

55

139

101

A

MacArthur Pine

32 Argonne Experimental Forest

45

6

8

Peshtigo River Trail

Crandon

8

32 Laona

32

55

Q

W

32

Wabeno

47

52

DD

Quartz Hill Trail and McCaslin Mountain

C

C

F Holt and Balcom Logging Camp No. 1

32

55

Cathedral Pines State Natural Area

Lakewood

45

52

Jones Spring Area

Mountain Fire Lookout Tower

W

64

64

W

32

Mountain

6 Miles

In mid-October, my amber-orange-red-gold
adventure turned soft white. *John T. Andrews*

12 Northern Highland-American Legion State Forest

HIGH ENERGY IN THE HIGHLANDS

Rarefied Air

"Grizzly Adams — that's who I wanted to be when I was a kid," says Tony Martinez, the Northern Highland-American Legion State Forest trail coordinator. He's referring to the character made famous in the 1974 film *The Life and Times of Grizzly Adams*, which later became an NBC television series. The shows were based on the real life of James (or John) Capen Adams, a woodsman who fled to the Sierra Nevada Mountains in the 1850s to live among the animals. The TV Grizzly Adams had a best friend who was, of course, a grizzly bear.

Tony and I are sitting in the heart of the forest, in a Boulder Junction coffee shop, on a Saturday morning in mid-October, and it's snowing. I had planned a fall visit to the state's largest land holding to see the colors, but it turns out my amber-orange-red-gold adventure will be tinged more toward soft white. Today, Tony has maintenance work to do on the trails before winter really sets in, but he's not averse to staying a little longer for another cup of coffee and a bit more conversation about the forest and the outdoors life he loves.

"I worked in a basement in Milwaukee for six years," Tony says. "It was for a screw factory, and I made the parts for soft-tip darts used in electronic dart games. When cutting, the drills on the automatic screw machines would often heat up. If the oil flow on the tools was not adequate, some of it would burn off, causing a wisp of smoke. Because of the poor ventilation in the basement," he explains, "the smoke would build up, making a blue haze in the air. Later, I moved up to first floor where I could open a window."

But a window alone wasn't enough to quench Tony's need for fresh air and outside places. Whenever he got some time off, he escaped to northern Wisconsin.

"I spent most of my free time and money coming up to the Northwoods every chance I could," says Tony. "My boss would hire temporary workers for the busy periods, and then lay them off when it slowed down. I asked my boss if I could be one of the people he laid off. I used that time to move up to northern Wisconsin for good."

According to Steve Petersen, the superintendent of this 223,283-acre Goliath of a forest, there is definitely something supercharged in the air here. "The Northern Highland-American Legion is the state's most frequented forest," he states. "What you sense when you arrive here is an overabundance of energy."

Ground Cover

Part of that energy, no doubt, is generated by the more than two million visitors who come to this forest every year. Proximity to Minocqua and Woodruff — two tourist destinations in themselves — probably adds to the forest's popularity. "Summer is vacation time up here," says Steve. "I can't believe how many people I see on our bicycle trails that meander into the woods. They're not only biking, but walking and even inline skating on these trails' smooth surfaces."

It's hard to imagine this place packed with folks from where I stand today, outside in the almost-deserted coffee shop parking lot, with a light snow falling. And yesterday, on the undulating, wavelike Lumberjack Trail, I had the wetlands and this immense forest all to myself — or so it felt. The tall trees along the footpath kept even the wind out. Steve knows exactly what I'm talking about.

"One of my most unforgettable memories is hiking the Raven Trail with my family in the fall when I was a five-year-old child," says Steve. "I felt like we were the only ones in the world. We camped close to the trail at Clear Lake a lot when I was a kid. I don't know why people park their rigs after Labor Day. It's like, 'You can't wear white after Labor Day, and you can't go camping,'" muses Steve. "What are people thinking? They're missing out on the best time

On the Lumberjack Trail, I had the wetlands and Concordia Creek all to myself, or so it felt.
John T. Andrews

of the year in the forest! It gets dark early so you can have a nice campfire. And it's cool and quiet; no bugs. Fall is a wonderful time to walk in the forest. And with almost a quarter million acres, there's a lot of ground you can cover."

Lakes and Legacies

I hoped to cover a lot of that spread-out acreage in the next three days of exploring and discovering what it is that makes this forest a "highland."

"Energy" is not just a modern construct here; it seems that it has abounded in this forest for eons. Going back almost two billion years, that energy took the forms of erosion and friction. Once, granite mountains — some as high as the Swiss Alps — made up the Wisconsin landscape. Hundreds of millions of years of erosion wore down the mountain peaks, leaving behind a rolling granite plain. Seas invaded the depressions, and they deposited their own thick layers of limestone and sandstone on top of the granite base.

More recently — until ten thousand years ago, in fact — glacial ice groaned and ground forward and backward over these rock stratums. When the ice melted, it dropped tons of hitchhiking boulders and gravel on top of the granite, limestone, and sandstone layers, creating "highlands." The unevenness of the glacial ice melt created swells and swales, knobs and kettles, moraines and lakes — more than 930 of them in this place that would later become the Northern Highland-American Legion State Forest.

Today, the forest contains one of the world's densest concentrations of lakes. At only three other locations in the world — in Minnesota, in Ontario, and in Finland — do lakes occur as frequently as they do here. Sixty of the lakes have been given official Wilderness Area and Wild Area protection (a designation as a Wild Area means the land is managed for scenic values, but it is not as well protected as lands actually designated as Wilderness Areas).

So thanks to all of that energy embedded in that ancient glacier, today we have the lake, wetland, meadow, grassland, and northern timber forest country known as the Northern Highland-American Legion State Forest. This geography is so rare that it was identified by the Wisconsin Department of Natural Resources, partner organizations, and citizens throughout the state as one of the special places that make Wisconsin "Wisconsin." In the *Wisconsin Land Legacy Report* published by the WDNR in 2006, the highlands were named one of 229 Legacy Places. They were also listed as one of the sixteen types of distinctive ecological landscapes found in the state:

- Central Lake Michigan Coastal
- Central Sand Hills
- Central Sand Plains
- Forest Transition
- North Central Forest
- Northeast Sands
- Northern Highlands
- Northern Lake Michigan Coastal
- Northwest Lowlands
- Northwest Sands
- Southeast Glacial Plains
- Southern Lake Michigan Coastal
- Southwest Savanna
- Superior Coastal Plains
- Western Coulee and Ridges
- Western Prairie

For me, before coming to this forest, the term *highlands* had always called to mind tour-brochure images of northwestern Scotland: conifers that stretch on and on under cloud-filled skies; reflective, cool *lochs* too numerous to count; and unpredictable weather that could change dramatically every ten minutes.

Scotland, I think, isn't so far off.

OBSERVING ORCHIDS

SEEING ORCHIDS IN THE WILD EXCITES flower lovers more than almost any other plant observation. With exotic names like lady's tresses, moccasin flowers, rattlesnake plantains, and ram's-head lady's slippers, they thrive in a wide range of Wisconsin habitats, from humid cedar bogs to dried-out limestone swales. There are forty-two native orchid species in the state.

In the Northern Highland-American Legion State Forest, several hundred pink lady's slippers may be found along the Trout Lake Nature Trail in the upland sands under jack pine and in the bogs. And bringing vibrant colors to the 435-acre Rice Creek State Natural Area within the Vilas County portion of the forest are at least seven species of orchids. Here, a two-mile stretch along Rice Creek is populated with heartleaf twayblades, bluntleaved orchids, early coralroot, and striped coralroot orchids.

All orchids have three petals, three sepals, and leaves with parallel veins. What distinguishes one orchid from another is its "lip." A modified petal, the

(continued on next page)

There are forty-two native orchid species in the state, seven of them in the Rice Creek State Natural Area. *Wikimedia Commons*

OBSERVING ORCHIDS

(continued from page 249)

lip may look like a pouch or shoe, such as with the "moccasin" of the lady's slippers; or like fringes, as on some of the rein orchids. Usually the lip is below the other petals, but in orchids like the grass-pink, the lip is above.

Another astonishing feature of orchids is their ability to produce millions of dustlike seeds that can float for distances of up to twelve hundred miles. Germination, however, is tricky; most orchids require very specific habitats and the presence of specialized fungi for their roots' environment. Blossoms may take another dozen years to appear after initial germination. Once established, though, orchids may live for a hundred years or more.

Pink lady's slippers (also known as moccasin flowers) seem to prefer the sandy pinewoods, while yellow lady's slippers thrive in hardwood forests. June is their flowering time. Bogs are home to the grass-pink, the rose pogonia, and the purpley dragon's mouth orchids, which also flower in June.

Wisconsin prairies are lit up by small white lady's slippers, which can take thirteen years to flower, in late May to June; by prairie white-fringed orchids in late June through July; and by white, spiraling common lady's tresses from mid-August through September.

Unfortunately, orchids are declining in number due to habitat loss and their collection by forest visitors. Remember that orchids are most beautiful in their own homes and are worthy of our awe — and our protection.

I'll Take the High Road

The Northern Highlands may have been identified as a distinct ecological landscape in the state, but as far as the seasons go here, I can find no line of demarcation.

On Sunday morning, the day following my coffee shop meeting with Tony, I decide to venture out on one of the trails he cares for and see if I can channel my own inner Grizzly Adams. I have never seen a black bear in a forest, but maybe the recent talk of Adams will bring me some luck.

The yellow loop of the Escanaba Trail is fully cushioned underfoot with fall's brown, crisp leaves. I walk through stands of balsams, maples, and aspens; in fact, almost a full third of the trees in this forest are aspens. Although the whole trail circles its way around five lakes — Escanaba, Lost Canoe, Mystery, Pallette, and Spruce — my brief two-and-a-half-mile trek will take me to a strip of land between the shores of Escanaba Lake and Pallette Lake.

Approaching the sandy outline of Escanaba Lake, I realize I've reached the place where time and the seasons overlap. On the opposite shore, snow dusts the limbs of almost-bare trees. It's winter over there. But here on my side,

The Northern Highland-American Legion State Forest is a "working forest"; logging does take place here. But loggers aren't the only ones harvesting trees, as these "beaver chews" attest.
John T. Andrews

fall's orange and yellow leaves still color the summer-brown sand. And on the ground, just ahead of the toe of my left hiking boot, lies one still flexible, vivid-green leaf amid the orange and yellow ones. It's telling me that even spring is hanging on in some form here.

As I bend to examine that one yet-supple leaf, I discover a footprint in the sand that certainly doesn't belong to me. The four-toed-and-clawed impression matches the wolf footprint in my animal-tracking guidebook. I've seen photos of wolves hiding behind trees in the woods, photos of wolves standing on mountains, photos of wolves running in the snow — even photos of wolves with the actor who played Grizzly Adams. But I'm having trouble seeing in my mind wolves playing on a snowy beach.

It's incongruous, just like the seasons here.

Where Forestry Was Born

Seeing the wolf track gives me a sudden chill that makes me involuntarily shiver in a quick moment. It's thrilling to be this close to something so wild. It could be said that the idea of preserving Wisconsin's forests for wildlife such as wolves and bears, for biologic diversity, and for aesthetics took root here in what is now the Northern Highland-American Legion State Forest, for this is the birthplace of Wisconsin forestry.

In 1903, Wisconsin passed its first comprehensive forestry law. Before that time, many people failed to see the need to conserve the state's natural resources. The term *conservation* wasn't even a part of the national vernacular until 1907, when President Theodore Roosevelt made his seventh annual message to Congress and stated, "The *conservation* of our natural resources and their proper use constitutes the fundamental problem which underlies almost every other problem of our national life."

The state's first forestry law prohibited the sale of state lands (with the exception of swamplands, farmlands, and woodlots of fewer than eighty acres that adjoined farms). Remaining state lands became part of the state forest reserve. The 1903 legislature also created the Department of State Forestry, under the control of the Board of State Forest Commissioners, which consisted of the attorney general, the secretary of state, the state treasurer, and two public members appointed by the governor. In 1904, the board appointed Wisconsin's first superintendent of forests, E. M. (Edward Merriam) Griffith.

Griffith's background included schooling at Yale as an engineering student and forestry training in Germany. Once on the job in Wisconsin, Griffith devoted much of his time and energy to convincing the legislature to pass laws and provide funds for an adequate fire-suppression and fire-fighting system. He developed a reforestation program to rectify the legacy of the state's logging boom, and he established the first tree nursery at Trout Lake — now within the Northern Highland-American Legion State Forest — in 1911.

The first official state forest in Wisconsin with definite boundaries was established in 1925 to protect the headwaters of the Wisconsin, Flambeau, and Manitowish Rivers. It was named the Northern Highland State Forest, and it originated from forest reserve lands that the state had set aside in 1904 in Forest, Oneida, and Vilas Counties. Between 1925 and 1938, six more state forests were designated: American Legion (1929), Flambeau River (1930), Brule River (1932), Kettle Moraine (1937), Point Beach (1937), and Council Grounds (1938; reclassified as a state park in 1978).

E. M. Griffith held the position of Wisconsin's state forester from 1904 to 1915. He was the first professional forester to use airplanes as an aid in detecting forest fires. *Courtesy Wisconsin Department of Natural Resources*

The Northern Highland and American Legion State Forests were managed as separate properties until 1968, when they were combined into one administrative unit. Now, at almost a quarter of a million acres, the Northern Highland-American Legion State Forest is the largest state forest in Wisconsin and almost two and a half times larger than the next biggest, the Flambeau River State Forest.

According to a state forest statute (s. 28.04, Wis. Stats.), forest superintendents are to manage forests to "assure the practice of sustainable forestry and provide a full range of benefits for present and future generations." Those benefits include "soil protection, public hunting, protection of water quality, production of recurring forest products, outdoor recreation, native biological diversity, aquatic and terrestrial wildlife, and aesthetics."

Forest superintendent Steve Petersen says that the Northern Highland-American Legion State Forest is living up to that mandate. "More than at any other place I've worked [Bearskin State Trail, Potawatomi State Park, Richard Bong State Recreation Area, Nelson Dewey State Park, the state parks central office, and the Brule River State Forest]," says Steve, "this forest is a dominant, energetic force in its local economy. It provides many jobs for community residents, averages about $3 million in annual forest product sales, and hosts two hundred thousand campers — and those two million visitors — every year."

At the Junction

And a whole bunch of those people stay right in the heart of the state forest, in the town of Boulder Junction, the Muskie Capital of the World.

The town's nickname gained popularity in the 1930s because, it is said, more muskies (a.k.a., "muskellunge") are caught in Boulder Junction's lakes every year than in any other similar-sized area in the world. It became official on June 8, 1971, when the United States Patent Office awarded the town the U.S. trademark on the phrase.

Every autumn, anglers congregate in this little burg in the forest and dream of catching the great muskie (or musky). The prime season is from May to November, but many swear that October is the optimal time. Even in my snowy October here, I can sense the "muskie obsession" in the atmosphere.

To get acquainted with this forest's finny object of desire, I visit the Arthur A. Oehmcke Fish Hatchery, located across from the Wisconsin Department of

Every autumn, anglers congregate in Boulder Junction — located within the forest's boundaries — and dream of catching "the big one."
John T. Andrews

Natural Resources office in Woodruff on Highway J. Originally established as a bass hatchery in 1901, today it is one of the largest muskie producers in the world. Muskellunge, walleye, white sucker, and lake trout are all reared here.

In early spring, millions of eggs and milt (sperm) from muskies are collected by capturing mature fish in the wild and then gently pressing their abdomens. After expelling the eggs or sperm, the fish are released unharmed back into their natural habitats.

Fertilized eggs are then transferred to the hatchery and placed into jars. A computerized water-temperature control system allows technicians to mix the hatchery's main water supply from Madeline Lake with hot or cold water from Clear Lake. Sixty to 95 percent of these incubated eggs will hatch, as opposed to less than 0.1 percent in the wild.

The newly hatched fish (or "sac fry") live on a nutrient-rich yolk sac until they begin to feed on plankton. Muskies will swim out of their hatching jars in seven to ten days, after the yolk sac is gone. They then start feeding on zooplankton and white sucker fry.

Muskie fingerlings grow about one inch per week throughout the summer.

MUSKIES: MOBY DICK, WISCONSIN-STYLE

JUST AS ALASKA IS ASSOCIATED WITH GRIZZLY bears and Yellowstone is symbolized by the howling of returned wolves, there is no doubt that the Northern Highland-American Legion State Forest is muskie territory.

Catching a muskellunge, Wisconsin's state fish since 1955, is a highly sought-after bragging right. The much quoted conventional wisdom is that it takes "ten thousand casts to land a muskie," making this lean, brawny, and moody fish akin to that other elusive quarry, Moby Dick.

Usually, it takes more than fifty hours to catch a legal muskie (currently thirty-four to forty inches, depending on the specific location). Part of the reason is that muskies are thinly dispersed: typically one fish for every two or three acres. But the main reason it takes so long is that once hooked, the muskie is a formidable fighter. At an average length of thirty to forty-two inches and a weight of ten to twenty pounds, this giant can keep you reeling for up to forty-five minutes. The state — and world — record is a sixty-nine-pound, eleven-ounce giant that measured 63.5 inches, captured by Louie Spray in 1949 from a dammed section of the Chippewa River near Hayward.

The torpedo-shaped muskie is solid as a rock, with pointed pelvic and pectoral fins set close together. Its streamlined anatomy gives it great speed, estimated at anywhere from thirty-five to sixty miles per hour. Known for its leaping ability, a muskie has an awesome jaw that wraps halfway around its head. It has the largest canine teeth of any freshwater fish — teeth

that are sometimes used to attack birds and mammals as large as a muskrat.

In coloration, a muskie has dark vertical markings on a lighter background, which ranges from silvery green to light brown in older fish. One way to distinguish a muskie from a northern pike is by the lack of scales on the lower half of the gill cover. Both the muskie and the northern pike have scales on their faces above the cheek and behind the eye, but the northern pike will also have them near the jaw. When eggs of a female muskie are fertilized by a male northern pike, a hybrid "tiger muskie" results.

Prior to stocking by the Wisconsin Department of Natural Resources, begun back in 1899, muskies were in gradual but constant decline in the state's waters. Today, probably one-quarter of the current population has been raised through stocking, much of it in the Northern Highland-American Legion State Forest.

The catch-and-release trend has also ameliorated the muskie decline. Because these fish are mostly trophies and not particularly "good-eating" fish, mano-a-mano muskie battles and near misses are enjoyed and talked about as much as actual catches. And by releasing a muskie, you allow it to grow larger and live longer to give other anglers their own big-fish stories to tell — most fishermen today yearn for the "fifty-incher or beyond."

Best of all, if you supply a photo and measurements, there are several companies that will make a graphite replica of your muskie to commemorate your inner Ahab.

By the time October comes, they are eight to twelve inches long and ready to be stocked into the lakes.

As a cool-water hatchery, the Arthur A. Oehmcke Fish Hatchery is also able to raise lake trout, a coldwater species. In November, technicians spawn adult lake trout and place the eggs in jars until they hatch in January. Approximately one hundred thousand of these trout may be stocked into lakes each year.

On Little Crooked Lake

As any good Boulder Junctionite should, Noel Malicki knows about and can tell some great tales on the subject of muskies. He lives with them — and their avid fans — day in and day out. Noel resides at and operates the Evergreen Lodge in Boulder Junction, his family-friendly rental compound on the 154-acre Little Crooked Lake. Noel tells me he only has three rules for his guests around the nightly campfire: no flashlights, no boom boxes, and no

According to Boulder Junctionite Noel Malicki, northern fishing off the Little Crooked Lake pier is excellent even in a snowy October. *John T. Andrews*

Fishermen need to develop a lot of patience — and come equipped with a strong line — if they hope to land a mighty muskie.
John T. Andrews

throwing live frogs on the fire. Apparently, that last one is for the kids who don't know any better. I hope.

It's said that if you ask a dozen fishermen how to land a muskie, you'll get a dozen different answers. But almost all will agree that patience is the most important trait for anyone dreaming of hauling in one of these monster fish. Patience and a strong line, that is.

Noel says his lodgers are used to practicing patience; often, they'll cast all day. "What they do," says Noel, "is go out on the lake in the morning on their boats. When they get cold and tired, they come back to the lodge and have a few beers or some coffee. Then in the afternoon, they fish off the pier using live bait. But, you have to be able to see your bobbers at all times," he says, "that's the law."

In fact, according to Wisconsin's fishing regulations, you must be within one hundred yards of your line at all times and be able to respond immediately to an indication of a bite.

"Even later," says Noel, "they might go back out on the boat and cast a few more hours until sunset."

ENCOUNTERING EAGLES

WITH ITS ANNUAL 2.25 MILLION VISITORS, the Northern Highland-American Legion State Forest is bursting with activity. But another species also gives this forest a "lift": bald eagles (*Haliaeetus leucocephalus*). You almost can't help but encounter them soaring overhead on a spring, summer, or fall visit here.

More than sixty pairs of nesting bald eagles call the forest their home: this landscape composed primarily of lakes and some of the tallest trees in the Northwoods makes it the perfect eagle habitat. Seeing one of these large birds of prey — with their unmistakable white heads, necks, and tails against a brown-black body — take off from a towering pine across a wilderness lake is a sight that emblazons itself on your memory.

The bald eagle has been the national symbol of the United States since 1782. It is an impressive thirty-one to thirty-seven inches in length, with a wingspan of more than eighty inches. An eagle will eat a wide variety of fish, but favorites are muskies, bullheads, northerns, and suckers. Live fish are captured with the bird's strong, sharp talons; dead ones may be scavenged along shorelines. Skilled hunters with keen eyesight, eagles will also take waterfowl, muskrats, and turtles. An eagle consumes and digests all of its prey; only the biggest bones will remain. Carrion, such as road-killed deer, may also be a part of their diets.

Many nesting pairs of bald eagles grace the Northern Highland-American Legion State Forest. *Bob Leggett*

A pair of adult birds will build a nest and defend a territory, which could include a small lake, several lakes, or a bay. Its eyrie is a large pile of sticks up to 150 feet above the ground, usually in a tall tree near water. If a nest proves successful for rearing young, it will be used again and again. Each year it will be renovated and added to, increasing in size — at times reaching up to one thousand pounds — until either its own weight or a winter storm brings it down.

One to three off-white eggs are incubated by both parents for up to thirty-five days. Chicks leave the nest around ten weeks after they have hatched. Immature bald eagles are colored mottled brown and white until they reach sexual maturity at four or five years of age. Only then do they acquire the distinctive white feathering on their heads.

While biologists don't know where Wisconsin's bald eagles overwinter, they suspect the birds move south where there is open water, concentrating along the Mississippi and Lower Wisconsin Rivers.

Driven to near extinction due to DDT poisoning and illegal killing, bald eagles were placed on the Wisconsin Endangered Species List in 1972 and on the Federal Endangered Species List in 1973. By 1997, however, with the population's rebound, eagles were delisted, and they are now a "species of special concern."

ENCOUNTERING EAGLES

Eagles are sensitive to disturbance by humans. When in the forest, stay clear of their nests and give them room to fish and raise their families. The Wisconsin Department of Natural Resources maintains an Adopt-an-Eagle-Nest Program. Your donations to the program are used to protect nests and rescue and rehabilitate sick, injured, or orphaned eagles.

The October Sunday I visited Noel, one of the fishing groups at the lodge was just finishing up a good weekend. "You should have been here yesterday," says Noel, as he points out the lodge's huge dining room window that faces the lake, "off the pier there, these guys caught a twenty-six-inch northern, a thirty-four-inch northern, and a thirty-nine-inch northern. And on the boat, they caught a thirty-six-inch northern. They were really happy," he says proudly.

However, I couldn't help but notice that the mighty muskie had eluded them.

Perhaps it's because all the while people are fishing for muskies, muskies are fishing for something else.

"I've lived here nineteen years," says Noel. "We always have loons on this lake. Every year, they have two chicks. A year or two ago, I guess it was, one pair of loons here had three chicks. Then one day, they showed up with only two. A Department of Natural Resources employee who lives up the road told me that loons can defend only two chicks at a time. Either the eagles snatch them, or the muskies do."

Jumping for Air

The common loons Noel mentions are one of about a hundred nesting pairs in the Northern Highland-American Legion State Forest. Not only are they quite frequently seen on Little Crooked Lake, they are often encountered on one of Tony Martinez's favorite trails here, the Fallison Lake Trail. Weaving around its namesake lake through a pleasing mixture of coniferous and deciduous trees, the trail passes several tamarack bogs while winding along its way and entices the eyes with new patterns and natural textures at every bend.

"While it is a beautiful trail," says Tony, "it's not one of my favorites to

The Fallison Lake Trail loops through a hemlock glade and several tamarack bogs, teasing your senses with striking visual patterns and natural textures.
John T. Andrews

maintain. It has 538 wooden steps, which at one time or another, all require repairs!" Tony laughs.

I ask him to think about the whole immenseness of this vast forest, to think about all the miles of trails he has to take care of, and then boil down for me to a single thing what it is that makes this particular trail such a special one in his heart.

He says, simply, "I like to sit by the lake on a warm, clear-blue spring day, and watch the trout jump."

But this time, it makes me happy to think, when Tony speaks of blue skies, they have nothing to do with being in the unventilated basement of a screw factory.

Northern Highland-American Legion State Forest

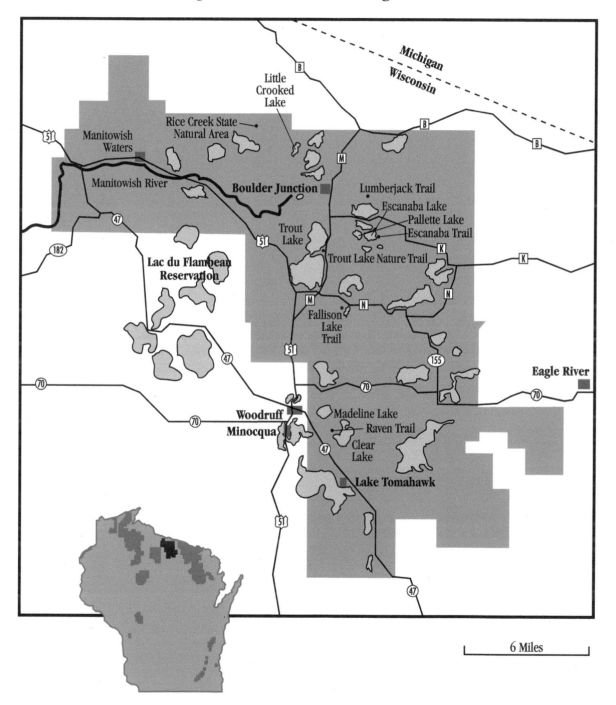

Michigan
Wisconsin

Little
Crooked
Lake

Rice Creek State
Natural Area

51

Manitowish
Waters

Manitowish River

47

182

Boulder Junction

Lumberjack Trail

Escanaba Lake
Pallette Lake
Escanaba Trail

Trout
Lake

Trout Lake Nature Trail

Lac du Flambeau
Reservation

Fallison
Lake
Trail

Eagle River

70

70

155

70

Woodruff
Minocqua

Madeline Lake
Raven Trail
Clear
Lake

Lake Tomahawk

47

51

47

6 Miles

The Johnson Falls portion of the Peshtigo River provides important habitat for many rare reptile and amphibian species. The banks contain mature forests, as well as forested seeps that can harbor rare plants. *John T. Andrews*

13 Peshtigo River State Forest

THE BIRTH OF A FOREST

It Almost Wasn't

It's a baby, really. But the birth almost didn't happen.

Established in 2001, the Peshtigo River State Forest is the newest addition to the state forest family, making it the tenth in Wisconsin (Black River, Brule River, Coulee Experimental, Flambeau River, Governor Knowles, Havenwoods, Kettle Moraine, Northern Highland–American Legion, and Point Beach are the others). In that year, the state's Natural Resources Board approved purchasing roughly nine thousand acres of land from Wisconsin Public Service Corporation for $25 million. The money came from the Wisconsin Stewardship Fund, which is formally titled the Knowles-Nelson Stewardship Program to honor Warren Knowles and Gaylord Nelson, the Republican and Democratic Wisconsin governors who pioneered public land acquisition. In 2004, the final land transfer was completed. It was the first new state forest in almost thirty years. Today, the Peshtigo River State Forest includes 9,200 acres of land, 3,200 acres of water, seventy miles of shoreline, and about twenty-three miles of the Peshtigo River — which contain a five-mile free-flowing stretch.

The forest is located northwest of Crivitz and about sixty miles north of Green Bay. It encompasses the waters and islands in the Caldron Falls and High Falls Reservoirs and in the Johnson Falls Flowage as well as the forested uplands that surround them. Downstream, twenty miles southeast of the main forest, is another portion of the state property: the 771-acre Potato Rapids Flowage.

While protecting the Peshtigo River watershed, this young forest also serves to provide wood products. It is open to the public for hunting, fishing, trapping, hiking, biking, camping, and swimming. Many of the roads and trails in the forest — about thirty-five miles of them — may be used for horseback riding. The forest waters are available for several types of boating: quiet-water paddling, rafting, and powerboating and waterskiing. There are fifteen boat landings in the forest: seven on High Falls Reservoir, five on Caldron Falls Reservoir, two on the Potato Rapids Flowage, and one on the Johnson Falls Flowage.

The Peshtigo River is noted for its exceptional fly fishing on its free-flowing portion and rapids, and for spin fishing on its flowage waters. During the wintertime, snowmobilers and ATVers can ride on twenty miles of trails, and cross-country classic and skate skiers will find eight miles groomed for their sport. The forest headquarters is located in the neighboring 2,600-acre Governor Thompson State Park.

Leon Popp, the owner of Popp's Resort, which sits comfortably on the shores of the High Falls Reservoir, was one of those who were present at the forest's birth. In fact, he was there long before, fighting to bring this baby into the world.

To get to know the child, I needed to see the man.

It Came from the Water

"You have to see the Peshtigo River State Forest by boat," Leon Popp tells me, when I call to ask him about which trails to hike and which spots to visit.

"The way people see this forest is from the water, more so than they see it by walking or by car or by any other way," states Leon. "I think the way the water meanders through the center of the forest and the fact that there are so many boat landings and so many water-access points make this forest totally unique from the others," he tells me.

It's true that boating is the most popular activity in this state forest. So upon reaching it on this hot July afternoon, I swap out my hiking boots for deck shoes and find myself standing outside Popp's Resort, ready for a forest excursion by pontoon. It even sounds funny to say. But Leon Popp and his wife, Bonnie, have the boat all primed and ready.

As we pull away from the dock and into Popp's Bay, I ask Leon about his family resort's history. He tells me:

Popp's Resort sits comfortably on the shores of High Falls Reservoir. "You have to see this forest by boat," says Leon Popp.
John T. Andrews

In 1886, my grandfather and his brother owned a bed-and-breakfast hotel in Crown Point, Indiana. But times were tough, and they lost the business. So my grandfather moved up to Crivitz, Wisconsin — originally called Ellis Junction — to homestead the cutover land following the logging era. When he moved here, he tried farming, but the soil wasn't good for agriculture. So he started cutting trees for the timber companies, since a bit of logging was still going on in this area. He cut trees in the winter and farmed a little in the summer to get enough together to feed his family. In 1904, my grandfather got his homestead papers signed by Teddy Roosevelt. I still have them.

It was about at that same time that work began on the dam that eventually created the High Falls Reservoir. "A power company owned some of the surrounding property, and they started to purchase more," says Leon. "I came across a receipt that stated that my grandfather sold forty acres to the company for a total of $4.96. It sounds kind of crazy by today's standards!" he laughs.

By 1911, the dam was completed. By then, Leon's grandfather had established a small, restaurant-bar-grocery store. Says Leon:

Leon's grandfather — like the men in this photo — worked for a logging company when he came to the Crivitz area in the late 1800s. *WHi Image ID 2884*

It was located on the site where my bait shop sits now. But as soon as the water started to come up, my grandfather also started a bait business where the Twin Bridge crosses High Falls. He had a floating boathouse out of which he sold bait and rented boats. When the water came up far enough, he and some others employed a horse and a little slush bucket to dig a channel. A slush bucket is dragged by a horse in a harness — much like the blade of a plow — and it moves the muck away and out. By building that channel, my grandfather could move his bait-and-boat-rental business from the floating boathouse to where his restaurant-bar-grocery store was — and where my bait shop continues to be. As early as 1926, he started building cottages. We're still renting some of those original cottages. Of course, they've been remodeled once or twice since then!

Popp's Resort was then passed down from Leon's grandfather to his father, and now it belongs to him. During all of that time, boating and fishing have been the big attractions to the waters of what is now the forest. The High Falls Reservoir, on whose shores Popp's Resort sits, holds trophy bass, northern pike, walleyes, and muskies. The Peshtigo River, especially between Johnson Falls and Spring Rapids in the southern section of the forest, is well known for its trout. And the 1,200-acre Caldron Falls Reservoir has healthy populations of muskies, smallmouth bass, walleyes, northerns, and all species of pan fish.

"When I was a kid," says Leon Popp, "I started out working at the resort bailing boats and selling worms. Worms were my thing — going into grade school, selling worms was how I earned my income. I guess you could say being a 'worm connoisseur' was my start as a businessman."

The Peshtigo River, especially between Johnson Falls and Spring Rapids in the southern section of the forest, is a well-known trout stream.
John H. Gaukel

And perhaps the start of a love for and connection to the land that would later translate into his considerable work and effort to make a state forest.

A River, Reservoirs, and Lakes

This new forest seems to require a new terminology. Leon knows every ripple and rock on the High Falls Reservoir, and as he motors me around, he describes the flowage's physical features and their local names.

"Here, we call the reservoirs 'lakes,'" says Leon. "And toward the southern end of the High Falls 'lake' we have the South Narrows and the North Narrows. We call the Caldron Falls Reservoir and the Johnson Falls Flowage 'lakes,' and we also call the Sandstone Flowage just outside the southern boundary of the forest a 'lake.'"

Whether it's officially a "reservoir" or commonly a "lake," being on a boat in the center of High Falls, with its tannin-stained water, granite outcrops, forested islands, and plentiful waterfowl, feels like being on a northern Canadian adventure.

The five-mile, free-flowing stretch of the Peshtigo River below the Johnson Falls Dam is just as impressive. Here, it runs a few rapids. The river provides important habitat for many rare reptile and amphibian species — such as

SWIMMING CHAMPS: WISCONSIN'S NORTHERN RIVER OTTERS

River otters are well adapted for enjoying the forest's largest recreational asset. *Bob Leggett*

THE PESHTIGO RIVER STATE FOREST IS dominated by its river and its reservoirs, and that makes it very appealing to the only native Wisconsin mammal with *river* in its name: the northern river otter (*Lontra canadensis*). And even more so than us, this animal just may be the most well adapted for enjoying the forest's largest recreational asset — its waters.

Unlike beavers or muskrats, the Northern river otter is a smooth operator when it comes to water activities; it barely makes a ripple when it swims or a splash when it dives. Nearsighted above water, an otter has excellent underwater vision. Its ears and nose have valve-like skin that closes to form a watertight seal. River otters can dive to depths of more than forty feet, swim at an average speed of seven miles per hour, and remain underwater for up to eight minutes.

This slender, sinuous, and slinky furbearer is red or gray-brown to black on its back, with paler silvery or gray-brown fur on its underside. Its cheeks and throat are silver or yellow-gray. An otter is three to four feet

in length, with a tail that may make up to 50 percent of that measurement. Weighing twelve to thirty pounds, an otter has short legs and webbed feet. Stiff, white whiskers two to four inches long help to detect food in murky water. Their petite, diamond-shaped noses are quick to detect the scent of other animals.

The river otter is the most playful member of the mustelid — or weasel — family. Otters like to run, hop, and slide over snow, wrestle and chase other otters, and play catch-and-release with live prey. They will grunt, growl, and snort while playing, but will make a shrill cry when threatened. Mates and siblings may elicit a squeak or a chuckle.

Home might be in a shore thicket, in a riverside burrow under a pile of rocks, or in a beaver lodge. Otters maintain a territory of three to fifteen miles.

Otters eat fish, which they catch by day. However, in areas disturbed by humans, otters become more nocturnal. Frogs, lizards, snakes, and insects are also on the menu. Occasionally, otters will take an aquatic mammal or bird, such as a water vole or a duckling.

SWIMMING CHAMPS: WISCONSIN'S NORTHERN RIVER OTTERS

Although river otters may be found in the state's western and central counties, they mostly reside in northern Wisconsin. Leon Popp of Popp's Resort is lucky to have seen the secretive animals. In the early decades of European settlement, unrestricted trapping depleted the state's population of otters, which were prized for their luxurious, warm fur. Loss of habitat and food also caused otters to disappear from many areas.

Wisconsin's otter population will probably never be as high as that of beavers or muskrats because of the otter's need for a large territory and a large amount of food. The Wisconsin Department of Natural Resources collects trapping information each season to help set limits. With this and other monitoring programs in place, hopefully we will always have otters — part of our natural, wild heritage — in our northern rivers.

This could easily have become a more urban landscape. Now, luckily, Wisconsinites have another natural state forest to treasure.
Candice Gaukel Andrews

wood turtles, Blanding's turtles, four-toed salamanders, and bullfrogs. The banks contain mature forests, as well as forested seeps that can harbor rare plants.

The Peshtigo River begins in Forest County near Argonne and flows 148 miles to the southeast, bisecting the Nicolet Land Base of the Chequamegon-

Nicolet National Forest before emptying into Green Bay, seven miles south-east of the city of Peshtigo. The river falls approximately 1,050 vertical feet in that distance, a drop in elevation that is faster than any other river in Wisconsin. A stretch of the Peshtigo River above Highway C (outside the forest) features one of the longest stretches of active whitewater in the Midwest.

The most significant alterations to the hydrology of the Peshtigo River in Marinette County are the five hydroelectric power dams owned and operated by the Wisconsin Public Service Corporation, four of which are in the forest.

The Peshtigo Fire

The river shares its name with the town of Peshtigo, which was destroyed by the deadliest fire in United States history on October 8, 1871. According to stories of survivors, many people fled to the river to escape what has been called an inferno. Some drowned while doing so.

In early October 1871, following a hot and dry summer, dozens of wooded areas and once-wooded areas around Lake Michigan burned. Loggers and railroad builders had left piles of slash that were tinder-dry, and farmers often burned their land to clear it. They frequently set fire to their pastures, too, believing it would result in better crops. In a tempest of October wind that blew up, the city of Chicago caught fire. Twenty-seven hours after the conflagration started, the metropolis lay in smoking ruins.

On the same night as what is now known as the Great Chicago Fire, the booming lumber town of Peshtigo was also engulfed in flames. A cold front moved in from the west, bringing strong winds that fanned smaller fires in the area and escalated them to massive proportions. A "firestorm" — a wall of flame, a mile high, five miles wide, traveling almost a hundred miles an hour — roared through the city. Hotter than a crematorium, the fire burned every building, consumed 1.5 million acres (an area more than one and a half times the size of the state of Rhode Island), and caused the death of more than twelve hundred people (the death toll in Chicago was about 250). Rail cars and houses were thrown into the air. Dead fish clogged the surface of rivers and streams. Green Bay was blanketed with dead birds that had burned in flight and dropped.

The Peshtigo Fire was the start of the end for the great white pine in this area of Wisconsin. Second-growth forests, just getting underway after heavy

On October 8, 1871, the same night as the Great Chicago Fire, a much larger firestorm swept through northeast Wisconsin. Later called the Peshtigo Fire, it killed more than one thousand people and destroyed more than one million acres.
Harper's Weekly 1871

logging, were killed. The hot flames opened the door for the cones of the shorter and scrawnier jack pine, whose seeds germinate following a fire.

It is interesting to note that National Fire Protection Week, which takes place in October, was started to commemorate the economic loss of the Great Chicago Fire. Ironically, that fire was dwarfed by the less-remembered Peshtigo Fire and its human and animal toll. Less than a century later, however, the Peshtigo Fire would be referenced in a military maneuver known as the Peshtigo Paradigm. The combination of wind, topography, and ignition sources that created the Peshtigo Fire was closely studied by American and British troops during World War II. They recreated those firestorm conditions for bombing raids on Dresden, Germany, and Tokyo, Japan. Using the Peshtigo Paradigm in those countries resulted in civilian death tolls comparable to or exceeding those of the atomic bombings of Hiroshima and Nagasaki.

After the Peshtigo Fire in 1871, a wave of new immigrants and settlers began sweeping through northeast Wisconsin. Leon Popp's grandfather was one of them. While they began their labors to convert cutover and burned forestlands to agricultural purposes, others were constructing dams on the Peshtigo River.

Dam Building

The High Falls Dam was constructed between 1907 and 1911, when it began operation. The Johnson Falls Dam was built between 1922 and 1924, and the Caldron Falls Dam was completed in 1926. The Potato Rapids Dam didn't start operating until about 1959.

Due to the fact that the Peshtigo River has more and larger rapids for its length than any other river in Wisconsin and because of its high and rocky banks, it didn't take long after the postfire wave of settlers arrived for numerous dams to appear. The primary function of the dams was the generation of electrical energy for northeast Wisconsin.

"Power companies built the dams," says Leon. "And WPS still retains ownership of the property near the dams. What they did in the early 2000s is get rid of the property they really didn't need. And we were just lucky enough to deal with it as well as we did," concludes Leon. "It could have changed the whole face of the place up here."

Leon drives the boat close to the edge of the High Falls Dam. Today, I can see some fishermen near this oldest edifice on the forest's portion of the river.

Conceiving a Forest

"When Wisconsin Public Service decided they wanted to sell their real estate around the reservoirs," says Leon, "they originally planned to put it up for sale as house lots. A group of local people got together when we got wind of it and tried to come up with some plans on how we could conserve it as the natural area it is. We didn't want to see it divided into housing lots, even though that might have meant an economic boon to the area. Personally, I felt it would deteriorate the wild environs, remoteness, and quality of life here. So we tried to come up with different ways to purchase it," he remembers.

Leon and some of his neighbors formed the Wild Shores Preservation Alliance. They approached the Wisconsin Department of Natural Resources and asked if there were monies available to buy the WPS lands. The answer, unfortunately, was an unequivocal no.

"So, our next plan of action was to get one of our legislators involved," reports Leon. "We started a petition that was in support of the state buying up the WPS lands for sale, and we got a lot of signatures. Once we could show that the public was vastly in favor of our idea, the state of Wisconsin allocated some money from the Wisconsin Stewardship Fund, monies that are specifically set aside for purchasing land to preserve it for natural resources of one kind or another," he relates.

In the course of these efforts, a fortuitous event occurred. Leon explains:

To the north of me, on the Caldron Falls Reservoir, was another resort. Although we hadn't known it, the resort had been doing some quiet negotiating with the state, hoping to sell their land for the purpose of creating a park. When that news started to come out, it helped our situation, since the resort's land butted up to some of the WPS forestland. It gave our cause a little boost. But it got to be complicated when it was learned that WPS wanted to dispose of some of their property holdings without incurring a large tax burden.

Having good timing is always of utmost importance when it comes to real estate matters, and I ask Leon how he kept WPS from selling the land to another buyer during the months he was trying to come up with the money.

That's a really good question because that was a key part. We managed to sit down with the president of WPS, Larry Weyers. He agreed to give us a year to put a viable plan together. During that time, WPS also formed a committee of interested people to try to bring more information into the mix. They were very cooperative with us. WPS could certainly have proceeded and sold the land. But what we wanted and what they wanted to accomplish coincided. We all came up with a strategy whereby WPS could donate a portion of the property; and by donating it, they would receive a tax break. So that's eventually what happened: they donated about 50 percent of the property and sold about 50 percent.

Today, rather than large houses on the shores of this portion of the Peshtigo River, there are forests. Aspens, oaks, and maples with a smattering of pine plantations, grasslands, and conifer lowlands greet the eye, instead of cement driveways and manicured lawns.

Just as we swing around to a quiet cove and Leon cuts the boat's motor, I see a great blue heron standing on the shore.

THE PESHTIGO RIVER STATE FOREST: THE WATERFRONT PROPERTY OF GREAT BLUE HERONS

A BIRD OF THE MARSHES, PONDS, RIVER edges, lakeshores, and flooded meadows, great blue herons (*Ardea herodias*) are found in a variety of habitats throughout the country. And since they always choose to live near bodies of water, they find the Peshtigo River State Forest prime real estate.

Paddle the river, take a boat ride on the forest's reservoirs, or canoe-camp at the Johnson Falls Flowage, and there's a good chance that you'll see one of the blue-gray birds, the largest herons in North America. They measure between four and five feet high and have a wingspan of up to six feet.

If you don't see them wading in the waters, stalking fish with their long, scissorlike, yellow beaks or trying to spear snakes, frogs, or mice, you certainly won't miss them when they take flight. Their huge wings slowly beat the air, and their gangly legs trail out behind. Unlike the sandhill crane that flies with its neck held straight, the great blue heron takes to the air with its neck in an S shape.

Physically, a great blue heron has a more elongated body than a sandhill crane. The great blue heron has yellow eyes and a white head with a black stripe that extends into several long plumes off the back like a ponytail. In front at the base of the neck, feathers drop down in a kind of necklace.

In spring, great blue herons build nests or refurbish old ones in treetops up to a hundred feet above the ground near open water. They usually nest in the same spot from year to year in colonies of two hundred or more. A stand of trees with their nests can look like a lofty airport when the jumbo birds wheel in.

The males select a new mate each year, and together the two will incubate three to seven blue-green eggs for approximately a month. Eggs and chicks that sur-

Catching sight of a great blue heron may be the best development yet on a Wisconsin waterfront. *John T. Andrews*

THE PESHTIGO RIVER STATE FOREST: THE WATERFRONT PROPERTY OF GREAT BLUE HERONS

vive the dangers of predators such as ravens and crows are fed with regurgitated, predigested food from their parents. The oldest, biggest chick usually receives the largest share.

Chicks prepare for their first flights by walking near their nest's edge, stretching their wings, and cleaning their plumage. Weaker chicks may fall from the nest and die from starvation. But at eight weeks, the one to four chicks that remain will start taking short flights between nearby trees and soon begin fishing on their own. They may live to be seventeen years old.

A blue heron will bark like a dog when startled. To avoid disturbing parents who are caring for their young, never enter a great blue heron rookery while birds are present. Adults will abandon entire colonies if there are too many intrusions, so stay well offshore from their roosts.

Catching sight of one of Wisconsin's great blue herons, standing graceful and tall near the shore, may be the most stirring and best development yet on a Wisconsin waterfront.

Keeping It Natural

The sighting of the magnificent blue heron and the intense color of the dark water and heavily forested shores makes me feel lucky to be here, fortunate to see what might have disappeared forever. This could easily have become a more developed landscape. Now, for ours and many future generations of Wisconsinites, three State Natural Areas totaling 672 acres, designated in 2007, are also in place in the Peshtigo River State Forest: Kirby Lake Hardwoods, Lake Lackawanna, and Johnson Falls.

Below the Johnson Falls Dam, the Johnson Falls State Natural Area in the south-central portion of the forest sits on a sandy outwash, along both sides of a 1.5-mile section of the Peshtigo River. Here, mature forests hold oaks, white pine, and some white cedar that exceed fifteen inches in diameter. Balsam fir, black spruce, white spruce, paper birch, black ash, red maple, basswoods, and hemlocks populate the steep sandy slopes and old river terraces.

On the forest floor, sharp-toothed jewelweed, low-growing and moisture-loving naked miterwort, and tall wild sarsaparilla mingle. Here and there, sphagnum moss weaves an extensive, thick carpet. Springs and seeps give life to dense masses of a variety of ferns and golden ragwort wildflowers.

Within the Johnson Falls State Natural Area on the northeast side of the

Peshtigo River are slabs of granite. Northern pin oak, red maple, white oak, white pine, and jack pine encircle the rocks. In open spaces, the rare, tall, and delicate Deam's rock-cresses stand straight. Big and little bluestems push up from the floor, and lichens and mosses create a velvety sheen over the exposed bedrock.

Island Retreats

Back on the boat, however, there are other massive rocks that Leon is calling my attention to. And these ones are surrounded by the "lake."

"There are several islands on High Falls that are fairly large in size," says Leon. "Up ahead is Chocolate Drop Island. Three well-known artists have painted it," he says with a touch of pride in his voice that comes from showing off your home to an outsider.

In fact, three artists did one painting of it. In a work titled *The Honeymooners*, Don Kloetzke, Jerry Gadamus, and Scott Zoellick depicted a mating pair of loons circling Chocolate Drop Island as a full moon rises in the background. A cozy, pine-sheltered campsite sits quietly on the shore. Some have speculated that the island got its name from its unique shape; the white pine growing on its top suggest a giant Hershey's Kiss.

We pass Chocolate Drop Island and soon Leon is pointing out another, Teacher's Island. "I think this one got its name because a high-school teacher used to come out and stay on it every summer, which went on until the late 1950s," says Leon. "I believe his family sold the island to WPS, reserving the right for the teacher to use it until his death," he states.

I notice that high above the island, in its tallest treetops, there are several nests of bald eagles.

It Goes Back to the Water

With all of the emphasis on boating and water activities, I ask Leon if it's possible yet to hike on any developed trails in the forest. He says:

We do have two systems of trails designated for cross-country skiing in winter and hiking during the rest of the year. Both are in the southern section of the forest. There are five miles of loops on the Spring Rapids

The Peshtigo River was put into service to provide electrical energy for northeast Wisconsin. The High Falls Dam was constructed between 1907 and 1911. *John T. Andrews*

Trail and three miles on the Seymour Rapids Trail. Both have some pretty steep hills and beautiful overlooks of the river below. But a lot of our trails were developed through a cooperative plan with Wisconsin Public Service and our local Iron Snowshoe Snowmobile Club. We were just recognized as one of the top five snowmobile destinations in the state.

In the summer, those snowmobile trails can also be used for hiking, especially in the fly-fishing area below Johnson Falls. The snowmobile trails aren't officially named, but the most well-known of them is the one we call the River Trail. It follows the descent of the river from Johnson Falls Dam all the way down to the foot of Seymour Rapids, which is all part of the fly-fishing area. The scenery from the high bluffs is really awesome, and a lot of eagles hang in that stretch of the river year-round.

Because he's lived here all of his life — well before this area was even envisioned as a state forest — I ask Leon to talk about the ways in which he has gotten in touch with the natural aspects of his home landscape over the years. Of course, while he has some great land-based memories, it all comes back to the waters of the Peshtigo.

"When I was younger," says Leon, "I had some good bird dogs and did a lot of grouse and duck hunting. I also hunted deer. But in the summer," he says with a smile, "I'd have to say my favorite thing to do would be waterskiing. Waterskiing has been a big part of my family's life. My daughter has been a state-champion, three-event skier. From that, she's gone on to water-ski all over the world. And we have a water-ski club on the reservoir that puts on weekend shows."

A Bigger Boat

As we pull off the High Falls Reservoir — Leon's "lake" — and back into Popp's Bay for docking in front of the resort, I realize that although this forest is just a baby, so to speak, it has long-time connections for many people in Wisconsin.

"We've got one family that has been coming to the resort for more than fifty years — in fact, fifty-four years this summer," says Leon. "It started out with the grandfather's visits, then the father's, and then the son's. Now they're on their fourth generation that has been coming up to spend part of their

Many of the roads and trails in the forest — about thirty-five miles of them — are open for very scenic horseback riding.
Candice Gaukel Andrews

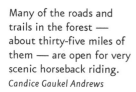

summers with us. They stay a week, and usually come one or two times in between. They come for fishing and swimming, mostly.

"In the past," continues Leon, "up until eight or ten years ago, it was very common for people to go back to the same resort year after year. A lot of people have been with us for thirty or forty years, and a lot of them who aren't as steady will say, 'Oh, yeah, I stayed at your place thirty years ago.' There's just a connection you feel when you come to this place that calls you back."

I ask Leon what he thinks that connection is, and he immediately speaks about the water — and something that runs a little deeper.

There are areas around the reservoir where the Peshtigo River State Forest stretches out about a mile — but that's about the widest point. So the water does cast a big shadow on this forest. Just as it is for the returning guests and for me, people get attached to things that meant a lot to them when they were young. I grew up here on the reservoir, so this forest, river, and lake have always been part of my life one way or another: swimming, waterskiing, hunting, or fishing. As a kid, ten or twelve years old, I had a little boat with a five-horsepower motor, and I was out there all the time.

Leon still is. Only now, it's usually on a pontoon.

THANK-YOU TO A VERY SMALL ECO-WARRIOR

OFTEN REFERRED TO AS WISCONSIN'S "STATE bird," mosquitoes are alive and well in all of our forests for almost three seasons of the year. In fact, our state has fifty different species of mosquitoes. Since mosquitoes breed in water and most of our Wisconsin forests have at least one river, stream, marshy puddle, or undrained depression, it's not surprising that you encounter them on your walks, hikes, and rides in the woods. But as pesky as these tiny, 0.06-inch insects are, I find it comforting to remember some good things about them.

First of all, remind yourself that mosquitoes are a part of nature and provide a major food source for birds, bats, dragonflies, and spiders. Would we really want a world without birds or bats or dragonflies? (I admit I might be able to do without the spiders.)

Secondly, only half of the mosquito population bites. And although it pains me to say this, it's the ladies that come looking for us. While a male sips nectar from flowers, a female must find appropriate food for her babies — thousands of babies. In her lifetime, she will lay about ten separate two-hundred-egg batches. To make all of that embryonic tissue, mom mosquito needs a rich source of protein. Unfortunately, that usually turns out to be mammalian blood — which includes ours.

Female mosquitoes hunt their blood host by detecting carbon dioxide and octenol in human and animal breath and sweat. So far, DEET and picaridin have proven to be the most effective mosquito repellents, since they inhibit the detection of odor cues in the insects.

Thirdly, as David Quammen, an award-winning science, nature, and travel writer, suggested, mosquitoes are the staunchest defenders of our wild and undeveloped lands. Robert Krulwich, a correspondent for National Public Radio's "Science Desk," puts it this way:

> Knowing, as we all do, that humans for eons have been moving into forests and plains and shores and river valleys and hills, pushing animals, vegetables, and minerals around in their very human way, destroying more and more life forms, and knowing, as we also do, that we are down to precious few places on Earth where there is still a rich diversity of species, have you ever wondered why, even into the twenty-first century, there are still large tracts of equatorial rainforest that have somehow survived human exploitation? Who or what has defended those last outposts of ferns, butterflies, beetles, and ants from humankind?

Krulwich and Quammen would posit that the lady mosquito deserves some credit. "Every time human settlers stepped into those areas in serious numbers, they got bit, then they got sick, and then, until very recently, most of them backed off," writes Krulwich.

So while you're spraying on the picaridin; or applying aloe vera, lime juice, or peppermint oil on your skin; or rubbing dryer sheets up and down your legs and arms; or trying the other million and one homegrown mosquito deterrents out there, take time to say a little thank-you to a tiny, fierce eco-warrior.

Peshtigo River State Forest

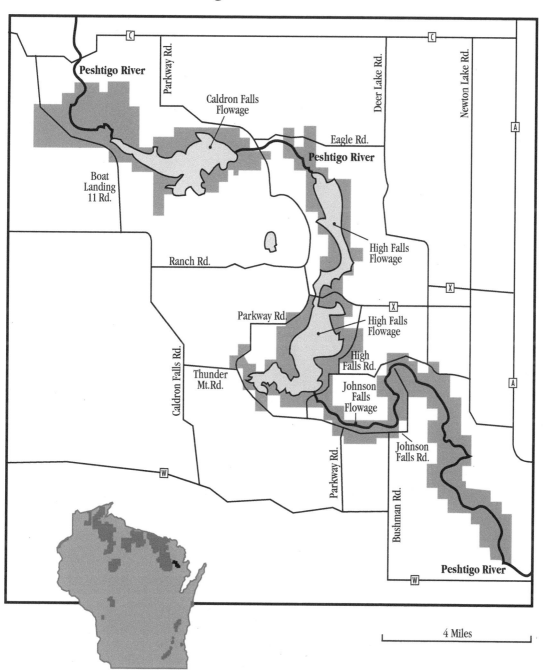

Parkway Rd.

Deer Lake Rd.

Newton Lake Rd.

Peshtigo River

Caldron Falls
Flowage

Eagle Rd.

Peshtigo River

Boat
Landing
11 Rd.

High Falls
Flowage

Ranch Rd.

Parkway Rd.

High Falls
Flowage

Caldron Falls Rd.

Thunder
Mt.Rd.

High
Falls Rd.

Johnson
Falls
Flowage

Johnson
Falls Rd.

Parkway Rd.

Bushman Rd.

Peshtigo River

Peshtigo River

4 Miles

There's a little forest that sits on Wisconsin's Lake Michigan shoreline that gives the impression that it is more beach than trees. *John T. Andrews*

14 Point Beach State Forest
BRIGHT LIGHTS AND MOVIE STARS

All Tanned, and Ready for a Close-Up

There's a little forest that sits on Wisconsin's Lake Michigan shoreline that gives the impression that it is more beach than trees; more sand reeds than pine stands. Petite at only six miles long and thin at just a mile and a half wide, it resembles a Hollywood movie star more than it does one of our Wisconsin Northwoods icons. And just like a famous film actor, its slender shape suggests that this forest belongs to a dietetic coastal culture rather than to a burly, mid-nation, lumberjack society.

It's true that within this forest there are thousands of red pine, white pine, and spruces. And it is one of the few remaining undeveloped and wooded tracts along Lake Michigan, a home for true forest dwellers, like white-tailed deer, mink, red and gray foxes, thirteen-lined ground squirrels, coyotes, wood-chucks, and rabbits. But this pretty, parklike parcel of 2,903 acres is visually dominated by latte-colored sand dunes and cappuccino-frothy waves. And standing tall above its beach swales and ridges is the white Rawley Point Light-house, an elegant reminder that just as with some movie stars, this forest has a lot of flash.

What Lies Beneath: Part I

On a cold Saturday in February, I make my introduction to the Point Beach State Forest by way of a hike along the beach and a short side trip to the Raw-ley Point Lighthouse. The winds off Lake Michigan are aggressive, and more than once they attempt to blow me off course. I button up my field jacket to

Beneath the dark waters of Lake Michigan, just beyond the sands of Point Beach State Forest, several ships still rest.
John T. Andrews

the neck and pull my fleece hat down tight against the best the great lake throws at me. How different this sandy-beach forest must appear in the summer, I think, when the lake draws swimmers and sunbathers from as far south as Chicago and as far north as Michigan's Upper Peninsula. But then, would I even be able to see the beach? Today, I have the whole shoreline — this stretch of it, anyway — to myself. While summer visitors need to keep an eye out for rip tides, I keep a sharp lookout for remnants of shipwrecks.

There are rumors that the large, steel boiler and engine cylinder heads of the bulk freighter and wooden steamship *Continental* can still be seen in the shallow water less than a half-mile out. The ship was driven ashore by a severe blizzard on December 13, 1904. Two of her crewmen managed to trudge through the storm for two days to report her stranding. Although the wind that is pushing against me is strong, my winter day here involves only a dusting of snow on the sands — nothing like what those two men must have encountered on this beach. While no loss of life was reported, by the time the tugs reached the *Continental* on December 14, she was already broken in two. Peering into the wind, I search for her remains, but I cannot positively identify her body.

SAND AND SNOW: THE BEST TRACKING MEDIUMS

How different this forest must appear in summer, when visitors come from as far south as Chicago and as far north as the Upper Peninsula of Michigan. But then, would I even be able to see the beach? *John T. Andrews*

TRACKING ANIMALS IS A WAY TO EXPERIENCE the "thrill of the hunt" — without the killing. There's a deep satisfaction that comes from successfully ferreting out a snippet of the wild; sharing just a few moments with an animal on his own terms; on his own home turf. With acute senses, most animals are experts at evading us, and sights that aren't commonplace are the ones we tend to put a higher value on.

Many mammals are nocturnal, and tracking is a way of finding them through their actions. Point Beach State Forest in winter is an excellent place to go tracking: wet sand is second only to snow as a footprint-leaving medium.

But footprints are far from the only clues a tracker uses: scat, nesting or denning sites, matted-down vegetation indicating an overnight bed, food rem-

nants, and rubs on trees are just some of the signs that can be used to help us understand the lives of mammals beyond our everyday world.

Winter does provide the best wide-terrain tracking opportunities because if there's fresh snow, there will be footprints. Animals need to eat, and that requires moving from place to place. One of the best ways to ensure you'll get off the beaten path and follow where the animals go is by wearing snowshoes. Whether wooden or aluminum, snowshoes leave a trail in soft snow that is virtually impossible to miss on the way back out.

To become a good tracker, you must learn to think like the wild animals, who respond primarily to their stomachs and their hormones. They have three basic

(continued on next page)

SAND AND SNOW: THE BEST TRACKING MEDIUMS

(continued from page 285)
drives: to eat, to avoid being eaten, and to reproduce. Predator species usually have to travel significant distances to locate prey, and prey need to remain close to cover for safety.

Amateur trackers can start to hone their skills by first learning to narrow down tracks to a small group of possibilities:

Rodent family. Four toes on the front foot and five toes on the hind foot (such as mice, voles, shrews, chipmunks, squirrels, or woodchucks).

Raccoon, weasel, and bear families. Five toes on the front and hind feet (such as weasels, badgers, skunks, fishers, otters, black bears, beavers, muskrats, porcupines, opossums, or mink).

Deer family. Two toes on a hoof (such as white-tailed deer or moose).

There are other factors that can be considered, such as whether claws are present and the length and shape of a footprint. Taking along a good guidebook can help in positively identifying the animal, but remember that tracks in the real world rarely look exactly like they do in a book.

While you'll find that out in the field some stories can be clearly read, others will offer a challenge. The pleasure of tracking, however, is often in trying to unravel the mystery. But maybe even more important is just going out to poke about in the forest, to explore, and to be part of the natural world again.

Before there was a lighthouse on this point that juts into Lake Michigan, twenty-six ships sunk or were stranded here: twenty schooners, one barge, two steamers, and three brigs. The ships carried a variety of cargo, including leather, wheat, wagon tongues, ballast iron, marble, furniture, Christmas trees, and passengers. One of the most tragic sinkings occurred on October 29, 1887, when the *Vernon*, one of the largest steamships on the lake at the time, went down in a gale. She broke up immediately, taking thirty to sixty crew and passengers with her (only one list of the passengers and crew was kept, and it went down with the *Vernon*). The reason she sank still remains a mystery; however, the only surviving passenger, Axel Stone, said he believed it was because the ship was overloaded. Scuba divers like to search for pieces of the *Vernon* and those other ships, too, south of the Rawley Point Lighthouse.

In 1912, the *Rouse Simmons*, en route to Chicago and laden with some ten thousand Christmas trees, sank off Two Rivers in a Lake Michigan storm.
WHi Image ID 6083

In fact, an organized group of scuba divers was sent to look for one particular ship in 2006. It was in another cold winter — in November 1912 — that the *Rouse Simmons* sank off this point. The schooner, loaded with Upper Peninsula Christmas trees, set off on her final trip of the season. After a long time

Diving to the *Rouse Simmons* is like touring an underwater museum. Much of what was in her cargo hold lies untouched since the ship went down in November 1912. *Courtesy Wisconsin Maritime Archaeology Program*

away from home sailing the Great Lakes, Captain Herman Schuenemann was looking forward to returning to his family in Chicago.

But, sadly, the *Rouse Simmons* never made it to the windy city. She — and everyone onboard — was lost somewhere on Lake Michigan. No one knew exactly the place or the cause. Fifty-nine years later, she was found — lying in 170 feet of water northeast of Two Rivers. She was mostly intact, and neatly stacked in her hold were the Christmas trees. Today, after nearly one hundred years beneath the cold, freshwater depths of Lake Michigan, the *Rouse Simmons* and her well-preserved trees still rest.

The Wisconsin Historical Society's Maritime Preservation and Archaeology Program sent a group of expert divers, maritime enthusiasts, and volunteers on a mission to explore the *Rouse Simmons* site in 2006. During a two-week period, the group braved the chilly waters to document the shipwreck, learn how the vessel was constructed, and search for clues that might explain why she went down.

Through an initiative called Wisconsin's Maritime Trails (www.maritimetrails.org), a partnership between the Wisconsin Historical Society, the University of Wisconsin Sea Grant Institute, and the Wisconsin Coastal Management Program, you can access the state's collection of maritime resources and research findings by Web site, public presentations, shipwreck moorings,

A dark, evergreen background provides contrast for the white, airy Rawley Point Lighthouse and keeper's home in a Point Beach State Forest winter.
John T. Andrews

and other venues. But here, today, standing in the wind on the shore of Lake Michigan, my dry, stinging eyes see no signs of phantom vessels.

An elongated, gray, winter cloud begins to obscure the sun, and soon two other, more competent "eyes" take over the chore of sweeping the lake. Every fifteen seconds, the two Rawley Point Lighthouse beacons alternately illuminate the darkening waters and warn boats of a potential stage for disaster and death.

The lighthouse is the third to guard this piece of shoreline and forest. The first on the point was a temporary one, located one and a half miles from the present site. Built in 1853, it was uncomplicated, consisting of four poles approximately seventy-five feet high, with a lantern at the top. The lantern was raised and lowered by rope and pulley. In 1873, a permanent, brick lighthouse and keeper's home were constructed at the current location. In 1894, when a new, steel tower was installed, the upper part of the brick lighthouse tower was dismantled, and the remaining structure was roofed and integrated into the keeper's house.

The new tower, 113 feet high, was made in France and was part of the French exhibition at the Chicago World's Fair in 1893. With eight corner posts and a complex network of diagonal tie rods and horizontal struts, the lighthouse is designed with a central cylindrical iron staircase that accesses the top lantern room and gallery. From 1894 to 1920, the seven-foot tall, French-manufactured Fresnel lens used vapor lamps for illumination. In 1920, the lighthouse was wired for electricity. An airport beacon light then took the place of the Fresnel lens until the present optic system was installed in 1987. Today, the lighthouse is fully automated.

The slender, airy lighthouse and accompanying white keeper's home, framed by evergreens, have become favorites of photographers in Wisconsin. Despite the winds, I stop to take a few shots myself. Under such a dramatic, cloudy sky, it is very clear why the structure was listed on the National Register of Historic Places in 1984.

Four Stars in Two Rivers

The Lake Michigan winds have made me crave a hot cup of coffee, and I drive in to nearby Two Rivers to get warm. One of the few places open on this winter Saturday is the Washington House Museum on Jefferson and Seventeenth Streets. It is there I bump into actor Charlton Heston.

Heston is the last person I expect to see in this little Wisconsin town. But there he is, staring out at me from a glossy, black-and-white photo propped up inside a dark-wood-and-glass cabinet, the kind for keeping curios in. Charlton Heston, the man — more so, probably, than anyone else on the planet — who

I meet Walter Vogl (left) and Bob Schaefer (right) at the Washington House Museum in Two Rivers. Bob's grandfather sold some of his land to create the Point Beach State Forest.
John T. Andrews

personified the likes of Moses and Ben-Hur. But what, on Earth, is his connection to Two Rivers?

"Charlton Heston married a local girl named Lydia Clarke," I hear a proud voice say from behind me. I turn to see that it belongs to eighty-year-old Bob Schaefer, a Washington House Museum host and tour guide, who kindly offers me a place out of the elements to linger. "At the time, she was an outstanding actress who had performed in many plays on Broadway," he continues. "Her father, L. B. Clarke, was principal of Two Rivers Washington High School for many years."

A ten-year volunteer at the museum and still going strong, Bob shows me around a veritable time capsule in a building that was Two Rivers' first hotel, built in the 1850s. The rooms are now bursting with vintage toys; decades-old dresses, shoes, and hats; band instruments that have seen better days; dishes you'd remember from your grandmother's kitchen; and winter sleds and cross-country skis from a time when those things were made out of wood.

"Please. Take your time looking around," Bob urges me. It was just what my still-numb ears wanted to hear.

As I wander these wonderful overfilled old rooms, I am surprised to find not only a Wisconsin connection to Charlton Heston but a long-time bond between Point Beach State Forest and Bob. It almost seems as if the forest winds shoved me here with a purpose in mind. At the end of my tour, Bob asks me to sit down with him and another visitor to the museum that day, Bob's good friend Walter Vogl. Walt is Two Rivers Historical Society's past president and current Washington House Museum administrator. I couldn't have run into two more knowledgeable and enthusiastic keepers of the area's and forest's history. Fate has put me in the presence of the forest's real notables — and I'm not talking Charlton and Lydia.

Bob's bond with Point Beach comes from a parcel of land that had been in the Schaefer family for four generations. And, quirkily, all four patriarchs were named Philip Schaefer.

Says Bob, "Point Beach State Forest is north of Two Rivers only about four miles. My grandfather, one of the Philip Schaefers, owned acreage in that vicinity. When the government was trying to create a state park, he sold some of the family land for that purpose."

In 1856, the first Philip Schaefer bought forty acres of land in the Point Beach State Forest area for $85. He bought eighty more acres in 1876 for

Point Beach State Forest is one of the few remaining undeveloped and wooded tracts along Lake Michigan.
John T. Andrews

$500. In 1937, a few local merchants, residents, and the president of the Community Club (now the Chamber of Commerce), Joseph Soit, decided that a recreational area close to Two Rivers might draw more tourists and business for the town. The Wisconsin Conservation Commission approved spending $10,000 to buy two hundred acres of land to get the project started. Eighty-five of those two hundred acres were Schaefer land, which Philip sold to the state for $50 an acre.

In that same year, an influential man named Charley Broughton, the editor and owner of the *Sheboygan Press* newspaper, persuaded the U.S. Congress to turn over to the state an eighty-acre surplus of land that the federal government owned at the site of the Rawley Point Lighthouse. One of the stipulations was that the state would establish a park there.

Not long after, Frank Kaufman, who owned much of the land around Molash Creek, offered to sell 350 acres to the state and donate another 100 acres of woodlands. The Manitowoc County Board, the Wisconsin Conservation Commission, and the city of Two Rivers appropriated the money for the additional land purchase, and in 1937 the Point Beach State Forest was officially established.

Originally, Point Beach was to be called a state park, but it became a state forest due to the fact that the land was actually acquired under the state's forestry law. It was all beginning to make sense to me, this apparent parkland that was masquerading as a forest.

In 1939, the forest really got underway when Works Progress Administration crews were assigned to clear trees for roads. A lodge was constructed with stones brought in from a quarry in Valders, Wisconsin; shakes from a prison camp in Rhinelander; and lumber cut from the woodlands. More than 475,000 trees were planted, the majority of them red pine, along with 5,000 white pine and 2,000 spruces.

By 1948, the state held 1,550 acres of land for the forest. A decade later, almost 587,000 trees had been planted. Some of those same trees I had seen today on my walk.

What Lies Beneath: Part II

According to Bob and Walt, all of those trees needed to be planted to recreate a "forest," because it turns out that the depths of Lake Michigan are not the only subsurface places where Point Beach has had a devastating history. Underground fires would have to play a prominent role in any film version of this forest's life.

"Our family farm that is now part of the forest burned in the 1800s," says Bob. "The fire was so great, my relatives had to bury their things in the earth and walk the four or five miles to Two Rivers. A couple days later, after the fire, they came back to the farm and found everything gone," he tells me, "even the items placed underground. So my great grandfather had to start from scratch. He worked awfully, awfully hard during his lifetime."

"It was like that," agrees Walt. "Fires were burning from Two Rivers through Door County for six weeks before the Peshtigo tragedy."

Walt tells me that while most people have heard stories about the October 8, 1871, Great Chicago Fire and some know of the Peshtigo Fire on the same date, very few are familiar with the fires that struck Manitowoc, Calumet, Brown, Kewaunee, and Door Counties during September and early October of that same year.

ALIENS INVADE POINT BEACH STATE FOREST

JUST BECAUSE YOU'RE AN ALIEN DOESN'T mean you're bad. It's when you out-compete the natives that things in the forest can start to take a negative turn.

"Non-natives" or "aliens" are species that have been moved from their natural habitats to a new environment. For example, the majority of the foods grown in home gardens are non-native plants.

The definition of an invasive species, however, is one that is "non-native to the ecosystem in which it is found *and* is likely to cause environmental, economic, or human-health harm."

Most invasive species arrived here from Europe or Asia, either purposefully or accidentally. These aliens then become invasive because without their natural enemies (predators, insects, fungi, or disease), they cannot be kept in check. They dominate, overwhelm, or wipe out the native species, which indigenous insects and animals are dependent on for survival. Thus invasives reduce the numbers of native plants and animals and the biodiversity of a community.

Black locust trees are an example of an invasive species that was introduced on purpose. A deciduous tree that grows thirty to eighty feet tall, black locust is native to the slopes and forest margins of southern Appalachia and the Ozarks. They were introduced throughout Wisconsin in the early 1900s because of their durable wood, which was suitable for — among other things — fence posts. The trees also provided nectar for honeybees. However, the black locust's aggressive growth patterns and dense stands shade out most understory, native vegetation. Recently, with

funding from the Division of Forestry, Point Beach State Forest has been able to reduce the acreage with black locust trees from about ten down to one. The goal is to eliminate all black locust trees from the Point Beach forest.

Another invasive species of concern to the forest is garlic mustard. Probably introduced by early European settlers for its uses in cooking and in medicines, garlic mustard is an early bloomer that shades out spring wildflowers and other native understory herbs before they have a chance to develop. At Point Beach in recent years, garlic mustard has been reduced by 50 percent in the campground areas, but it invades new campsites every year. Compounding the problem is that its seeds are viable for many years. And while the invasive spotted knapweed has also been reduced by 50 percent, it is spreading faster than it is being eliminated in the sensitive sand dunes. Because knapweed has a taproot, it decreases erosion control when it crowds out native grasses with fibrous roots. Lyme grass, yet another invasive plant, also threatens the dunes.

During the past two hundred years, it is estimated that almost 180 exotic species have found their way into the Great Lakes from foreign ships and surrounding terrestrial areas. Since invasive species are often spread via seeds, check the places they could hide before traveling through the forests. Bicycle and ATV tires, hiking boots, and pants cuffs are favorite places for seeds to hitch a ride. For more information on how to prevent the spread of invasives, contact a local Wisconsin Department of Natural Resources office.

"I think the fact that there was no rain from August to October started the fires," says Walt. "Every so often, you'll hear that high winds carried burning leaves from Green Bay to the west side of Manitowoc. But I don't believe it's possible for a leaf or ember to fly that far. Wood-burning stoves, sparks from trains, woodlots that were almost contiguous — all of these things could have contributed to why a fire that started north of Two Rivers was able to travel through five counties. Remember, everything was tinder dry at the time."

Walt is correct. In 1871, the last of the rain had fallen on August 3, and snowfall was rare during the previous winter. Streambeds had dried up, as had many of the shallow, hand-dug wells. And during the late summer and early fall, dry, highly combustible materials had sometimes just burst into flames.

Those flames traveled the plank roads and ate them up, and people frantically jumped in the rivers to try to escape. Farmers ripped down their rail fences to prevent fire from coursing along them and igniting their buildings. Because of the water shortage, milk that had soured was dumped on burning fences to douse the ravenous flames. Fire even traveled underground through dry peat, and followed and consumed tree roots, causing one-hundred-foot white pine trees to topple without warning. Potatoes were baked in the ground in these strange, subterranean fires, and even the possessions Bob's family and others like them had buried were not safe.

Finally, on October 9, a two-hour rain fell. The fires subsided. But multiple stands of tamaracks, pines, hemlocks, and hardwoods had been destroyed. And with them went the area's tannery industry, a direct spawn of the forest.

"The fire closed down the tanneries for all intents and purposes," says Walt. "That's an industry that had been growing since 1861 when the Pfister and Vogel Leather Company was built at Two Creeks, about seven miles north of Point Beach State Forest," he says.

Before the fire, Two Creeks had been a thriving Lake Michigan shore community, with a sawmill, planing mill, port, wagon maker, and the tannery. It employed three hundred men.

"The reason the tanneries were here was because of the hemlock forest at Point Beach," Walt goes on. "The sale of hemlock bark had been lucrative because it was used in tanning skins. When my great grandparents bought our 160 acres in 1868 — acres I still own — the deed indicated there were one hundred cords of hemlock bark in the woods not included in the sale, it was so valuable," he muses.

The fires of 1871 and the resultant loss of the hemlocks did indeed contribute to the shutdown of most of the area's tanneries by 1875, including Wisconsin Leather Company in Two Rivers.

"Just a few years ago," notes Walt, "charred white pine stumps could still be found in the Point Beach State Forest."

On a winter hike along Point Beach, the winds off Lake Michigan attempt to blow me off course, but I have the whole shoreline to myself.
John T. Andrews

A Forest Facelift

If the disappearance of the lines of fire of almost 150 years ago is regarded as a positive thing, there are other old lines on the face of this forest that should always be valued and protected.

Lake Michigan, the eastern border of the forest, is the sixth largest freshwater lake in the world. It was created by a glacier about fourteen thousand years ago, when a lobe of ice began to pull back (see pages 175–177). Today, this great lake is 925 feet at its deepest, with an average depth of 279 feet. Those who venture into the Point Beach State Forest today will find the fishing in its waters good: Chinook and coho salmon; rainbow, brown, and lake trout; yellow perch; and smallmouth bass are just some angler favorites.

As the ancient lake that was Lake Michigan's predecessor gradually receded and lowered, it left behind wave-caused ridges of sand, the remnants of beaches deposited at different times during the last eight thousand years. The ridges now range from a foot and a half to twenty-six feet in height. The water-laid

Even on a February day, the dune grasses pushing through the snow make a lasting impression about this unique forest's ridge-and-swale topography.
John T. Andrews

sediments were topped by wind-blown sands and became dunes. At Point Beach State Forest, eleven alternating ridges and swales paralleling Lake Michigan are now exposed, but similar ridges extend under the lake for a substantial distance. On the forest's beach cordwalk, I can walk over these bumps and bottoms.

The diversity of northern trees I see growing on the ridge formations is striking and even more apparent on a winter day. On the eleventh swale west of the lake stand black ash and tamaracks, and the ninth ridge is forested with white pine, white cedar, yellow birch, and hemlocks. On the eighth ridge to the fifth, red maple and white birch trees thrive. But the farther east I go, the more the flora becomes less like a forest and more like a coastal beach. Several sand plants, junipers, and bearberry stabilize the second ridge. And ridge one and the shoreline east of it are vegetated with the specialized flora of lake beaches and dunes: sand reed, clustered broomrape, dune thistle, and dune goldenrod — all plants listed on the state's threatened species list.

The forest is located under a major migratory corridor and flyway for birds and is a site on the Great Wisconsin Birding and Nature Trail.
John T. Andrews

The swales — those narrow, low wetlands between these old beach ridges — hold thick peat (partially decayed plant material) at their bottoms; some deposits are up to five feet deep. While most of them dry out during late summer, some contain water year-round. Sedges, wildflowers — including orchids — aquatic plants, and several types of ferns flourish here during the warmer seasons.

A few months from now, these quiet swale wetlands will be alive with wood frogs, spring peepers, and red-backed and blue-spotted salamanders. In this sort of habitat, these species find a protected place to lay eggs and for their offspring to grow and mature. If I was walking here in spring instead of winter, my steps would be buoyed by frog songs as loud as guitar-heavy, hard rock music.

However, these low, wet environments also make a perfect breeding ground for mosquitoes — twenty-seven different varieties of them — and that thought makes me happy that my introduction to the forest has occurred in winter. While mosquitoes are a bother to us, they are an important food source for birds and bats. Given the numbers of migratory birds who stop here, it seems that mosquitoes, like Lake Michigan and the tanned sands, also draw a certain "breed" of visitors to this forest. (See the sidebar "Thank-You to a Very Small Eco-Warrior," page 280.)

In Wisconsin, this ridge-and-swale topography is found only along Lake Michigan's western shore. Other than at Point Beach State Forest, there are only three places in the state where you can see it: at the Jacksonport Ridges and Bailey's Harbor Ridges in Door County, and at the Woodland Dunes Nature Center in Two Rivers. This rare sort of beauty is why 175 acres of the forest were designated a State Natural Area in 1971 and a National Natural Landmark.

There are some wrinkles, ridges, and lines that no cosmetic intervention should ever be allowed to erase.

With Stars in Their Eyes

If anyone could appreciate the rhythm of the undulating and alternating ridges and waves, and the candlepower and timing mechanism of the Rawley Point Lighthouse, it's Bob Schaefer.

"I retired from Paragon Electric Company almost twenty years ago," says Bob, as I button up my coat once again to brave the Lake Michigan winds. "We made timers and time switches. With timers you have to be so careful. Just one little thing wrong with the mechanism will screw up everything."

It's not surprising then, that Bob's favorite exhibit item in the Washington House Museum has to do with rhythm and timing.

"I guess my favorite exhibit is the Gloe-Naidl Orchestra display," says Bob when I ask him to choose. "I set that one up more than five years ago, and Arthur Gloe was my uncle," he explains. "In the 1920s and 1930s, his orchestra was very popular. In those days, they played in this area and went as far as Door County."

I smile. Of course, in the twenties and thirties, Door County from Point Beach would seem far. The world has shrunk in the decades since. We tend to travel faster now. But I'm sure by the tone in Bob's voice that the boys of the Gloe-Naidl Orchestra had felt they had hit the "big time."

I look at the creased old photograph of the band members in their

GREAT BIRDS ON THE GREAT WISCONSIN BIRDING AND NATURE TRAIL

POINT BEACH STATE FOREST NOT ONLY HAS ITS unique dunes underfoot; overhead, its skies have their own special and unusual character. The forest is located on a major migratory corridor and flyway for birds.

More than 130 species of migratory and resident birds have been spotted in the forest. Green-backed herons, great blue herons, pileated woodpeckers, great crested flycatchers, indigo buntings, wild turkeys, northern harriers, white-throated sparrows, white-breasted nuthatches, and pine warblers have all frequented Point Beach State Forest.

As an added attraction, various shorebirds, songbirds, and vireos arrive in massive numbers during the spring migration. Avian visitors such as wood ducks, blue-winged teal, sandhill cranes, spotted sandpipers, and Caspian terns appreciate the ponds, dune ridges, and forest trees that provide shelter from the mighty winds off Lake Michigan. Scaup, bufflehead, and goldeneye ducks stop here on the bays, en route to their boreal breeding grounds. In late May, whippoorwills are often heard letting out their three-syllable, tremolo calls. But the warbler migration may be the most spectacular of all.

By early May, many birds have already returned to the Upper Midwest. Most warblers, however, prefer

Bufflehead ducks are one of the many species of waterfowl that stop to rest on the waters of Lake Michigan off Point Beach State Forest during spring and fall migrations. *Courtesy Wisconsin Department of Natural Resources*

to wait until the insect hatch is sure to have already occurred. When the winds start blowing from the south, all at once the warblers seem to race to their northern nesting sites. Because they are some of the last birds to return to Wisconsin, their arrival denotes the final climax of the spring's winged invasion.

Warblers are seldom more than five inches in length and only a third to a half an ounce in weight, making what these tiny birds accomplish quite a feat. For example, a blackpoll warbler — a bird that has been spotted in the Point Beach State Forest — flies from Central and South America to its northern breeding grounds in central and northern Canada, covering at least 2,500 miles.

Wood warblers are some of the most colorful birds in the forest, and the Blackburnian warbler, also known as the torch bird, is unmistakable. Perched on the highest tips of a tree, with the sun behind him, a Blackburnian shows a fiery orange throat that almost seems ablaze.

Point Beach State Forest is a site on the Great Wisconsin Birding and Nature Trail. The trail consists of waypoints on a mapped auto tour that will reach into every area of the state when it is complete. As of

(continued on next page)

GREAT BIRDS ON THE GREAT WISCONSIN BIRDING AND NATURE TRAIL

(continued from page 299)

now, the Great Wisconsin Birding and Nature Trail encompasses five regional trails:

- Central Sands Prairie Birding and Nature Trail
- Lake Michigan Birding and Nature Trail
- Lake Superior/Northwoods Birding and Nature Trail
- Mississippi and Chippewa Rivers Birding and Nature Trail
- Southern Savanna Birding and Nature Trail

For the best possible chance of seeing the birds of Point Beach State Forest, visit before the leaves fill out the woods canopy, usually before mid-May. To follow the Great Wisconsin Birding and Nature Trail, look for the signs with the sandhill crane logo. More information on the trail can be found at www.wisconsin birds.org/trail.

uniforms. I see stars in the eyes of these young men. It seems that Point Beach State Forest has always been a place for big dreamers and treasure seekers — from the past's enterprising and seafaring Europeans with their cash cargos to today's scientists who come to study the unique ecology; from the scuba divers who search for sunken riches just offshore to the winter hikers like me who hope to glimpse a long-ago foundered ghost ship.

It's even a place where a small-town, local girl can dream of meeting and marrying a movie star — and have it all come true.

There are secrets under the rhythmic, roiling waves at Point Beach: rip tides and remnants of shipwrecks.
John T. Andrews

Point Beach State Forest

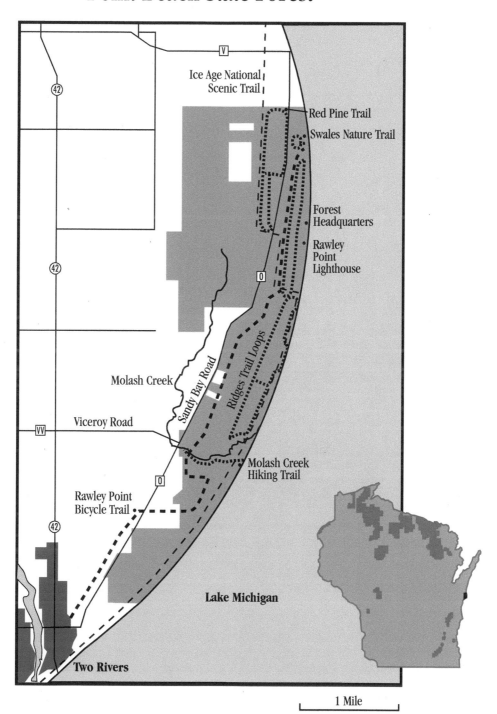

Ice Age National Scenic Trail

Red Pine Trail

Swales Nature Trail

Forest Headquarters

Rawley Point Lighthouse

Molash Creek

Sandy Bay Road

Ridges Trail Loops

Viceroy Road

Molash Creek Hiking Trail

Rawley Point Bicycle Trail

Lake Michigan

Two Rivers

V

42

42

42

O

O

VV

1 Mile

John T. Andrews

Appendix A

When Wisconsin State and National Forests Were Established

Forest	Established
Northern Highland State Forest (Since 1968, part of the Northern Highland-American Legion State Forest)	1925
American Legion State Forest (Since 1968, part of the Northern Highland-American Legion State Forest)	1929
Flambeau River State Forest	1930
Brule River State Forest	1932
Chequamegon National Forest (Since 1998, part of the Chequamegon-Nicolet National Forest)	1933
Nicolet National Forest (Since 1998, part of the Chequamegon-Nicolet National Forest)	1933
Kettle Moraine State Forest	1937
Point Beach State Forest	1937
Black River State Forest	1957
Coulee Experimental State Forest	1960
Governor Knowles State Forest	1970
Havenwoods State Forest	1980
Peshtigo River State Forest	2001

Appendix B

WISCONSIN'S TREES

Although creating an all-inclusive list of every tree type that at any one time stands in the forests of Wisconsin would be difficult (the experts don't even agree on a single list!), below is a look at just some of those you may discover on your own forest adventures:

Alder, speckled *(Alnus rugosa)*
Apple, crab *(Malus* sp.)
Apple, wild *(Malus* sp.)
Ash, American mountain *(Sorbus americana)*
Ash, black *(Fraxinus nigra)*
Ash, blue *(Fraxinus quadrangulata)*
Ash, common prickly *(Zanthoxylum americanum)*
Ash, European mountain *(Sorbus aucuparia)*
Ash, green *(Fraxinus pennsylvanica)*
Ash, white *(Fraxinus americana)*
Aspen, bigtooth *(Populus grandidentata)*
Aspen, quaking (or trembling) *(Populus tremuloides)*

Basswood (American linden) *(Tilia americana)*
Beech, American *(Fagus grandifolia)*
Beech, blue (or American hornbeam or musclewood)
    (Carpinus caroliniana)
Birch, paper (or white) *(Betula papyrifera)*
Birch, river *(Betula nigra)*
Birch, yellow *(Betula alleghaniensis)*
Bladdernut, American *(Staphylea trifolia)*
Boxelder *(Acer negundo)*
Buckeye, Ohio *(Aesculus glabra)*
Buckthorn, European *(Rhamnus cathartica)*
Butternut *(Juglans cinerea)*

Catalpa, northern *(Catalpa speciosa)*
Cedar, eastern (or northern) white *(Thuja occidentalis)*
Cedar, eastern red *(Juniperus virginiana)*

Cherry, black *(Prunus serotina)*
Cherry, choke *(Prunus virginiana)*
Cherry, pin *(Prunus pennsylvanica)*
Chestnut, American *(Castanea dentata)*
Chestnut, horse *(Aesculus hippocastanum)*
Coffeetree, Kentucky *(Gymnocladus dioica)*
Cottonwood, eastern *(Populus deltoides)*

Dogwood, alternate-leaf *(Cornus alternifolia)*

Elm, American *(Ulmus americana)*
Elm, rock *(Ulmus thomasii)*
Elm, Siberian *(Ulmus pumila)*
Elm, slippery *(Ulmus rubra)*

Fir, balsam *(Abies balsamea)*
Fir, Douglas *(Pseudotsuga menziesii)*

Gum, black *(Nyssa sylvatica)*

Hackberry, northern *(Celtis occidentalis)*
Hawthorns *(Crataegus* sp.)
Hemlock, eastern *(Tsuga canadensis)*
Hickory, bitternut *(Carya cordiformis)*
Hickory, shagbark *(Carya ovata)*
Hoptree, common *(Ptelea trifoliata)*

Ironwood *(Ostrya virginiana)*

Juneberry *(Amelanchier arborea)*

Locust, black *(Robinia pseudoacacia)*
Locust, honey *(Gleditsia triacanthos)*

Maple, Amur *(Acer ginnala)*
Maple, black *(Acer nigrum)*
Maple, mountain *(Acer spicatum)*
Maple, Norway *(Acer platanoides)*
Maple, red *(Acer rubrum)*
Maple, silver *(Acer saccharinum)*
Maple, sugar *(Acer saccharum)*
Mulberry, red *(Morus rubra)*
Mulberry, white *(Morus alba)*

Oak, black *(Quercus velutina)*
Oak, bur *(Quercus macrocarpa)*

Oak, chinquapin *(Quercus muehlenbergii)*
Oak, northern pin (or Hill's or jack) *(Quercus ellipsoildalis)*
Oak, northern red *(Quercus rubra)*
Oak, swamp white *(Quercus bicolor)*
Oak, white *(Quercus alba)*
Olive, Russian *(Elaeagnus angustifolia)*

Pine, Austrian *(Pinus nigra)*
Pine, eastern white *(Pinus strobus)*
Pine, jack *(Pinus banksiana)*
Pine, ponderosa *(Pinus ponderosa)*
Pine, red (or Norway) *(Pinus resinosa)*
Pine, Scotch *(Pinus sylvestris)*
Plum, American *(Prunus americana)*
Plum, Canada *(Prunus nigra)*
Poplar, balsam *(Populus balsamifera)*
Poplar, Lombardy *(Populus nigra)*
Poplar, white *(Populus alba)*

Redbud, eastern *(Cercis canadensis)*

Serviceberry, roundleaf *(Amelanchier sanguinea)*
Spruce, black *(Picea mariana)*
Spruce, Colorado *(Picea pungens)*
Spruce, Norway *(Picea abies)*
Spruce, white *(Picea glauca)*
Sumac, poison *(Toxicodendron vernix)*
Sumac, staghorn *(Rhus typhina)*
Sycamore *(Platanus occidentalis)*

Tamarack (or eastern larch) *(Larix laricina)*

Wahoo, eastern *(Euonymus atropurpureus)*
Walnut, black *(Juglans nigra)*
Willow, black *(Salix nigra)*
Willow, laurel *(Salix pentandra)*
Willow, pussy *(Salix discolor)*
Willow, weeping *(Salix babylonica)*
Witch-hazel *(Hamamelis virginiana)*

Appendix C

Uses of Tree Species

Species	Primary Uses	Secondary Uses
Ash, white	Oars, baseball bats, tool handles, veneer cabinets, furniture, flooring, crates	
Aspen	Lumber, veneer, pulpwood, particleboard, pallets, matches	
Basswood (American linden)	Lumber, Venetian blinds, sashes, door frames, molding, woodenware	Veneer, pulpwood, wood carving
Beech, American	Flooring, furniture, handles, veneer, woodenware	Railroad ties
Birch, paper (or white)	Toothpicks, tongue depressors, ice cream sticks	Spools, bobbins, toys
Birch, yellow	Furniture, boxes, woodenware, doors	Veneer
Butternut	Lumber, veneer	Furniture, cabinets, paneling
Cedar, eastern (or northern) white	Poles, cabin logs, railroad ties, lumber, decorative fencing	Boats, woodenware
Cedar, eastern red	Fence posts	Chests, wardrobes, closet linings, flooring, pencils, small boats
Cherry, black	Furniture, veneer	Caskets, woodenware, paneling
Cottonwood, eastern	Lumber, veneer, pulpwood, firewood	
Elm	Furniture, veneer, decorative panels	
Fir, balsam	Pulpwood	Lumber, Christmas trees

Species	Primary Uses	Secondary Uses
Hemlock, eastern	Lumber, pulpwood	Pallets, crates, boxes
Hickory, shagbark	Tool handles, ladder rungs, athletic goods, poles, furniture	Pallets, smoking meat
Maple, red	Railroad ties, boxes, pallets, furniture, veneer, woodenware	
Maple, sugar	Lumber, veneer, syrup	Flooring, furniture, cabinets, cutting boards, pianos, billiard cues, bowling alleys, dance and gymnasium floors
Oak (black/northern pin/ northern red)	Lumber, railroad ties, mine timbers, fence posts, veneer, pulpwood, firewood	Flooring, furniture, caskets, woodenware, handles, railroad cars, boats
Oak (bur/white)	Lumber, railroad ties, mine timbers, fence posts, veneer, firewood	White oak: Planking and bent parts of ships and boats, furniture, flooring, pallets, railroad cars, truck floors, furniture, doors
Pine, eastern white	Lumber	Sashes, doors, furniture, interior woodwork, caskets, toys, shade and map rollers
Pine, jack	Pulpwood, pallets	Railroad ties, mine timbers, poles, posts, firewood
Pine, red (or Norway)	Lumber, cabin logs, pulpwood	Poles, posts, firewood
Spruce, black	Pulpwood	Framing material, general millwork, boxes, piano sounding boards, bodies of string instruments
Spruce, white	Pulpwood	Christmas trees, framing materials, general millwork, boxes, piano sounding boards, bodies of string instruments
Tamarack (or eastern larch)	Pulpwood, railroad ties, lumber, mine timbers, firewood, fence posts, poles	Framing materials, tank construction, boxes, pallets
Walnut, black	Furniture, architectural woodwork, decorative panels	Gunstocks, cabinets, interior woodwork

Appendix D

WISCONSIN FORESTS CONTACT INFORMATION

Black River State Forest
910 State Highway 54 East
Black River Falls, WI 54615
(715) 284-4103
http://dnr.wi.gov/forestry/StateForests/
  SF-BlackRiver

Brule River State Forest
6250 South Ranger Road
Brule, WI 54820
(715) 372-5678
http://dnr.wi.gov/forestry/StateForests/
  SF-Brule

**Chequamegon-Nicolet National
  Forest–Chequamegon Land Base**
Forest Headquarters Office
1170 Fourth Avenue South
Park Falls, WI 54552
(715) 762-2461
www.fs.fed.us/r9/cnnf

**Chequamegon-Nicolet National
  Forest–Nicolet Land Base**
Forest Headquarters Office
500 Hanson Lake Road
Rhinelander, WI 54501
(715) 362-1300
www.fs.fed.us/r9/cnnf

Coulee Experimental State Forest
Wisconsin Department of Natural Resources
3550 Mormon Coulee Road
La Crosse, WI 54601
(608) 785-9007
http://dnr.wi.gov/forestry/stateforests/
  SF-Coulee

Flambeau River State Forest
W1613 County Highway W
Winter, WI 54896
(715) 332-5271
http://dnr.wi.gov/forestry/stateforests/
  SF-Flambeau

Governor Knowles State Forest
325 State Highway 70
P.O. Box 367
Grantsburg, WI 54840
(715) 463-2898
http://dnr.state.wi.us/forestry/StateForests/
  SF-Knowles

Havenwoods State Forest
6141 North Hopkins Street
Milwaukee, WI 53209
(414) 527-0232
http://dnr.state.wi.us/org/land/parks/specific/
  havenwoods

Ice Age National Scenic Trail
National Park Service
700 Rayovac Drive, Suite 100
Madison, WI 53711
(608) 441-5610
www.nps.gov/iatr

Kettle Moraine State Forest–Lapham Peak Unit
W329 N846 County Highway C
Delafield, WI 53018
(262) 646-3025
http://dnr.wi.gov/org/land/parks/specific/lapham

Kettle Moraine State Forest–Loew Lake Unit and Pike Lake Unit
3544 Kettle Moraine Road
Hartford, WI 53027
(262) 670-3400
http://dnr.wi.gov/org/land/parks/specific/
    findapark.html#loew
http://dnr.wi.gov/org/land/parks/specific/pikelake

Kettle Moraine State Forest–Northern Unit
Forest Headquarters
N1765 County Highway G
Campbellsport, WI 53010
(262) 626-2116
http://dnr.wi.gov/org/land/parks/specific/kmn

Kettle Moraine State Forest–Southern Unit
Forest Headquarters
S91 W39091 State Highway 59
Eagle, WI 53119
(262) 594-6200
http://dnr.wi.gov/org/land/parks/specific/kms/

Northern Highland-American Legion State Forest
Trout Lake Forestry Headquarters
4125 County Highway M
Boulder Junction, WI 54512
(715) 385-2727
http://dnr.wi.gov/forestry/StateForests/
    SF-NH-AL

Peshtigo River State Forest
N10008 Paust Lane
Crivitz, WI 54114
(715) 757-3965
http://dnr.wi.gov/forestry/stateforests/
    SF-Peshtigo

Point Beach State Forest
9400 County Highway O
Two Rivers, WI 54241
(920) 794-7480
http://dnr.wi.gov/org/land/parks/specific/
    pointbeach

Appendix E

To Volunteer for Wisconsin Forests

To volunteer for state forests, parks, trails, and recreation areas, contact:
Friends of Wisconsin State Parks
P. O. Box 2271
101 S. Webster Street PR/6
Madison, WI 53701
(608) 264-8994
http://fwsp.org

To volunteer for the Chequamegon-Nicolet National Forest, visit:
www.fs.fed.us/r9/cnnf/general/offices/index.html.

To learn about the Passport in Time Program (assisting U.S. Forest
Service employees with archaeological and historical projects), visit:
www.passportintime.com.

Index

About the Author

John T. Andrews

A former screenwriter for Paramount Pictures in Hollywood, Candice Gaukel Andrews now lives in her home state of Wisconsin and specializes in nature and travel writing. Her other books include *An Adventurous Nature: Tales from Natural Habitat Adventures*, *Great Wisconsin Winter Weekends*, *The Minnesota Almanac*, and *Travel Wild Wisconsin*. Visit her Web site at www.candiceandrews.com.

Praise for *Beyond the Trees*

"Nearly half of Wisconsin is forest, not a dark, monolithic stand of trees but a patchwork of diverse woods, each unique in makeup and history. Candice Gaukel Andrews takes us on a great ramble through the state's publicly owned forests, accompanied by ecologists and foresters, rangers and river guides, fire lookouts and local historians. *Beyond the Trees* penetrates the deep foliage to show us the biological diversity of our forests and their many recreational possibilities." — **JOHN HILDEBRAND**, author of *Mapping the Farm: A Family Chronicle, Reading the River: A Voyage Down the Yukon*, and *A Northern Front: New and Collected Essays*

"*Beyond the Trees* is important in a state where forests make major contributions to the economic, recreational, and aesthetic well-being of its citizens. Ms. Andrews's first-person narrative in each of Wisconsin's national and state forests provides readers with a taste of specific landscapes and familiarity with the specific people who molded that landscape — past and present." — **LOWELL KLESSIG**, professor emeritus of natural resources, University of Wisconsin–Stevens Point

"Candy Andrews's stories of Wisconsin's forests are the stories of the people who make them so special. Our state and national forests exist for the people, and the stories on these pages will make them live for present and future generations forever." — **STEVE PETERSEN**, superintendent, Northern Highland-American Legion State Forest